THE NEW BREED OF DRUG EXPLOITATION
PLAGUING OUR STREETS

COUNTY LINES

JASON FARRELL

JOHN BLAKE

Published by John Blake Publishing,
2.25, The Plaza,
535 Kings Road,
Chelsea Harbour,
London SW10 0SZ

www.facebook.com/johnblakebooks
twitter.com/jblakebooks

First published in paperback in 2020

Paperback ISBN: 978 1 78946 192 3
eBook ISBN: 978 1 78946 193 0

British Library Cataloguing-in-Publication Data:

A catalogue record for this book is available from the British Library.

Design by www.envydesign.co.uk

Printed and bound in Great Britain by Clays Ltd, Elcograf S.p.A.

1 3 5 7 9 10 8 6 4 2

John Blake Publishing is an imprint of Bonnier Books UK
www.bonnierbooks.co.uk

For Kerrie

CONTENTS

SLANG

Baby mama – young women who have children with gang-involved males

Bics – disposable children

Burner – disposable phone, used to run a line

Capping – shooting

Cheffing – stabbing with a long knife

Clean skins – children with no criminal record, also called 'tinys'

County line – branded phone number used by dealers as a drugs order line

Cuckooing – taking over the home of a vulnerable person to deal drugs

Gang-associated – interacting socially with gang members

Gang-involved – not a member but intermittently co-opted, willingly or not, to participate in some of its illegal activities

COUNTY **LINES**

Going country, 'Going cunch', 'OT' – running drugs to areas outside of the main city

Links – young women in casual sexual relationships

Plugging – concealing drugs internally, either in the rectum or vagina, or storing 'wrapped' drugs in cheeks, which can be swallowed if approached by police

Rep – reputation and status

Runners and Shotters – usually aged between twelve and fifteen, moving or selling drugs

Savage – drug addict or aggressive person used to conducting violence

Splashing – stabbing repeatedly until someone is bleeding heavily

Talent – a known threat to the gang, also known as 'Other'

Trap – any place where drugs are being exchanged

Trap House – a house where drugs are prepared and sold

Youngers – generally aged under eighteen. Usually street dealers who will report directly to the elders

Wannabes – aspirants who, whilst subscribing to gang norms, values, dress code, signs and signals, have not been accepted into the gang

Wifey – girlfriend

1.

SUFFOLK SHRIMP –
AN INTRODUCTION

Dr Leon Barron looked at the reading on the liquid chromatography mass spectrometer (LC-MS). It didn't make sense. He conferred with his colleague, Dr Thomas Miller, who couldn't believe it either. They'd been tasked with examining the environmental impact of certain farming techniques in East Anglia. Their teams had collected shrimp from the streams and rivers such as the Stour and the Gipping that run through rural communities and villages in Suffolk. The tiny crustaceans were delivered in Perspex boxes to the King's College laboratory in south London. The shrimp were then freeze-dried, extracted into alcohol and cleaned up to remove pigments and dyes. After that they were placed in small test tubes and shelved into what resembled a giant photocopier attached to a desktop computer. Then came the process called 'solid phase extraction', where a heart monitor-style line runs along the screen, moving in waves as the spectrometer detects certain substances within the shrimp.

The scientists were looking for the masses of more than a

hundred chemicals to monitor what is called a fragmentation pattern. The purpose of that day's test was to establish whether banned pesticides were still being used by farmers and possibly being absorbed into river-borne creatures. These chemicals could be having unforeseen effects on the local eco-system. But the LC-MS machine doesn't just test for pesticides – it can detect all sorts of substances, and one that Dr Miller and Dr Barron really hadn't expected to find was now evident on the monitor. A sharp peak rising upwards on the screen confirmed the presence of cocaine.

They tested more shrimp. Every time, the same result. Further tests showed it wasn't just in shrimp harvested from the rivers running through larger Suffolk towns such as Ipswich, but also in those found in the smallest of streams, upriver. One of the most substantial substances in the shrimp was benzoylecgonine – the chemical created by a human body after it has absorbed cocaine. There was also a high presence of ketamine. They found fenuron too – an illegal pesticide. But more common than this was lidocaine – a cutting agent used by drug dealers when diluting cocaine. And, the most present substance of all, found in every sample and at greater quantities than any other foreign substance – was pure cocaine.

Across London, in a seemingly unconnected event, Handsome knocked on the door of a north London flat. He was holding a baseball bat. Like the scientists in their lab, the Iraqi Kurd was just doing his job. He'd been sent a photograph via Snapchat and the target looked fairly soft, certainly no match for a refugee who'd survived being tortured by Islamic extremists. He'd followed his target to the flat by placing a tracker on his car. He'd watched him go in. He'd be in and out quick. The pill Handsome swallowed would help numb the pain of any return punches.

Meanwhile, in Yorkshire, Helen had had to call in sick from her dinner-lady duties at the school. Her thirteen-year-old son Callum had gone missing. In recent months he'd become ever more disconnected from the family. This morning she'd woken to discover his bed empty. She called the police and had been out all day looking for him. Now, travelling along a country lane, she could see a figure in the road, staggering down the pavement and, as her car approached, Callum stepped in front of it, forcing her to slam on the brakes. Wide-eyed and screaming, he began to push against the bonnet.

In Southampton, fourteen-year old Lucy was in trouble. They'd said it would be straightforward – but then, as she came out of the station, it all went wrong. Someone robbed her. It was as if they'd known she was coming. As if they'd known what was in the bag. A punch, a grab – gone. She couldn't exactly go to the police. She stood in shock. And it wasn't the bruise on her face that caused her to shake, nor the cut on her hand as the bag was snatched away. It was the thought of explaining to the boss that she'd just lost his drugs.

Uncle didn't care about all of this. Uncle didn't care a jot. He just sat in his crack den playing with his Rambo knife and his roll of twenties. He had a problem with a rival in Reading – but one of the kids was dealing with it. After all, it's a dog-eat-dog world out there. Maybe someone would come for him one day. But he'd be ready. Uncle was numb to it. He'd seen so many things that he couldn't un-see. It didn't matter any more. It was just business.

In Ipswich, seventeen-year-old Tavis was outside some shops when he spotted the boys getting out of the van. He knew this was going to be trouble. His home was just down the street and he began to jog towards it.

There were what, five or six of them? Moving with purpose. The kids from J-Block, taunting as they ran, jabbering about revenge. Something must have happened. Tavis picked up his pace. His jog turned to a sprint. He was fit. But some of these J-Block boys were fast – and big. He could see the hedgerow leading up to the Baptist church. His heart was thumping. His enemies were on *his* street. They were closing in when he slipped. Disaster. He tried to get up but there was a shove. His face was slammed against the concrete. He twisted as they set on him. His ankle turned so hard his trainer came off his foot. Then two of them had him pinned to the ground.

Only for a second did he see the knife – a long blade in someone's hand. Then they were on him like he was a piece of meat. He felt a searing pain in his leg, his stomach, his chest. Blow after blow. His body filled with terror and adrenaline. What had he done to deserve this? Hang out with his mates? Appear in a YouTube drill video? Then they were running. He was on his feet – there was a white flash, an almighty thud. Something cracked against his head like a block of ice. Only it wasn't a block of ice. Blood and glass splattered over his clothes. A parting gesture – a bottle smashed over the crown of his head. But he was still upright. He was staggering now – still trying to get home. Would he even make it to the top of the road? He reached for the gaping hole in his head. His hand was dripping red. His white T-shirt was also soaked with blood. His life was draining away from him, seeping into his clothes, and for what?

A short while later, in the River Gipping, there was a

plop on the water surface, and a knife, the knife used to kill Tavis, sank to the bottom of the river. The same riverbed that happened to be inhabited by cocaine-infused shrimp. Indeed, it was the same month that King's College published a report in *Environmental International*, which found that 'the most frequently detected substances in the Suffolk shrimp include cocaine and ketamine'. And that cocaine, in particular, was found 'in all samples tested'. Dr Leon Barron from King's concluded: 'Such regular occurrence of illicit drugs in wildlife was surprising. We might expect to see these in urban areas such as London, but not smaller more rural catchments.'

Eight days after the murder of Tavis Spencer-Aitkens, a police frogman brought the knife to the surface.

This all happened in the eighteen months before this book was written, and these multiple narratives are connected, of course – not just the shrimp and the murder weapon – all of it.

It's hard to imagine that the London hitman and the Yorkshire dinner lady are in any way linked, but they are – by a business that is spreading its tentacles into towns and villages everywhere. It is flooding through our rivers, pumping in the veins of addicts, and cutting through the social fabric of the UK. 'County lines' drug dealing has already arrived in a town near you. It brings with it a wave of gang culture, addiction, knife crime, heartache and the trafficking and murder of children. Like the King's College scientists, if you probe into it, you'll be surprised by what lies beneath the surface of our small towns and rural villages.

In this book, we are going right into the heart of the county lines operations. We will meet 'Uncle' in his crack den,

'Handsome' the hitman, 'Lucy' the runner, and many others, be they dealers, gang members, addicts, prostitutes, police, youth workers – everyone involved in or touched by this industry will have their say in explaining what county lines is, how it affects them and how we should be tackling it. These are real people and real stories. And what we will learn from them is that the war on drugs is being lost.

You can count that defeat in the 44,076 knife crime offences in England and Wales in the year to June 2019[1], or the record number of homicides in London in 2018, or the fact that drug-related deaths in Scotland topped 1,000 last year, making it the worst number of deaths per capita in Europe. Or you can look at the sewage water in Bristol, which currently tops London, Barcelona, Amsterdam and every other European city for its levels of benzoylecgonine. In other words, we are pissing more cocaine down the toilet in Bristol, per head of population, than in any other city in Europe. It is perhaps unfair on Bristol, as the tests haven't been done in other UK cities, but what if they were? We get an indication of the answer from the cocaine-imbued shrimp in Suffolk.

Even in the criminal underworld, they don't really know what to make of it. Many of them are shocked, too, by the way things are turning. In particular, the exploitation of children and the levels of violence. I'll admit it has disturbed me too. I am merely an observer. I don't have to live this life. If you're looking for an authentic voice from the street, I'm not it. But that also means I don't colour what I see by my own experience. I find I can meet anybody and talk to them. That's what I can do. And, as much as possible, I'll let the characters

---

1 Office of National Statistics

speak for themselves – because to understand this, I think we need to hear from everyone. Although, forgive me if I draw a few conclusions from time to time.

Some of this research I have done as part of my work as home editor for Sky News, so I may occasionally refer to cameramen and producers who have shared this journey with me. But now I want to share it with you. Turn the page and come with me into the deeply disturbing world of county lines drug dealing.

2.

MUMMY MULE

'In a place like this, trouble finds anyone and everyone.'

Linda walks across the concourse of Liverpool Street station carrying a couple of Topshop bags. Just a face in the crowd, she looks like any other woman returning home from a day's shopping, but normality is her camouflage. Aged forty-seven, black hair, black ripped jeans, high-heeled boots and a dark denim jacket, Linda is a drug mule. She has agreed to show me one of her routes. I want to start off by getting a sense of the impact of county lines on a marketplace, and what better way to go OT (Out There) than with a runner. So, Linda is taking me to one of her drop-off points – Southend-on-Sea.

We don't talk much before getting on the train, but once we find an empty carriage, and it starts to move, she explains in a soft voice: 'I'm involved because my son got involved. I'm helping him.'

She's a nervous woman. She exists in a natural state of high tension. Her eyes flicker about beneath thick eyeliner. We've agreed that she won't be carrying drugs on this particular trip. I just want her to show me the route, explain what she takes, where to and how she got involved. But she's on edge, as if her bags *are* loaded with drugs. Maybe it's meeting a journalist that makes her nervous. It's the first time Linda and I have met in person. We travel with a person known mutually to both of us, and my Sky News producer Andy Hughes.

Once it's clear that no one else is in earshot, Linda begins to open up. She tells me she has been running drugs errands for ten years. It had started when her son was going through a particularly disruptive period – bunking off school, not coming home, hanging out with some dodgy mates. They lived in the Tottenham area of London and Linda was an unemployed single mum. She was unaware of her son's drug dealing until one day he just came out and told her about it. He said he was worried about threats made against his sister by other gang members. He needed her help.

'He'd got involved in bad company,' Linda says. 'I didn't know at the beginning. Only that his behaviour changed. He was becoming nervous and shouting a lot and then, in the end, he told me. And he asked me to help him. So, I've been helping him ever since.'

It was an extraordinary decision by Linda to join her son's criminal network, but she insists she did it to protect him and the rest of the family. 'I got involved because I thought, I don't want nothing to happen to my son. They could maybe kill him. You don't know with these people.'

Either her son's life *is* at risk, or he's got Linda thinking it is. Like students who come home just to get their clothes washed by a slavish mum, Linda's son is taking advantage of his mother's devotion. And it's not like it's a one-off favour – she's been acting as his mule for ten years, unpaid.

'He asks me to take the stuff. I just deliver it. I take the stuff,

I deliver it and I leave. I don't even talk to them because I'm scared of them.' Linda speaks with the softest of voices, so she's sometimes difficult to hear over the screeches, rumbles and whistles of the train. But one thing that comes across loud and clear, because she keeps saying it, is this: 'They are bad people. Not nice people.'

She describes the packages she is given as small and very tightly wrapped. Enough packaging, she hopes, so that a sniffer dog wouldn't be able to detect what's inside.

'I do worry that I'll get caught. I'm scared every time I do it. My heart beats and I think it's the end of me. But I have to do it for my son.'

'Because you'd rather *you* were doing it than he was doing it?' I ask.

'Yeah.'

'Do you think you're less likely to get caught?'

'Well, every time I do it I'm very scared, because every time you do it you think, I'm going to get caught. Once it's over you feel relieved.'

The urban landscape turns to countryside as we talk – occasionally we flash though towns and industrial areas, but the horizon is opening up and flourishing with green. Soon, I'm looking out on hills, forests and farmland. This is a journey similar to those made by hundreds of dealers supplying what has become known as county lines. The term is used when drug gangs from big cities expand their sales to smaller towns, using violence to drive out local dealers and exploiting children and vulnerable people along the way. UK drug-trading routes have been around for decades, but aspects of county lines are relatively new, only properly defined in the last few years. And the menace is growing fast.

One characteristic is that, once establishing a possible market, the dealers use mobile phones, known as 'deal lines', to take orders from their new-found users. A deal line can develop its own brand among clients. In a national assessment by police in 2015, only seven police forces reported knowledge of county lines in their area; then, by November 2017, there were 720 'lines' or networks known to the police. But by November 2018, Sky News reported the number had more than doubled to over 2,000. With each line averaging an annual income of around £800,000 a year, the net worth of this industry is half a billion pounds. The controllers of these lines can remain in their central location, a good distance from their market. The National Crime Agency (NCA) has tracked lines running as far as London to Scotland. The further these operations expand, the more drug runners are needed to transport the drugs and collect payment – and with large sums of money or valuable merchandise travelling such distances, these networks have to be controlled with a certain degree of menace.

Hence, the next characteristic of county lines is the exploitation of young people by the gangs. Police estimate up to 10,000 children may be involved in county lines operations. Often, they act as the runners, moving drugs and cash under the radar of the police, acting as if they were Amazon delivery drivers dropping off their purchases. But these children are exposed to physical, mental and sexual abuse, and, in some instances, will be trafficked to areas a long way from home to become part of a network's satellite operations.

The Children's Commissioner's office reports that at least 27,000 children are members of criminal gangs – most of which are involved in selling drugs. The rule of thumb is that the more vulnerable the child, the more likely they will be preyed upon by a gang. Someone running away from home, for example, is a prime target. But it isn't just vulnerable children at risk – nor indeed is it just children. There are many vulnerabilities that criminal intent can probe and push at – youth is just one of them. Linda's decision to do the running for her son is perhaps unusual – but then again, an ordinary-looking woman in her late-forties is another good disguise to evade detection.

'You don't look like a drug dealer,' I say to Linda.

'Well, I'm not – it's not me.'

'But you are part of the system.'

'Yeah.'

'How does that feel?'

'Not very nice. Not nice at all. I worry because I don't know where this is going to stop or how it is going to stop – or *if* it is going to stop. I don't know what to do. You can't go to the police because they'd [the gang] probably kill us if we did. They would come after us. They've got contacts everywhere. It's not just one person or two.'

For someone so anxious about what she's doing, Linda seems unquestioning and extremely naïve about the money situation. 'I don't get paid,' she says, although she sometimes carries money in an envelope back to London. She doesn't know whether her son gets paid for her drops, and all she seems to get in return is that he 'helps me out', paying off the odd bill. Basically, Linda is getting a raw deal here, risking prison, risking her health with the anxiety, and travelling to towns as far as Birmingham to deliver drugs to people she feels threatened by.

She won't say exactly where she does the drops in Southend, but she describes what sounds like a 'trap house' – a place where drugs are stored and prepared for sale – often by younger gang members. She says it's a rundown property that has frequently changing inhabitants of different ages. One shared characteristic they all have: 'The people look sick – they don't look well.'

In many cases, a county lines gang will take over local properties, up to a dozen locations for each route. These normally belong to a vulnerable person or a drug addict. The practice is called 'cuckooing', where a property is turned into a trap house and sometimes lodgings for the out-of-town dealers. It's often children who are housed in these properties to run the drug supply. In one week in 2019 police rescued 400 children in operations across the UK – some had effectively been kidnapped and locked up to serve the dealers in trap houses.

Police have carried out numerous raids on trap houses in Southend. It's often difficult for them to distinguish between the users, the ones being exploited and those running the operation. When faced with this problem, Essex Police have sometimes used disruption tactics rather than prosecute. For example, in the summer of 2018 a woman from east London appeared to be involved in taking over flats and turning them into trap houses.

Ciera Hulatt, twenty, was accused of cuckooing, and police described her as working for the 'Knuckles' gang, based in east London. However, they didn't have the evidence to link Hulatt directly to the sales operation; they just kept finding her in properties whenever they did the raids. So, rather than charge her for dealing drugs, they instead made her subject of a court order barring her from entering Southend.

'You are now arriving in Southend,' says the train's recorded voice. Linda and I walk out of the station and, just outside in a pedestrianised square, is the unmistakable slouch of a homeless man bent double on a stone seat. I leave Linda to do her own thing for a while, and sit down next to him. He's a lot younger than I first thought – maybe in his twenties. He's just out of rehab, but says it was pointless. He got clean just to be thrown back into street living. He'll be back on the drugs soon, he confesses. Some others come and join him – friendly enough to chat to. They say Southend is the best place to be homeless in Essex. It has the best provisions, soup kitchens, a hostel, if you can get in. People come from other towns in East Anglia to be homeless in Southend.

A young woman, Lucy, aged twenty-one, says she's been on the streets for four years and tells me to watch out for fake beggars. 'A lot of them aren't really sleeping rough like us,' she insists. 'They're just pretending to be homeless.'

I want to know where to find the dealers and she points me to a group of teenagers who she says supply the drugs in the area. 'It's pretty blatant,' reckons Lucy. 'Sit here for a few minutes, you'll see it going on.'

I approach the teenagers, but the four of them tell me they are not selling. They say they've been asked to sell drugs by gang members from London, but not got involved. This group are all aged about eighteen, and say it's the younger kids I should be talking to. 'There are kids nowadays who will walk around the town centre with a bag of drugs, a knife and a knuckleduster and think it's appropriate – and these kids are twelve or thirteen,' says a young woman called Chloe.

She adds, 'I've lived in Southend my whole life and it's turned into somewhere you don't want to live. You walk around and you see crackheads everywhere, drug dealers, people carrying knives. It's a horrible place to live in.'

Another of the teenagers, called Po, says he's been tempted to sell drugs. 'It's really enticing to become a drug dealer at points,' he admits. 'You see them have all these fancy clothes, and all that money.'

A young man called Kofi tells me people visiting from London had offered him the chance to sell drugs. He also admitted he carried a weapon. He says Southend has become a place in which he feels the need to have one.

'There are times I've felt like I've had to because of problems I've had with people and certain threats,' he says. 'I'm not going to look to use it, but if I'm in a situation where my life's threatened, then I will use one. In a place like this, trouble seems to find anyone and everyone.'

Almost as he says it, there is a disturbance: two boys on bikes, no older than thirteen, start shouting at another boy who looks about eighteen years old. The bikes hit the floor and it seems certain a fight is about to break out. Community officers quickly step in. Suddenly the eighteen-year-old is surrounded by three officers and is screaming his head off. 'I'm the victim in this, I'm the victim!'

The officers talk to him calmly and it turns out he has been told to stay away from the town centre. 'You shouldn't be here,' says a female officer.

The same banning order used on the woman found in the trap house is also sometimes used on people involved in selling drugs where there is a lack of evidence for a full prosecution. Essex police create 'no go' areas for known gang members – often town centres – making it more difficult for them to conduct street sales. It's not clear whether this is the case here, but officers are telling the young man he should avoid the area. He continues to rant: 'This is a joke. I'm the one who got stabbed in the head.' The other kids are now also being spoken to by officers.

After a while, things calm down and I get a chance to speak to the older boy. He's furious. 'They are just kids. They call themselves 12-Block. They think they're serious but they are really not.'

'So, what happened? Why were you shouting about being stabbed?'

And I get the story. He didn't want to be identified, so let's call him Lee. Of course, Lee's issues all boil down to county lines.

'Last Monday I was standing outside of my block with my boys and this twenty-six-year-old man came up behind me and stabbed me in the head with a cut-throat razor blade.' Lee pulls back his dark-grey hoodie to reveal a still-healing red gash across the top of his shaven head.

'Look, six centimetres long, three centimetres into my head. He stabbed me in the fingers, armpit, shoulder, arm and back.' He points to the locations and it's apparent he is wearing the sweatshirt he had on when he was attacked. There's a hole in the back where the blade cut through.

'Ruined my top. That's the worst of it.' Lee says this without even a flicker of jokiness. He really is more furious about his knife-torn hoodie than the punctures in his flesh that will heal.

'Why did he stab you?' I ask.

'Some kid owed me twenty quid. So I took it. But it was his runner. So this kid who I got my money off – he was selling drugs for this older person. But he owed me twenty quid. So this bloke was making threats and then he came and stabbed me.'

'So, he did it to protect his runner?'

'No, just to show principle.' Then Lee looks at me as if there's something I'm really not getting. Something painfully obvious. So he puts me straight: 'This is Southend, bruv. Everyone gets stabbed in Southend.'

I'm suddenly struck by the fact that I've been in Southend for less than an hour and already I'm in the thick of it. I know I've come looking for it, but still. The first person I saw was an addict and, ever since, I've only spoken to kids who, if not dealing themselves, are certainly involved in the violence that envelops county lines. It feels like you could throw a stone in this town centre and likely hit someone who has in some way been impacted by it. As I carry on walking down the high street, just as the homeless girl Lucy said, I find beggars on every corner and I can't distinguish who the real rough sleepers are.

It was of course an exaggeration for Lee to say that *everyone* gets stabbed in Southend but, later, when I go looking for members of the gang he mentioned, 12-Block, I discover there are plenty of other kids who can show me stab wounds. One, claiming to be a member of 12-Block, pulls up his T-shirt to show a wound that has an entry and exit scar either side of his armpit. The other kids laugh and jeer as he shows it off, but I can tell a certain level of respect is granted him for his badge of honour.

I also tracked down one of the younger boys who had been involved in the altercation with Lee. He was thirteen and fairly new to Southend, having moved up from London after his father went to prison in Colchester. For a child, there was something disconnected and hateful about him. I'm sure he had a tough life, but I've rarely met someone so full of menace. When I asked him about the fight, he said Lee was a 'snitch' for going to the police about the stabbing. There was real hatred, like he just couldn't believe that someone would actually report something like that – to the police! 'That kid,' he said, (and this is a thirteen-year-old talking about an eighteen-year-old), 'that kid will be dead by the end of the year.'

I think back to what Chloe said, the first girl I met in Southend, about how the town had changed. For a young person to be walking down the high street thinking, *Now I'm at risk* – that is a real change. I grew up in Essex and I don't remember anywhere that felt like that.

But maybe for many local residents, the adults, this change is still fairly imperceptible. It all seems to be going on under the noses of the average middle-class man and woman. If you happen to live on a street where you know drugs are being dealt, and you are highly observant, then you may notice a few new faces. Or if you live next to a vulnerable person or an addict on an estate, the normally quiet, unassuming character may suddenly seem rather popular and have lots of visitors to their flat who you've not seen before. On a visit to the park there may be young people gathered around a playground or a skate park; and if you ventured off track you might find needles or small metal spoons used for preparing drugs. But for most people who commute every day from Southend to London for work – they just wouldn't know that there's now a different kind of commuter travelling in the opposite direction with a bag of class A drugs.

A National Crime Agency and National Police Chiefs Council report in August 2015[2] noted that coastal towns with declining economies provide suitable markets for metropolitan dealers: there's a high availability of cheap rental accommodation in converted hotels, attractive for prisoners on release; there

2   https://news.npcc.police.uk/releases/county-lines-urban-drug-gangs-target-coastal-communities

are often housing re-allocations from the capital, which is suffering from chronic home shortages. Southend's proximity to London means those dealing drugs often have family or community links that make entry to the area easier.

Deprivation in seaside towns is frequently mentioned as a contributing factor to them becoming county lines hotspots, but Southend is by no means an economic backwater. The high street, like many in the UK, has too many boarded-up shops, and the town's population of 182,500 has a 3.6 per cent unemployment rate, which is higher than the national average – but it's not dramatically worse than any other UK town. There's actually a fair amount of affluence in Southend, and higher-than-average home ownership. Perhaps the biggest attraction is the town's transport links to London. Both road and rail provide easy access.

It's one of the first places where journalists picked up on the phenomenon of county lines. In 2016 Max Daly, a reporter for *Vice*, came to Southend. He met a former sex worker, Debbie, who 'hosted' dealers from different London gangs at her home in Southend for several years. She told Daly: 'I relied on them because the more addicted you are, the more vulnerable you are. If I complained they shut me up by giving me drugs. I was scared of losing my property, which was all I had. In the end, I had a total breakdown.'

It was a perfect description of cuckooing – before the phrase had been established. And what's more, she had a string of young houseguests. She told Daly that some of the boys housed in her property were as young as fourteen: 'They were kids, but they never talked about normal teenage things. They were shutdown people, always silent. They were mentally drained.

'They used to lie on my settee and sleep with the phone by their head, working twenty-two hours a day, eating in McDonald's and sleeping on my sofa. A couple of times they would have a treat, like buying a new pair of trainers. They were putting on an act, trying to pretend they were the big boys, but they were young kids getting exploited.'

Even in 2016 Daly observed that Southend had seen its drug trade almost completely taken over by London-based gangs. He spoke to two men called Patrick and Nick, who worked as drivers for the dealers and told of regular trips at the wheel of BMW and Mercedes hire cars between London and Southend.

Daly wrote: 'Patrick, who used to work for the RAC, was paid £120 cash on top of bags of crack and heroin to drive from 9am to 9pm. He regularly drove the boss of one London crew, an Asian dealer in his twenties who is now in jail, back to London's East End to pick up large amounts of crack that had been imported into the UK as liquid cocaine inside the bodies of live tropical fish. According to Patrick, who built a close rapport with his boss, the gang made on average £2,500 a day on each of its six county lines, which also included Swindon and Stevenage. Before costs, this meant the firm was bringing in £450,000 a month from selling outside London.'[3]

Patrick told Daly: 'I've seen knife-slashings and people have been shot. I've had my windscreen smashed with an iron bar. Most of them have no regard for killing or shooting people. It's all about greed.'

The other driver, Nick, had been a crack and heroin addict for more than fifteen years and was paid £500 for every twenty-four-hour driving shift. By the time he'd finished a shift, most

---

3 'VICE investigation: The Inside Story of London's Drug Dealers – 'Going Country'
Max Daly, 24 November 2016

of his wages had gone on crack to keep him awake. He describes the dealers from London as 'Dogsbodies, young, a bit rude, full of bravado, *blud* this and *blud* that, who all have knives but wished they had guns.

'It's a big glory thing for them, and they listened to songs that idolised drug dealing,' he says. 'Even though they're spending their lives sitting in a car with someone like me, who's at the bottom of the pile, they think they are the bees' knees because they are living a "trap life".'

My visit to Southend leads me to suspect these networks have become even more entrenched. Local sources tell me that two rival gangs from Tottenham have been fighting for dominance in the town for a number of years. It's clear they not only import their own runners to prepare and sell drugs in trap houses, but have realised there are some established postcode rivalries – and a pool of easily turned kids who can do much of the running in the local area. So, mules like Linda, who I came here with, simply have to drop the drugs and there's a network of youngsters to take it on from there.

The town's council and local police force are well aware that they have a problem. And they are conscious of its threat to children in the area. In 2018, they ran a joint campaign called #SeeTheSigns. It warned parents with a slogan – 'Do You Know Who Is Controlling Your Children?' The image on posters and online was of a child, with 'mule' written on her dress, hanging from strings like a puppet.

It urged parents and carers to find out more about how the criminal groups operate, and offered advice on how to spot signs that a child may be involved in drug dealing. The campaign warned that children as young as eight to twelve years old and 'into adulthood' were being exploited. And that they were targets 'across all economic, ethnic and social groups, and the associated violence, drug dealing and exploitation has a devastating impact on young people, vulnerable adults and local communities'.

Signs parents were asked to look for included:

- A child persistently going missing from school or home and/or being found out-of-area
- Unexplained acquisition of money, clothes or mobile phones
- Excessive receipt of texts/phone calls and/or having multiple handsets
- Relationships with controlling/older individuals or groups
- Leaving home/care without explanation
- Suspicion of physical assault/unexplained injuries.

Parents and carers were also being asked to keep up with the language involved: 'Young people will rarely say that they are running a "County Line" or "Country Line". They are more likely to say that they are "Running a Line", "Going Cunch" or "Going O.T." (which stands for Over There, Out There or Outta Town).'

Councillor Helen Boyd, cabinet member for children and learning in Southend said, in an article in the *Southend Echo* on October 18th 2018: 'It's easy for us to believe that these issues only affect other people, but this kind of criminal gang activity is happening across all walks of life. There is no one type of child that is being targeted, and this campaign highlights the fact that all parents need to be aware of this issue.'

Chief Inspector Neil Pudney, district commander for

Southend, said: 'Essex police officers are out on the streets everyday tackling gang violence. Last year we secured 109 years imprisonment for drug dealers, seized drugs with a street value of £220,000 and arrested 232 people suspected of drug and gang crime.

'Young people can fall into gang lifestyles in different ways, but vigilant and loving parents can spot issues and get help before they develop. Gangs recruit young people by portraying a glamorous lifestyle but the reality is far different: you will be at risk of serious injury, arrest or having to commit awful acts of violence.'

A campaign was also launched by Essex police and the council to target recreational drug users over the Christmas period of 2018. #MerryMuletide was the message telling festive drug users that their fun-time drug use was having catastrophic consequences on the lives of Southend children. The advert, which was plugged on social media, showed a man snorting children's sweets through a rolled-up note.

Councillor Mark Flewitt, cabinet member for public protection, said, in the article in the *Southend Echo* on 18th October 2018: 'Recreational drug users may not realise the effect their drug taking has on children. They may care about the plastic they use, and how much they recycle. But, if they're tempted to perk up a Friday night party, many don't know about the young children forced into working for violent gangs that supply their drugs. This campaign is purposefully uncomfortable to look at, but it has to be to get this message across.'

That same article in the *Echo* reported on how Southend's children were being targeted to move drugs and money through the borough and up and down to London.

'Schoolchildren are being forced to deal Class A drugs by

gangs,' it warned. 'The council and police are urging members of the public to remove the demand for drug dealers in the area by avoiding using them completely and taking away the market.'

The *Echo* spoke with a parent who discovered her thirteen-year-old son had been groomed to sell drugs and, after reporting this, the paper was contacted by other parents with the same problem. One had been forced to move out of the town after being intimidated by the dealers.

Councillor Helen Boyd said: 'Worse than just being "couriers", our children are purposefully targeted by criminal gangs. They are tricked into carrying small packages, and then opened up to a world of extreme violence and control. They are often sent miles from home, made to stay in squalid conditions and even forced to commit acts of violence themselves. They are set up on trains to be robbed of the money they're carrying, so feel indebted to these criminals and unable to leave. More and more we are seeing criminal gangs target children across all towns, socio-economic backgrounds and ages. Children as young as twelve years old are being used to traffic drugs around and in and out of our borough.'

The two campaigns are commendable and streaks ahead of other councils that are still coming to terms with county lines. Many don't acknowledge their problem, or know about it but don't have a strategy to deal with it. However, it's not recreational cocaine users who enjoy a line at the weekend who are the lifeblood customers of county lines dealers. While these networks do sell powder cocaine, cannabis and pills, the majority of their sales are crack cocaine or heroin. The typical customer is an unemployed addict who is not going to change his or her habit because of a poster campaign.

Take Louis, aged fifty. He is a crack addict living in Southend. He is black, with close-trimmed hair, and he walks down the street in what looks like an out-of-world stupor. He's dressed in ill-fitting clothes that might have looked smart if they'd not been worn over many days and nights and subjected to the elements. Given his circumstances, he is probably the friendliest homeless guy you'll ever meet. His face creases into an endearing smile as I approach. A friend of his later tells me he is always smiling and he'll always ask very politely if you have any spare change.

'I started weed when I was sixteen,' he tells me. 'I was twenty-five when I first tried crack cocaine. My friend introduced me and since then I've been on it.'

'Were you addicted straight away?' I ask.

'No. I didn't like the first one.'

'So why did you do it again?'

'The first one was too weak.'

'Right.'

'When I took the second one, it was better.' He gives me the biggest grin yet.

'What do you think about when you take the drugs?'

'I think about godliness.'

'What?'

'Godliness. I feel good inside.'

'What about when you don't have it?'

'I feel okay.' He simply can't stop smiling at my questions.

'So, what's been the impact on your life?'

'I have to go out and hustle money to get it. I don't steal. I ask politely for money. Sometimes I ask for food.'

'What proportion of your money goes on drugs and what proportion on food?'

'Most of it goes on drugs. But I don't go hungry.'

'Do you regret it?

'No. No!'

'Why not?'

'I think about godliness, innit. When I listen to reggae music, I think about godliness. Because the music is about godliness and it's better under the drugs. I dance when I listen to the music.'

I think of the famous image of Bob Marley and his reefer. The reggae artist converted to Rastafarianism from Christianity in the mid-1960s, well before he achieved any international fame as a musician. He became the most celebrated symbol of his Jamaican culture and religion. Rastafarians famously use marijuana as a sacred herb to aid meditation and apparently achieve greater mystical insight into the nature of the universe. Marley attributed the drug to his musical creativity, and it seems Louis feels greater appreciation of music when he's off his head on crack. For Louis, crack is the most important thing in the world.

'Isn't is a bit dangerous, the world you live in?' I ask. Some of these drug dealers don't seem very pleasant.'

Louis smiles once again. 'People I ask for money are more aggressive than the drug dealers. They say, "Get away from my car." But I'm always polite.' He is too. But despite the happy smile, his tired eyes and emaciated frame are no advert for crack cocaine.

A bit later I catch up with 'mummy mule' Linda in Nando's. We talk a bit more about her son who has coerced her into becoming a mule. I feel like I need to put it out there: is her son really someone she needs to protect, or is he just as dangerous as everyone else in his gang?

'I don't think he's a danger to other people,' she insists. 'He's just got involved with them. He doesn't know how to get out of it. It's difficult to get out of it, once you're in it.'

Linda thinks about this to herself. I can tell she's asking herself, *Is there a way out of this terrible life?* Then she adds, 'I could say, "I'm not going to do this any more". But that means my son will be doing it. I keep on telling him to find a way out. I've told him to go to the police to get out. But he is scared. They won't just go after him, but probably the whole family.'

He has her on a hook. I suppose it's easy to be cynical about this, but Linda's son probably isn't the kingpin of the organisation, and the life he leads means he probably is in danger. He has undoubtedly surrounded himself with some unsavoury characters. His mother is perhaps right to be afraid of them – but I suspect her son has overplayed the threat of walking away from the life he is leading. I suspect he's told quite a few whoppers on that matter.

But meeting Linda leaves me wondering about what's going on at the origin of all of this, in places like Tottenham, not far from central London. On one level, surely there is nothing new about dealers travelling from urban cities into smaller towns to supply drugs. But there is something different with county lines. It's not just the phone lines: it's also the exploitation, the ambition, the organisation, the fear and the conflict. To get to the heart of this, I need to go to the centre of it.

3.

THE DEALER

'There's no love any more.'

Cody is an old-school drug dealer who has been operating in Tottenham for well over a decade, serving his local area and keeping business as simple as possible. But he's noticed things are changing. The gang structure is falling apart. Young people are getting restless and unpredictable. 'There's no love any more,' he says.

It's hard to remember a time when there was ever much love in Tottenham. The north London area has a reputation for lawlessness. It is one of the most deprived places in Britain, blighted by gang culture, drugs and gun crime. It is also a crucible for mass disorder. Two notorious riots kicked off here: the Broadwater Farm riot of 1985 and the London Riots of 2011. For decades, police have tried and failed to counter numerous 'postcode' gangs – most notably Tottenham Mandem (TMD), whose feuding and drugs wars have resulted in scores of deaths.

Every type of illegal substance is readily available on

Tottenham's streets from dealers like Cody, but it is specifically the heroin trade that has put the area on Britain's crime map. The Turkish Mafia, based in Haringey, has been estimated to control around 90 per cent of the country's heroin market in the past decade and remains the dominant group in this trade. It is one reason why dozens of the UK's estimated 2,000 'lines' are run from this one London suburb to other towns and cities across the country. It seems this is as good a place as any to properly launch our journey into the source of the brutal county lines business.

However, I'm not going to be able to just walk into a Tottenham crack den and get criminals to open up about how it all works. Not yet anyway. So, I'm starting with Cody, a small-time local dealer and a former member of TMD, who works for himself. A muscular black man in his mid-thirties, he is too young to remember the infamous Broadwater Farm riot, but he was very much involved in the riots of 2011, which exploded into a national crisis. We'll come to that later. Right now, Cody has other things on his mind.

'Things ain't how they used to be.' This is the thing Cody wants to tell me, and he isn't happy about it. 'Everybody is using each other, or attacking each other,' he says. In his youth, older people on the estate watched out for the younger ones – now they exploit them.

'That's the thing that I hate. We never used to do that. This is a new thing and it pisses me off. They're not actually helping their kids. They're using them. If you're helping your little brothers because they're suffering and they've got no way to make money, that's different. But if you're using them, I find that devilish. To tell the truth, I don't like it. I've never used little kids. Apart from anything else, I don't trust little kids not to talk. I'd rather just do it myself. So, if I get arrested, I get arrested. It's my fault. I've got a daughter. She's only eleven. If someone tried to give her drugs to sell, that would make me sick.'

'How were you treated by your gang as a kid?' I ask.

'When I was growing up the elders used to look after us. That was above anything. They wouldn't be sending you to go and sell drugs for them, or nothing like that. If you decided to do anything like that, you did it yourself. Some of the stuff I hear now about people using the little kids… it's not brotherly.'

It was August 2018 when I met Cody in a recreation ground that had been parched yellow by a long hot summer – a heat that also helped energise rising violence in Tottenham. An increase in stabbings always seems to coincide with warm summers; fewer people go killing in the cold and damp. At that time, Tottenham had 5,500 violent offences committed in just 12 months – that's 15 a day, in a population of 112,000 people. Knife-related injuries were up 90 per cent over the previous 6 months – making it the most dangerous suburb of London to be a teenager. The borough of Haringey, which incorporates Tottenham, accounted for 9 of London's 135 homicides of 2018. The murders were mostly stabbings of young men, but there were also 3 fatal shootings, including that of 17-year-old Tanesha Melbourne-Blake. She was gunned down in a drive-by shooting, despite having no apparent gang affiliation.

Cody's concern about the exploitation of young people was shared by the authorities. It became a much-talked-about feature of the county lines phenomenon. At a gangs strategy meeting in March 2019, Haringey Council identified the following issues:

1. Serious youth violence was up 33 per cent in 12 months
2. The recent practice of county lines drug dealing was luring children into criminal networks
3. There was a prevalence of so-called 'zombie' knives being carried by young people
4. Historic tensions between Wood Green- and Tottenham-based gangs were bubbling
5. The area had 10–11 active gangs, several peer groups, and one organised crime network
6. There were 202 individuals on the Trident Matrix (recognised by police as affiliated to gangs), 139 in the community, 63 in custody
7. A significant proportion were between 18 and 24 years old, the majority Black African/Caribbean
8. A significant number had mental health issues including cognitive issues, depression, PTSD etc.

Cody's chosen park bench was in Lordship Recreation Group, which overlooks the tall, tombstone-like tower blocks that make up the Broadwater Farm estate, where his gang was based. He is still considered what they call an elder but, he says, he is not active in the gang. I wanted Cody to help me explore the Tottenham drugs world and get a basic understanding of what makes someone become a dealer. The good thing about Cody is he gets right to the point.

'Do you know what being broke is like? It's like being dead. What can you do when you're broke? Nothing. You might as well be dead. And everyone just wants to live. We all just want to live. That's it.'

But it's a dangerous way to live, always on the edge of death. Cody has been stabbed several times and has been shot at.

This, he says, is part and parcel of the job. 'That's gang life. It's a sad life. But, if you don't accept it, well, that's like someone committing crimes and not expecting to go to jail. If you do the crime, you gotta do the time. Don't be a baby. You can't expect all the pleasure and none of the pain.'

Like many people who've made the choices Cody has, it's quite easy to trace problems back to his childhood. His home life was punctuated by bouts of domestic violence from his dad against his mother. 'It's just stressful,' says Cody. 'It's the worst time for a kid. I think between seven and eleven is the time when you need a lot of peace as a child growing up. As a boy, it can determine how you feel for the rest of your life.'

Cody's mum and dad eventually split up and he stayed with his mother, moving from place to place to place. He was in London, Milton Keynes and Liverpool. Then he came back to Tottenham. Cody felt like he was on the move all the time. He can't remember staying in one house for more than a year or so. Then, aged eleven, he ran away from home. For about eight months he was on the road, until one of his aunts took him in, but only for a while. He preferred living on the streets around Broadwater Farm. In today's world, he would have been a prime target to become a county lines drugs runner. But he says the elders on the estate took him under their wing and never pressured him to do anything.

'I was with my friends. I didn't really join a gang as such. It was just our friends; we all grew up together, looked out for each other. At first, no one ever really classed it as a gang. But then people started saying, "Yeah, we're a gang." Our gang was the Tottenham Mandem. Then it got shortened to TMD.'

'What was the purpose of the gang?'

'We were just friends. You're talking about lots of guys with no father figures. The people we'd look up to were the boys who were making money, and treating us like their little brothers. Like I said, it's not like how I'm seeing it now. They weren't telling us to sell drugs for them. But you could see where the money was being made.'

Cody describes his elder gang members as 'big brothers', never asking for anything, simply looking after the community as a whole. He paints a picture of Robin Hood characters, and perhaps he has a rose-tinted view of them, but there's no doubt they formed his view of the world.

'So, at this point, criminals became your role models?'

'Yeah, because they're the only people around. Where are the doctors, or the accountants or the lawyers? I see it this way: I want to become something successful and they [the dealers] are all I see. I know there are kids from the estate who went on to get good jobs, but they move on. If someone becomes a doctor, and he's pushing a big Jaguar, he doesn't come back to the Farm [the estate] and say, "Look, you can get this just how I did it", you know. He doesn't tell you, "They can't take it off you. They can't do anything. It's all yours." He doesn't come back because he has moved on to a different life. No one thinks to come back.'

'And you think there are people who've done that?' I ask. 'They've left the estate, got good jobs and never looked back?'

'Yeah – I know now there are people like that. I just never saw them when I was growing up. They didn't come back.'

Reflecting on his youth, Cody's other complaint is that once you have a criminal record you are marked for life. He was fifteen when he was charged for smoking marijuana and he believes this made it very difficult for him to get legitimate work.

'They don't give you a second chance. You could have a

good CV, but you'll get rejected,' he says with a shrug. 'When I look at my friends, most of our first criminal things were smoking weed. That's it. I think it's a crime to ruin someone over that. Once you're done for possessing, it's much harder to do anything, because you're a criminal. You've been slandered. You have a criminal record and you're just a kid. You should just get a caution – you're smoking weed, not troubling anyone else. It's just your own lungs.'

Aged sixteen, Cody moved into his own place and needed money. 'I haven't got a mum that could give me money. I have no family. I can't get a job. I couldn't even buy a pair of trainers. And I don't believe in Jobseeker's Allowance. I don't know why they have it. People with disabilities should get unemployment benefits, but able-bodied people shouldn't be getting money from the government – they should be getting jobs. They should just get help doing that.'

'But that's what the Job Centre is there for,' I suggest.

'At the Job Centre, they don't actually want to help you. They know you can't get jobs, so they pressure you – sending you on courses and courses. Then they want you to work for free. If I do voluntary work, it's of my own free will. I'll go and volunteer in an old people's home. I'll go and volunteer with some young kids. But, with the Job Centre, I'm volunteering and doing a job that other people are getting paid for. That's not going to inspire me or pull at my heartstrings. It doesn't make me feel good.'

'And what about getting qualifications?'

'I got loads of qualifications. But who cares about them when you've got a criminal record? They don't see the qualifications; they just see a piece of paper with a criminal record on it. I have a youth work qualification. I did a health and social care qualification and I was practising to be a social worker. I was giving a lot of my time for free. I was promised a contract. Inspectors came in and gave us high reports and everything. But they didn't give us the contracts. So they just used me to do what they needed to do, then they discarded me. The system is just there to cheat you. So, sorry if we have no trust for these people. I have no trust for official people.'

Cody is a father now. He also has a decorating business, but says it's not enough to pay the bills, and if he wasn't selling drugs he wouldn't be able to afford his daughter's school uniform. In his view, the world is divided into haves and have-nots – and everything is tilted against the latter group.

'For example, nowadays, you can't take a child out of school to go on holiday. So you wait till the school holidays, but then prices are sky high. So, what they're saying is, poor people can't go on holiday any more. Rich people can go when they like, because they can afford it. But poor people – they can't go on holiday. If people weren't selling drugs, how the hell would they even go out?'

You're probably getting the sense that Cody feels the whole world is stacked against him. But there is this one outlet – a way he can make a reasonable amount of money. He makes it sound like the drugs industry is to Tottenham what tech is to Silicon Valley. In this enclave of London, narcotics is the biggest and most available industry to people like him. With drugs, he is the end retailer in a lucrative global supply chain. If you think about it, in his pockets is merchandise from two different hemispheres: heroin wraps that have travelled at least 4,500 miles from Afghanistan, and cocaine 'rocks' whose base ingredient has come 5,000 miles across the Atlantic from Colombia. At the top of the chain huge sums of money are being made. Cody says if he had that kind of money he would turn Broadwater Farm into a gated community, and keep the police out, but, like many drug dealers I've met – from Glasgow to Los Angeles – he envies the people further up the chain. Wherever you are in the chain you want to be one higher where the bigger bucks are being made. Even he questions how the drug barons are able to get away with it.

'We don't grow crack or cocaine here. I don't know any poppy fields in England. So how does it get in? That's all I want to know. Why don't they go after the big guys? They always go after people like me. Why stab at the body of a snake when you can go straight to the head? That's where you'd stop the problem. Whose fault is that? The government isn't protecting its civilians.'

You can tell that Cody has found many ways of blaming society and the system for *his* actions – and you are either nodding along or furious with him for his lack of self-accountability. This is a trait we will encounter time and again in the world we are entering. People who feel entitled to break the law – an absent morality around drug dealing can quickly morph into cold calculation towards stabbings and even murder. This, they convince themselves, is all the fault of society and authority. The actual offenders, the individuals, are absolved of responsibility. Why? Because no one ever cared for them.

This is a theme we will explore in more detail later – in particular the rewiring of a young person towards violence. Research shows, for example in Sue Gerhardt's 2004 book *Why Love Matters*, that even in babies and up to three years old the brain's emotions and immune systems are affected by stress and can become less effective, making a child more vulnerable to depression, anti-social behaviour, addictions or anorexia.

The mistrust of authority such as that demonstrated by Cody is endemic in Tottenham. If you need evidence, look to the riots of 2011. You'll excuse me if I go off on a tangent here, but the wildfire nature of the London riots acts as an interesting precursor to the spread of county lines. During that summer, London was plunged into crisis after the police shooting of a local Tottenham man. What began as a gathering of around 200 protesters demanding answers over the death of Mark Duggan, culminated twelve hours later in a full-scale insurrection that saw brazen looting spread across the suburbs, literally like a fire. Shops burned. Stealing was rife – trainers, food, electronics were smashed-and-grabbed by people, many of whom had been law-abiding until that point. This one questionable act from the police triggered a complete breakdown of the moral codes of a civilised society.

A Sky News reporter, Mark Stone, filmed youths yanking television sets off the walls in Dixons, and only escaped a beating after running into a nightclub with his footage. Personally, I witnessed a female photographer being punched to the ground, her camera smashed, for photographing someone who set fire to a vehicle. There were numerous confrontations between police and the public. Bottles were thrown. Two patrol cars were set alight. Riot officers on horseback, deployed to disperse the crowds, came under attack from fireworks and other missiles. Petrol bombs were also thrown. The London Fire Brigade dealt with 49 fires in the Tottenham area and received more than 250 emergency calls from the public. Then, the disorder spread to Hackney, Brixton, Walthamstow, Peckham, Enfield,

Battersea, Croydon, Ealing, Barking, Woolwich, Lewisham and East Ham. After that, it caught hold in other towns and cities across the UK, including Birmingham, Liverpool, Nottingham and Bristol. But it all started in Tottenham.

Cody was friends with the man who was shot. Mark Duggan was a twenty-nine-year-old black man, who, like Cody, was also a member of the Tottenham Mandem. They had both been in and out of jail. For Cody, the first time was for drug dealing, the second for an armed robbery. The shooting of Duggan would lead to Cody's third stint in prison. He won't be specific about what he did in response to the murder, as he feels it will identify him, but whatever his role in the chaos, he feels it was justified because of what the police did to his friend.

Police said they suspected Mr Duggan was planning an attack and was in possession of a handgun. Cody doubts this. He says: 'A lot of people feel it was murder – because they told so many lies. First, they told people that he shot at them. That he had fired a bullet into one of their officers. They said that to the newspapers.'

He's right about this. After initial reports that Mr Duggan had fired at officers, forensic tests showed the gun found at the scene had not been fired. The police watchdog was forced to admit it may have misled journalists into believing Mark fired at the police before he was killed. Ballistics experts found that a bullet, which lodged itself in one officer's radio, was police issue.

In a statement, the Independent Police Complaints Commission said: 'Analysis of media coverage and queries raised on Twitter have alerted us to the possibility that we may have inadvertently given misleading information to journalists when responding to very early media queries following the shooting of Mark Duggan by Metropolitan Police Service officers on the evening of 4 August.'

After this, what else were residents and relatives going to believe? 'This is why we will never trust the newspapers again, ever,' says Cody. 'Everything they said was a lie. So, whenever they write stuff, even about Taliban people, I don't trust them no more. I don't like people blowing other people up, but I can't trust anything the papers say about these people, because I heard what they said about my friend. They said he was the tenth most-wanted man in Europe. Flipping hell! How many drugs and guns do you have to move to meet that? What, they wanted him in Europe? So, France was looking for him? Wow! Thank you, liars! Big, big liars. I'll never trust them, ever.'

'Was he wanted?'

'No! He wasn't even the tenth most wanted person in Tottenham! How can he be most wanted in Europe? He was just like the rest of us – he had a criminal record. No one's perfect. We're not perfect to the world, but he wouldn't shoot at police officers. No one does that in our country, apart from that Cregan guy[4]. But apart from him, no one else does it. They said Mark had a gun. They said they found it. Apparently, he threw the gun away. But they shot him, and when you've been shot, your body goes into shock. You can't throw a gun away! The most you might do is drop something. Everything they said doesn't add up.'

In an inquest in 2014, lawyers representing Mr Duggan's family suggested police had planted the handgun, which was found on grass 14 feet away from his body, but the jury

---

4 In May 2012 Dale Cregan, a psychopath from Manchester, lured two female officers to his house with a hoax call. When they arrived, he ambushed them with a handgun and a grenade, killing both of them.

concluded that Duggan had discarded it as the minicab he was in was brought to a stop by police.

The inquest found Mr Duggan was lawfully killed. The police watchdog, which cleared officers of wrongdoing, said he was likely to have been throwing the weapon to one side as he was shot.

Conflicting witness accounts left his family unsatisfied, and in 2019 they decided to sue the Metropolitan Police. Civil proceedings brought by Pamela Duggan, Mark's mother, accused Scotland Yard of liability for the death. The family has now reached a settlement with the Metropolitan Police and the terms of the settlement remain confidential.

Mark Duggan's death is an important part of the cultural history of Tottenham. It is simply accepted in many parts of the community that the police killed him unlawfully and got away with it. Furthermore, it's assumed this sums up the attitude of police towards anyone involved in, or on the edge of criminality in north London: that they don't deserve to live – especially if they are black. In Cody's view, 'They're killers. But, because they work for the government, they could kill who they like. So this is why we walk around the street knowing that we're just basically dead. No, we're not alive. Who cares?'

I've reflected on Cody's words a lot during my exploration into county lines – this image of dead men walking, carrying appropriately named 'zombie' knives. It explains a lot of what I am about to describe. The people involved in this game have zero respect for the police, for society, the people they stab, and, when you dig deeper, for themselves. Selling drugs has just about given them something to live for, something to kill for, something to die for. But they are not so different to the addicts they are feeding with crack. There is something missing, and the drugs fill the void.

Is this all the fault of an uncaring capitalist ethos? Certainly, inequality is higher now than in the 1960s and 70s, but has remained fairly stable in the last 40 years. Even so, according to House of Commons figures in 2017–18, 42 per cent of all disposable household income in the UK went to the 20 per cent of people with the highest household incomes, while 7 per cent went to the lowest-income 20 per cent.

What's more, the most notable cuts in the government's austerity drive since 2010 have appeared to hit those on lower incomes, be it the freeze in many working-age benefits and tax credits, the two-child limit for benefit payments, or reductions in Universal Credit. In 2018, the *Guardian* calculated that the average lone-parent family lost a fifth of its net income, and this was especially hard on those with more children. Exactly the type of broken homes gang members come from.

They feel the world is against them, so they rebel. But this deep-rooted feeling of rejection and neglect from society hasn't led to a pulling together of this struggling group. Quite the opposite. Cody comes back to the subject that is bothering him most: the breakdown of traditional gang loyalty. 'There's no loyalty, no love, there's no common unity. You have people on their own estate warring with each other.'

When I think of the London riots – and I was in the thick of them as a reporter – it wasn't cohesive or self-affirming. Some protests really are, but this wasn't. It was frightening. It was each man for himself. It was selfish. Steal what you can. Steal from your local grocer. Burn what you can. Burn your local shop, burn your neighbour's car. Fuck the police but, quite frankly, fuck everything.

THE DEALER

Contrast this to the Brixton Riots of 1981. On the surface, the unfolding spectacle looked much the same – mostly young black men fighting the police and setting fire to buildings. But those riots were defined by a political purpose. Many young black men believed officers discriminated against them, particularly by use of the 'sus' law, under which anybody could be stopped and searched if officers merely suspected they might be planning to carry out a crime.

Lord Scarman's report, which responded to the factors that created the riots, was published in November 1981. It said there was 'no doubt racial disadvantage was a fact of current British life'. His report led to an end to the sus law, and the creation of the Police Complaints Authority, as well as new approaches to police recruitment and training.

The riots helped kick-start plans for a newspaper aimed at the black British community – *The Voice*. It was an impetus too, for black people to become politically active. In 1985 Bernie Grant became the first BAME (black, Asian and minority ethnic) leader of a London council (Haringey). Two years later he was one of the first four people from an ethnic minority to be elected to parliament (as MP for Tottenham).

Nothing positive came out of the 2011 riots. A year on, the only thing to show for it was nearly 1,300 prosecutions for disorder and theft, and a sense that an uprising over a suspect police shooting had been selfishly exploited by too many people as an excuse to shop for free. And so, in Tottenham 2019, drug dealer Cody is left perplexed: 'I don't know what's happened, but there's not much love in the streets no more.' He says: 'We've become an unfriendly place. I think it's because of how the kids have become and what they're learning from the adults now. As they're getting older they just want it all for themselves. They want the next pair of trainers. They want to compete with their parents for who has the most money.'

Boredom and few opportunities add to the picture. 'Or maybe there are opportunities, but for how many people? How many can get them? There's not enough jobs for sure, so now even kids who before wouldn't have been a part of this, are becoming a part of this. Some kids might even go to university and, after that, they just can't get a job. So, he's grown up in the area. He listened to everything his mum and dad said. He did everything the right way and now he still can't get a job, but his drug-dealer mates are making money and they're going raving and having all sorts of fun.

'They could do other crimes, but there's not much point the kids getting involved in street robberies and burglaries, because what money can you get stealing off people that live near you? They're broke as well. There used to be a lot of vandalism but even that is quite boring. So, they sell drugs.'

TV plays its part. Cody says: 'Then you get these petty little arguments, and, because they're watching telly, it glamorises gang stuff. They turn into what they see in the films. Everyone wants to be Mad Max. They want to be the baddest gang member. They're evolving and they getting colder. That's how the world is turning. I mean, these kids are so unfeeling now. Look at their YouTube videos. They just wanna kill each other. It's disgusting, it's organised, it's vicious. But to these kids it's real. I mean, they could just make money and focus on that, but they actually hate each other. And once a friend dies, that's it. That's why we really need to start thinking about prevention for these young people. Although, I'd say for this generation it's already too late.'

'Surely it's never too late?' I say.

'It is, and I'm going to tell you why. Because if they've lost a friend, then they hate already. Once they hate, it's too late. You can't stop hate. Ask a soldier when he goes to a war zone – they've got a job to do. But ask them what happens when they've gone out on their first patrol and one of their platoon dies. They actually hate for a little bit. They can't help it. They don't mean to. It's normal. They've just lost their friend. They hate the other side now, and this is what these little kids feel once they've lost their friend – they are gone. They are tribal now. Only, like I say, even the tribes are breaking up. Now it's just all against all. And even inside tribes there's fighting.'

It is desperate stuff. Utterly depressing. If these kids have lost faith in everything, even the brotherhood of their own gangs, what's left? During the 2011 riots, the scales fell from the eyes of cosseted, wealthier Londoners who lived cheek-by-jowl with the people who were burning their high streets. And what they saw was not just fury at the police but also despair: a lethal absence of hope among a whole section of society. Then the riots stopped and, over time, people sort of forgot about it. But this lethal absence of hope hasn't gone away. It hasn't improved through ten years of austerity and cuts to public services and stagnation in wages and increases in child poverty. It hasn't led to more rioting – not yet, anyway – but it manifests in something less dramatic and less obvious but even more devastating: what Cody describes as the death of love in his community.

'So, this change – do you think it's connected to county lines drug dealing?' I ask Cody.

'Sure, it's connected in the way the elders are treating the young people,' he says. 'And it's about money. There's too many dealers – everything is stagnating. So they start going out to different areas, outside of London, where it might be a little bit quieter and easier. But sometimes all those beefs [arguments] between the different groups in Tottenham get transported to the new markets. Your beef goes wherever you see your enemies. That's the truth of it. So, wherever they see each other – it may be jail, it may be a christening, it could be anywhere – if you want to kill someone, you think someone wants to kill you. You have to defend yourself. It's the one animal trait that everyone has. So, it's messed up.'

The phone rings. He looks at the number. 'Actually, I need to get this.'

'A deal?'

He nods. 'Yeah, I'm coming,' he says down the phone. Then to me, 'I need to go.' Then back to the phone: 'Okay. Cool, cool, cool.'

And off he goes. Just another drug deal in Tottenham about to take place. There are hundreds every day. In a short space of time, Cody has painted a bleak picture. He has touched on the pressures that might be contributing to county lines drug dealing. A growing sense of desperation, legitimate work opportunities running dry, more people, and younger people, turning to drug dealing – and being raised in a more brutal environment. At the same time, he suggests the market is stagnating in London, further fuelling the rivalry and violence between the postcode gangs. I'm keen to meet some of these kids – the ones in the thick of it. But before meeting the postcode gangs in Tottenham, let's explore the other question raised by Cody. Who are the guys at the top – the ones making the big money, bringing the drugs in?

4.

THE WHOLESALER

'Rip on, rip off.'

Klodjan Copja watched as police officers bust down the doors to his safe house in Earl's Court. It was okay, because he'd just snuck out and was being driven away in an old Ford Fiesta. As he glided past the front of the house and looked out of the passenger window, one of the officers, dressed in blue body-armour and a riot-helmet, turned and caught a glimpse of him – but it was too late. They didn't even know what he looked like. He was invisible to them. And though they had raided his crack dens, confiscated his drugs, seized weapons and arrested his couriers many times before, nothing led back to him.

A few days later he was back in the leather chairs under the canvas sun canopies of the Living Bar in Albania. His plush, legitimate business, where he ploughed his drug profits, is located on the Qemal Stafa Boulevard in his hometown of Elbasan.

Elbasan, Albania's third largest city, is one of most deprived cities in Europe. The old industrial metalworks from the communist era have ensured it is also one of the most polluted places on earth. The streets are covered with asphalt dust, tons of metal factory waste has been pumped into the air and rivers, and the soil is centimetres thick with contamination.

But the city's mountainous surround includes the Jabllanice National Park, which has breathtaking views – and anywhere looks good if you drive round it in a blood-red Ferrari, as Copja liked to. It didn't matter that the air was toxic. He was more toxic. Copja was feared and respected here. He owned this place. And all of this thanks to the £150 million he'd accrued from exporting drugs into the UK.

In the space of five years he had built up a network that smuggled cocaine into southern England, and from there he distributed it to organised crime gangs in London and Birmingham. Those gangs then subdivided the consignments and distributed to their own local networks in an activity the police were calling 'county lines'. That was the buzzword. It didn't mean anything to Copja; that was his clients' business. He was the wholesaler.

Wholesaling required logistics, business acumen and balls. It was high risk but, if you got it right, the rewards were even higher. Wholesaling was like county lines but on a bigger scale: it was all about getting the drugs in and the money out, without leaving a personal 'footprint' in the marketplace. Rather than a town, your marketplace is a country. And in that country you had to be untouchable, untraceable, preferably unknown to the authorities. For this reason, Copja had a plethora of false documents, multiple IDs and, luckily for him, no previous convictions. When in the UK, he was anything but the big man who lorded it around his hometown. In the UK, he was Mr

Nobody. He kept a low profile, renting an expensive but not too flashy modern flat in Wandsworth. None of his gang were showy, always using ordinary, nondescript cars. Copja himself would never drive. Nobody in his organisation made gangland YouTube videos.

He only allowed his wealth and status to become apparent when he was back home, and even then he wasn't like his hothead brother who'd been arrested for blowing up a rival in Albania. He was careful. And although gangsters dressed as policemen had sprayed a rival bar in Elbasan with bullets, killing three people and wounding seven, no one could link that directly to him. Even if that bar, just a few hundred metres down the road, was stealing his business.

Copja stayed under the radar and got filthy rich and, to be fair, a bit chubby. Enough that his nickname became 'fat Leonardo DiCaprio'. But of course, it's not always the big dramatic things that get you in the end. Copja had left one thing behind in his safe house in Earl's Court that would eventually catch up with him – his fingerprints.

A few months later he decided to try out some new fake ID at the border from Albania into Greece. The border guard was suspicious about the passport. Before long, Copja was in a back room being checked out. A fingerprint test was run through AFIS database, which is INTERPOL's identification system, containing 185,000 records of international suspects. The arches, loops and whorls unique to Copja's finger matched one placed on the system by UK authorities. Bingo! Customs officials realised they had a big fish on the line.

From here he was extradited to the UK on a European arrest warrant. Even so, nobody in the UK knew what he looked like. So, after a three-year surveillance operation on his business by the Met's Organised Crime Command, detectives didn't have a formal visual of Copja until they watched him being led from the plane in handcuffs. And not until they themselves had placed his fingers in black ink could they be satisfied they'd captured the boss. Once they'd done that, they had copious evidence to show he was the Don of a massive drugs ring. Copja was just thirty years old when he was finally jailed for drug trafficking, in August 2017. He was sentenced to seventeen years and four months in a British prison.

Copja's story is just one of many linking cocaine to Albania, and if you think about it, that's rather odd, as Albania is geographically in the wrong part of the world to supply cocaine, which is grown and produced in Latin America. The criminal gangs that emerged from the Balkans in the 1990s and 2000s appeared to be far more interested in growing marijuana and trafficking sex workers. Yet criminals from this low-income country, with a population of less than 3 million, now dominate the UK cocaine wholesale market. So how did that happen?

To answer this question, I'm recruiting the help of Tony Saggers, the former head of drugs threat and intelligence for the National Crime Agency (NCA). As Britain's most senior drugs cop until he retired in 2017, it was his job to oversee the UK strategy for combating supply lines coming into the UK. Tony's first encounter with the drugs world was as a nineteen-year-old uniformed PC, in 1989, when he arrested someone for selling a dozen gram 'wraps' of amphetamine in Newmarket. He then spent his early career working in the Suffolk drugs squad before graduating to big-league drug prosecutions, such as that of Curtis Warren, whose illicit earnings trafficking drugs were in the region of £198 million, so he knows more than most about the different criminal facets of the UK drug industry – in particular the subject raised by drug dealer Cody in the last chapter. How are all these drugs getting into the UK?

'The UK is Europe's biggest drug market,' says Tony. 'We consume around thirty tonnes of cocaine a year. That quantity has an estimated wholesale value of £1 billion, and a retail value of £4 billion.'

That's one third of Albania's total GDP. It's an attractive market for any criminal network. According to Tony, the drugs supply networks are ever evolving. There is a ruthless battle for control between different ethnic groups, and it is also transforming through technology.

'The world has become smaller because of transport, logistics and the ability to electronically move cash. Everything is much more fluid now,' he says. Networking is easier through technology, and organised crime groups are finding new ways to move and conceal the huge sums of money they earn.

Fluidity also applies to the backgrounds of the people involved. In recent decades Britain has become far more multicultural, but with this so too has the criminal demographic changed. In the 1980s and 90s, crime groups trafficking drugs into the UK involved British and foreign nationals from about six countries. Now there are between thirty and fifty nationalities, which means a wider range of supply routes from all over the world.

'Targeting this is much more complex,' says Tony. 'In the nineties you could stereotype to a high degree of accuracy the national backgrounds connected with importing drugs. With crack cocaine it was primarily Caribbean and white British, and for heroin it was Pakistani, Turkish and white British. Now it's a more complicated picture.'

In the late 1990s, thousands of Kosovan refugees fled Serbian ethnic cleansing to claim asylum in the UK. The war in the former Yugoslavia between 1998 and 1999 saw ethnic Albanian civilians become victims of terrible war crimes committed by ethnic Serbs and the government of Yugoslavia. But among the Kosovan arrivals in the UK were also many nationals from neighbouring Albania itself, who'd seen an opportunity to escape an impoverished country. Many claimed to be Kosovan in what has since been described as the biggest case of nationality switching in recent UK immigration history.

Criminal kingpins were already established in Albania. After the collapse of communism in Eastern Europe in 1990, there had been civil unrest in the country and widespread corruption. Around fifteen families had seized the opportunity to establish organised gangs, known as Mafia Shqiptare. Like the Italian mafia's law of *omertà*, or silence, members of Albanian criminal gangs live and die by a ruthless code of conduct. Their oath called *besa*, meaning trust, is the promise to defend with their lives the honour of the ruling family. Each family has an executive committee, or *barjack*, which selects a *krye*, or boss, who in turn appoints a *kryetar*, a second in command. There is no doubt that these structured gangs saw the influx of Albanians to the UK as a huge opportunity to get their workforce into a number of illegal marketplaces.

Some took jobs as door staff in the heart of London's sex and vice trade in Soho, at the time dominated by the Maltese mafia. But the Albanians were said to quickly take over London's prostitution rackets – their speciality was trafficking women. In the space of two decades they went from dogsbodies to Mr Bigs. Vice squads now estimate that Albanians run 75 per cent of the UK's brothels, having established a presence in every major town and city.

I should add at this point that the vast majority of new Albanian immigrants took legitimate work. I recall travelling to the Fens while reporting on the EU referendum and meeting a farmer who employed Albanians and Romanians by the tractor-load. I asked him why he'd use them rather than the disgruntled, unemployed British workers I met in the nearby local town. He took me to his turnip field and showed me the sheer determination with which those Eastern Europeans harvested root crops from the ground. 'Brits don't work like that,' he said. Having worked on a potato farm in East Anglia in my youth, I knew how backbreaking it was sifting mud from vegetables and lumping heavy sacks from a machine onto a pallet.

'I used to do it,' I told him. He examined my soft hands and somehow, correctly, doubted I was much good at it. But whether it be legitimate work or the black market, there's no doubt Albanians arrived in the UK with a voracious appetite for opportunity and an enviable work ethic. This was noted in the criminal underworld.

The Albanian gangs were forging links with crime gangs throughout Europe to smuggle counterfeit goods and weapons into Western Europe (the grenade Dale Cregan used in 2012 in Manchester to kill three people, including a policewoman, came from Albania). And while the first wave of Albanian gangsters operating in Britain was thought to have cornered much of the brothel market, a second wave was forging strong links with British crime syndicates.

Old-school British crime gangs became wary of the Albanians after the infamous Tonbridge Securitas robbery in February 2006. This joint UK-Albanian operation was the UK's biggest ever cash heist and more than half of the £53 million stolen was never recovered. This massive theft involved kidnapping the depot manager, Colin Dixon, his wife and child at gunpoint. According to Wensley Clarkson, in his book *The Crossing*, British gangsters believe the Albanians took more than their fair share of the loot, and what's more, some of the Brits involved met sticky ends.

One disappeared and is presumed dead, another was murdered in Spain, a third was knocked down in a hit and run, and a fourth killed himself after threats made against his family. A fair number of people involved in the heist were arrested and convicted, including two Albanians – but the ambitious robbery well and truly put the Albanians on the UK crime map, and Clarkson, who spoke to numerous underworld contacts, tells how, from that point, these Eastern European newcomers brutally removed many of the home-grown gangsters from their own backyards.

For example, he tells how one British gang who tried to push back against an influx of foreign drug dealers were taken into a field and 'played with' by their rivals with guns and knives. 'It was fucking terrifying!' said one, who'd had a gun shoved down his throat. 'None of us had the bottle to hit back again. We closed down the drug-dealing operation, abandoned all our spots and split up for good. They'd won hands down.'

Another villain told Clarkson: 'Most of the old-school Brits gave up the fight. There's no other way to describe it. We were facing a bunch of psychos and it wasn't worth it.'

At this time, the Albanians also managed cannabis farms in the Balkan hills and used their network to ship cannabis to the UK. In this market, they were up against Jamaican and Chinese drug gangs, but here again the crime group demonstrated its audacious levels of ambition to control a market. They began to grow potent strains of the drug, both in Albania but also in the UK, illegally importing bonded workers to look after cannabis grow-houses, often in the north of England, but in reality anywhere they could find a dark corner, out of sight.

In 2018, a group of cavers ventured 150 feet down into an abandoned Wiltshire mine and were struck by how, instead of the usual cold air and dank smell of dripping water, there was a warmth and sweet fragrance in the caves. As they went deeper into the 10 acres of caverns in Bethel Quarry, the explorers discovered it had been transformed into a sophisticated cannabis factory.

The caves, once used by Heinz to grow mushrooms for tinned soup, were now packed with more than a dozen agricultural black tents where hundreds of cannabis plants grew under specialist lighting and a powerful heating system. A nearby plastic swimming pool stored water for the crop, banks of propagators nurtured seedlings, and a drying room housed the harvest. The 'gardeners' even had a gymnasium next to their bedrooms.

The cavers fled when a baseball-wielding guard stepped from the darkness to accuse them of trespassing on private property. Once safely above ground, they alerted police who raided the factory in October of that year.

Two Albanians were arrested. One of the farmers told police his £100-a-day wage helped pay the £5,000 he owed people smugglers who brought him to Britain. They were both jailed for eighteen months for cannabis production, although the judge admitted they were 'cogs' in a 'far larger machine' thought to have been operating for three years.

Having established a criminal network and trafficking routes for smuggling people and marijuana, it made sense for the Mafia Shqiptare to somehow diversify into the UK's most profitable illegal drug – cocaine. There was one problem of course: getting access to the base material. Anyone distributing cocaine or crack cocaine around the UK has to have links, usually through a third party, to the cartels who control coca production in South America. Cocaine is produced primarily in Colombia, Peru and Bolivia. Devising the best transport route from the supplier to Europe's biggest market is a fiercely competitive enterprise. In the last ten years, Albanians have rapidly managed to prove that they have triumphed in this endeavour.

According to Tony Saggers and other sources at the NCA, the Mafia Shqiptare have utterly broken the traditional supply model. They started out, like other criminal networks operating into the UK, sourcing their drugs through wholesalers in Spanish, Dutch and Belgian ports. It makes sense to use the Atlantic-facing ports of Rotterdam and Antwerp for drug smuggling, as they also receive the highest volumes of legitimate commercial shipments from Latin America. Just as normal pineapples would travel through the Netherlands to the UK, so too would the hollowed-out pineapples that have been refilled with bags of cocaine.

Saggers explains: 'There are various reasons why these points of entry are so favoured by cocaine traffickers, not least the high demand within the UK for other goods that are making a similar journey. For example, Britain is the largest consumer of bananas in the EU (about 1.15 million tonnes a year), equating to 20 per cent of EU consumption. These are most commonly acquired from Central America (usually Costa Rica and Panama) and three of the Andean Pact countries

(Ecuador, Colombia and Peru). Using fruit, particularly bananas and pineapples, to conceal cocaine has long been a favoured method of traffickers trying to get the drug to the EU and beyond, or direct to the UK.'

The high volume of legitimate trade is an opportunity to 'hide in clear sight'. Fruit also has swifter clearance through border controls than non-perishable goods. The traffickers either create what is called a 'cover' business, where they will also genuinely trade the bananas, or use 'concealment' – where they hide their cocaine in someone else's load and then remove it before it's delivered.

'The process of inserting and then removing drugs is commonly done after security checks at port entry and before clearance at destination,' says Tony Saggers. 'This requires the placement or manipulation of corrupted port workers at both ends of the journey and is known as "rip on, rip off" or "rip in, rip out".'

In this way, cocaine arrives into these ports by the tonne-load before being broken down into smaller quantities for different European national markets. Numerous crime groups operate here: Dutch, British, Spanish, Colombians and Brazilians all have cocaine-wholesaling businesses going through Antwerp and Rotterdam. Many of the trade routes from these ports into southern Europe are controlled by the most powerful of the Italian Mafia, the 'Ndrangheta, while the Albanians appear to have quite recently secured the lion's share of UK trade. They did this in part through a reputation for ruthlessness, but mostly though good old-fashioned undercutting the market.

The Albanians began to push their way into the wholesale cocaine market around 2008/9 and started buying their drugs for the UK in the mainland European ports at the same price as everyone else, roughly £30,000 a kilo. But they noticed that crime groups trading wholesale into the UK were being quite greedy and marking up to a UK-wholesale price of £45,000 a kilo. So, they reduced their margins, and sold for £40,000 a kilo, in order to gain a sizable market share.

But criminal networks of any kind don't give up a lucrative market share without a fight. Like any threatened business, the other UK importers reacted to the interlopers and improved their quality and reduced their price too. But the NCA noticed that between 2010 and 2015 the Albanians kept cutting by £2,000 a kilo every year, until the wholesale price in the UK was down to £30,000 a kilo. It was an extremely aggressive market grab.

It seems unsustainable, but over that time what the Albanians had also done was bring down the wholesale price in the mainland EU ports. This was stage two of their market takeover – cutting out the middleman.

At first they shaved their margins by commissioning their own consignments through established importers and buying in bigger bulk, but they then decided to leapfrog the established players and go direct to the supplier. Delegations went to meet the Colombian cartels in South America.

This was by no means an easy task. For fifty years war has raged in Colombia over the drug trade. Guerrillas of the Revolutionary Armed Forces of Colombia (Farc) started becoming involved in coca production in the 1980s and gradually increased their presence after the death of drug lord Pablo Escobar in 1993. But Farc were also notorious kidnappers and just as dangerous as any cartel. Even after a peace deal in 2016, the violence continued to rage, as dissident rebel factions and right-wing paramilitaries battled for ownership of the coca-growing territory previously controlled by Farc.

It seems Copja and other Albanian crime lords built a relationship with one of these groups. They travelled to South America posing as Italians, making it near impossible for authorities to know exactly which players were involved and who they were dealing with. But it is clear they brokered agreements that would create a flow of drugs from the fields and laboratories deep in the Colombian jungle, down the San Juan and Naya rivers, through the country's main port of Buenaventura out on to the Pacific, then to Rotterdam and Antwerp, before being packed into lorries bound for Kent and distributed to dealers across the UK – an entire supply network from plantation to London city banker's nose.

During this time, data from the United Nations Office on Drugs and Crime (UNODC) showed that coca cultivation surged to a record high, with land used to harvest the coca plant increasing by 17 per cent between 2016 and 2017 alone. Over the same time period, despite the peace deal, hundreds more people continued to be killed in Colombia in territorial battles, and thousands of indigenous people were displaced from their farms and villages to make way for this additional coca production.

Tony Saggers says: 'What they [the Albanians] did was import, themselves, on a major scale into Rotterdam and Antwerp and started to systematically drive down the Dutch prices, which was unprecedented. It had never happened before. They drove down the price from £30,000 to £25,000 and lower. It was market forces combined with the reputation of having been through a civil war, having access to firearms, having a ruthless attitude to competition. The working relationship status went along these lines – "We want to get on with you but if you don't want to get on with us there will be consequences."'

Even though they were driving down the Dutch wholesale price, they were no longer paying even that reduced figure. Instead of £22–25,000 a kilo in the ports of Rotterdam or Antwerp, the Albanians could get their cocaine for a quarter of the price, at closer to $5,000 (£3,900) a kilo, in Colombia. The transport costs would have probably come in at another $5,000, and they'd need another $5,000 per kilo to pay off corrupt port officials, but the margins were still massive. And again, rather than go for immediate profits, they cut the price at the UK wholesale level and offered greater purity.

Again, I refer to Wensley Clarkson's in-depth exploration of how the ground war was played out between the 'old-firm' British criminal networks and the Eastern European newcomers. In his book *The Crossing* he explains how the Albanians had been eyeing up the potential cocaine profits of the UK criminal underworld for years. His story paints a picture of maturing British gangsters, semi-retired in the Costa del Sol, who lacked the hunger, inventiveness and brutality of the Eastern Europeans. Not only were the UK gangs marking up their price too high, they had been selling an ever-decreasing in quality product.

A pint-sized Albanian drug boss who Clarkson calls Bari explains: 'We (are) very professional proud of being efficient businessmen. That means selling good coke otherwise customers go someplace else. British gangs had been too greedy for too long before we got here. They cut the coke with so much shit that it had no actual cocaine in it. That is stupid and short-sighted. We made sure there was real cocaine in the stuff we sold on the streets. The customers come back for more and more. It makes good business sense, yes?'

The result was that the UK wholesale price of cocaine and crack cocaine has come down dramatically in the last decade, and is the cheapest it's been in the UK since 1990. Not all of that reduction has been passed on to the end user, however. The sub-wholesalers, who break the bulk down into their own county lines distribution networks are holding on to some of the profit. But generally, the purity of cocaine has improved. One explanation for the growth of county lines is simply a better product at a cheaper price – and a great mark-up opportunity at street level.

There have been successes in combating these imports. In 2018, Antwerp authorities seized 50 tonnes of cocaine – that is more than ten-fold the amount they were seizing only five years previously. They've also been making bigger seizures in the Netherlands, and UK Home Office statistics released in March 2019 showed Border Force officials confiscated more than 5,500 kilos coming into the UK in 2018, up a third on the previous year.

Either the authorities are improving their search techniques or the gangs are shipping more drugs. But things are always changing. The next thing to impact the UK's narcotics import market will be Brexit. Tony Saggers wrote an article in January 2018 for RUSI, the world's longest-standing think-tank on defence and security, in which he argued that Brexit will bring aspects of the drug trade closer to our shores.

For example, if the UK makes unilateral tariff changes under World Trade Organization rules on goods such as pineapples and bananas, we may cease trading through the large EU ports and instead transit them direct to the UK. Tony wrote in *RUSI* magazine: 'If it becomes less likely for UK-bound consignments to pass through the EU (due to tariffs, taxes or fees), this will have considerable implications for organised crime group (OCG) logistics, control and presence. After Brexit, it seems unlikely that OCGs targeting the UK will have the same opportunities to cover for or conceal their cocaine consignments via the EU. While the Latin America–EU–UK trade routes will inevitably continue, fruit is a probable casualty. This being the case, it is likely that fruit will be directly routed to the UK, together with the cocaine it conceals.'

He goes on to argue that if that happens it could bring with it 'high levels of corruption, security breaches, violent crime, murders and a concentration of multi-national crime bosses and logistics controllers'.

His point is that the Albanians and other crime groups will have to move some of their operations and resources into UK ports. They will need to bribe officials here, and fight off threats from other international gangs here rather than on the mainland. What has been a horrific problem for Belgium and Dutch authorities will, in part, shift its base and become a problem for UK police forces to deal with.

You might hope that UK entry points would not be susceptible to corruption, but only in April 2018, a gang of eleven, including two baggage handlers, were found guilty of smuggling cocaine through Terminal 5 at Heathrow. The NCA intercepted 100 kilos, but believe the 'rip on, rip off' system being conducted by the Heathrow handlers had been successful for some time. At the UK end it simply involved switching bags from the international to domestic carousels. An easy job for baggage handlers Joysen Jhurry, 41, and Mohammad Ali, 42, but in the end it cost them both fifteen years in jail.

So after Brexit we might 'take back control' of fighting the cocaine wholesalers within our own borders, but these efforts are always based on international intelligence sharing, and there are question marks over how that will continue between the UK and the EU once we have left. For example, utilisation of the European Arrest Warrant used to extradite Copja may be impacted, although you have to hope that is a hollow concern and police forces will continue to cooperate with each other.

There is one other question that has dogged Brexit since it was voted for in June 2016, but which is also of interest to drug smugglers: what kind of border will exist between Northern Ireland and the Republic in the south after the UK has left the EU? At the time of writing this has not been resolved, but all parties are agreed a hard border would be a terrible idea, as it could reignite old animosities. If it remains soft, however, the shoreline of Ireland could become an attractive option for traffickers as an entry point to the UK.

The changes to shipping port destinations could also lead to a greater use of what is known as 'coopering'. This is where a large ship from South America is met by smaller UK-based vessel mid-ocean in order to shift some of the consignment into a yacht that can then dock fairly innocuously anywhere along the UK coast. The Albanians don't tend to get involved in this, but if it becomes a more popular smuggling route due to Brexit supply-line disruption, the UK would have to invest in more offshore patrols and place greater emphasis on intelligence gathering upstream.

The UK's wraparound sea border offers a challenge to smugglers, but that doesn't mean it is easy to police. Smugglers have been known to use private light aircraft, helicopters and microlights to get drugs across the Channel, or they go for small boats, anchoring near beaches or docking at small marinas that clearly don't have the same level of focus as an international seaport or airport. The NCA relies on intelligence to cut these imports off.

It was an intelligence operation by four different European countries that led to the interception of a yacht off the coast of Cornwall in July 2018. Officers discovered dozens of bales of cocaine wrapped in plastic in a compartment beneath the decking at the stern of the boat – destined for the UK market. It was double the amount found in any previous raid off the south coast. Two Dutch nationals were arrested after their boat was escorted into the harbour of Newlyn, a popular Cornish seaside town.

Only a month later two British men and three Europeans were also arrested and escorted into Newlyn. Their 60-foot yacht, *Nomad*, had set off from Portsmouth. The catamaran was intercepted by border patrols in the western approaches off the southern Irish coast. Inside a hatch were three bales each containing 1,400 one-kilo packages of high-purity cocaine. As we've established, just one package on the black market would fetch some £30,000. So, the total wholesale market value of the cocaine on board came in at well over £100 million.

The crew included UK nationals Nigel Clark, 64, and Dean Waters, 59, who were living in Spain at the time. There was also an Estonian, Richard Must, 49, and 21-year-old Latvian Voldemars Gailis. The fifth member was Raymond Dijkstra, 27, from Holland. He would later claim in court that he'd only boarded the boat in Portsmouth as part of a pleasure cruise to Spain and Portugal. But in fact the boat had stopped mid-Atlantic to meet with a larger ship from South America. Dijkstra told the court that there were so many bales of drugs, initially stored upfront, that the boat's propeller 'lifted out of the water', and so the bundles had to be redistributed around the craft. It still didn't match the largest cocaine seizure in the UK. In 2015, a yacht raided off the coast of Aberdeen had more than three tonnes on board – at that time the estimated street value was £512 million.

You may have noticed that these boat seizures contain a mixture of nationalities, and none of them Albanian. In the last couple of years, the NCA believes mixed-nationality crime groups are making a resurgence into the market, and there's evidence that British and Western European gangs are forging their own links with Colombia in a way that they couldn't have imagined during the days of Farc.

In January 2018, two Britons, two Spaniards and an Italian paid £138,000 to hire a private jet to Colombia. They pretended they were managing a rock band going to a charity gig in South America. Before heading out to Bogotá, they stayed in upmarket London hotels and were driven to Luton airport in luxury cars with their fifteen suitcases – which happened to be empty.

Their plan was to create a direct chain of supply from its source in Colombia to the UK streets. Flight records would later show that they had at the very least done a dummy run – if not successfully already used the technique once before. The potential to get a direct source to street profit must have been tantalising and well worth the hire of a private jet. Indeed, it was worth a few investments.

In Bogotá, they used armoured vehicles to transfer the 500 kilos of cocaine to the plane where they had paid off officials and used fake uniformed police officers, with fake sniffer dogs, to pretend they were going through a search. The theatre was put on to fool the uncorrupted staff at the airport – and to hoodwink the pilot and crew of the aircraft, who had no idea about the cargo.

But an intelligence-led police operation in the UK was tracking their movements. When they landed at Farnborough airport, five people were arrested, as were the corrupt officials in Bogotá. The fifteen suitcases were filled with a total of half a tonne of cocaine. It ended with four men being jailed for a total of ninety-two years.

Direct flights are always going to be a temptation, and for years Border Force has tackled 'stuffers and swallowers' – often from Jamaica. Lawrence Gibbons, the current head of drug threat at the NCA, showed me X-ray photographs that would make anyone wince. Some mules appeared to have up to forty or fifty thumb-sized bundles rammed into their intestines – either swallowed or stuffed up – probably both. The image showed the bundles pressing up against the mule's ribcage.

'It only needs one of those capsules to split and it's lights out,' says Lawrence. 'The most a normal person can do is just under a kilo. But you've really got to count them in and count them out.'

He adds: 'The person organising the smuggling bombards the flight with numerous couriers. They work on the premise that if they get two-thirds through that's enough. Say there are sixteen couriers on one flight and four or five get stopped, they are still in profit.

On the whole, the Albanians appear to use a more straight-forward method of smuggling into the UK – and that is to continue the 'concealment' or 'cover' operation from mainland ports by putting the drugs into UK-bound lorries or containers alongside or contained within legitimate products.

The amounts will be broken down, as with the swallowers and stuffers – you don't put all your drugs in one container.

During Klodjan Copja's court case it emerged that one of his couriers was observed by police as he made weekly trips to a lay-by in Maidstone, Kent, where he would meet a lorry carrying imported cocaine from the continent. They learned that Romanian drivers were recruited to drive loads to rendezvous points where drugs were transferred to smaller vehicles and driven to safe houses. These were often drivers from legitimate firms looking to supplement their income.

Tony Saggers says: 'I've seen lorry drivers being paid £20,000 for taking one consignment of drugs into the UK, when their annual wage is £30,000. This is where criminals will always have the upper hand on law enforcement, because they've got access to all the money: £20,000 is profit from one kilo of coke. If you have a hundred kilos in the back of a lorry and you write off one to pay for a driver, that's a good investment.'

Copja also had a network of couriers from crime gangs around London and the south-east who would collect the drugs from safe houses and supply them to organised crime groups in London, Birmingham, Leicester and Nottingham. On one occasion, police stopped a Renault from Copja's gang in Oxford. They spent hours examining it, unable to find the drugs even though they had watched them going into the car. Eventually they discovered a secret mechanism that caused the whole dashboard to flip open – behind it were several kilos of cocaine.

In total, the authorities seized 204 kilos of high-grade cocaine from Copja's gang, but estimate this was a fraction of his consignments over the years. Police never recovered the cash from Copja's multi-million-pound drug deals. Detectives know all the money went back to Albania, but there the trail went cold. Much of the cash was probably transported out in the same way the drugs came in, either in lorries or concealed in secret compartments in cars.

While the Albanian wholesaling operation is now highly sophisticated and established, there are differing views on how interested they are in the street-level sales. There's no doubt they have people involved in this. The Hellbanianz are the most infamous gang based in Barking, east London, and like any street drug gang these Albanians often show off their guns, cash and flash cars on social media. In one rap video the gang insisted they were 'ready for war' and over the years members have been jailed for selling drugs and concealing arms, including sub-machine guns.

In July 2019, an Albanian street gang of ten men were found guilty of peddling drugs in London's square mile. In the same month, the *Sun* reported that 'Albanians now make up the second highest total of foreign nationals in UK jails at 760, 433 of who are in for drug offences – just a handful behind Poland on 787 despite only tens of thousands living in the UK compared to almost a million Polish.' And that is perhaps the problem for this particular crime group: they don't have the manpower to dominate the street-level market.

Tony Saggers says: 'The Albanians are dominant in terms of importation and the wholesale side of market, but it's a bit of a free-for-all once it gets in because they are not particular about who they sell to, as long as they are prepared to pay the price.'

So, gangs controlling their county lines networks are not really threatened by the Albanians at the retail end, but whatever their ethnicity, they are now using them more and more as wholesalers. The crack in dealer Cody's pockets may well have come from Albanians. And people like Cody can be thankful to these enterprising criminals for bringing the price down. As Tony Saggers says: 'They are giving a good slice of their margins to the customer.'

The wholesale market has changed dramatically in a decade – and in doing so appears to have made the lower-end markets more profitable. That in itself may be attracting more players. Having spent years combatting the top-level suppliers, Tony is back to looking at the retail end of the market and helping police forces combat county lines dealers. He believes this new form of drug dealing only began in its current form in the last five or so years. While dealers have always travelled from urban cities into smaller towns to supply drugs, what makes county lines different is the business model, the people involved, and the way it has developed.

Tony says: 'The bigger fish have busted in on the small pools, but that is usually someone else's market. The London, Liverpool and Manchester gangs have found groups of people who are already addicts. Part of the county lines dynamic is to go into an existing market and take control of the supply that was previously in the hands of someone else – so there's an instant competition and potential for a feud. However, with the background and reputation of London and its emphasis on violence and exploitation and carrying knives, which is common to the point of being the norm, they are intimidating to a lot of local drug dealers. So, some of those dealers are now actually working for county lines as the only option to maintain a position in the supply chain.'

The export mentality of some London gangs is not too different to Copja's larger-scale wholesaling business. They have sought out markets, firstly around the M25 corridor, then further afield, but always trying to ensure they don't leave a personal footprint. They get others to do the running and the dealing – often children.

County lines is also a system that has evolved through conflict. Both drug-dealer Cody and anti-drug cop Tony Saggers agree on this point. The Metropolitan markets, London in particular, were becoming saturated. Urban street gangs were trying to control territories in which there were too many suppliers and not enough customers, so they were rubbing up against each other. Competition led to friction, which spurred violence, and now that is spilling out of the big cities into smaller towns.

To understand the evolution of county lines, we need to go to back to ground level and meet the street dealers in the heart of London – the postcode gangs. Back to Tottenham.

5.

THE POSTCODE GANG

'If they want someone hurt, we get it done.'

Rocco doesn't look like a gang leader. He has taken some persuading to agree to meet up, and as he walks into the Abbey Tavern in Kentish Town, I can see why. He's wearing a collared blue shirt and carrying a smart bag, having just knocked off from work. It turns out Rocco holds down a perfectly respectable job in the office of a construction site, whilst also controlling a gang of youths involved in criminal activity in the Tottenham/Wood Green area of north London.

Rocco is twenty-five years old and has been in his gang since the age of eleven – like Cody, he is now what is called an Elder, but, unlike Cody, Rocco is active within the gang. On first impressions, he smashes the stereotype of a gang leader – he is in employment, and he is fairly well spoken. Apart from having to slip away to sell drugs down an alley next to the pub, you'd never know.

There are at least 200 different gang-zones in London, many defined by postcodes. In the south of the city, the high density of activity is around Brixton, Camberwell and Peckham. In the north, the concentration is in Finsbury Park, Green Lanes, Wood Green and Tottenham. In the space of one square mile, a dozen gangs rub, not very pleasantly, alongside each other. Their names include: the Red Brick Thugs, the Grey Gang, Meridian Bloodline, Selby, NPK, P-Block, Wood Green Mob, TMD, Risley Avenue, Scotland Green, Reed Road, Chestnut Estate Black Gang, Saltram & High Cross, and Broadwater.

The gang Rocco is taking me to meet is one of the above, but I have been told not to directly identify them, as speaking to a journalist is sometimes considered snitching. After a conversation establishing the ground rules, Rocco and I drive north to the postcode where his gang operates. It was September 2018 when I met them, and there had already been over 100 murders in the capital that year – a third of them 16- to 24-year-olds, most thought to be linked to gangs. The youths I was about to meet were very much in this high-risk category. They'd been involved in an ongoing feud with a neighbouring crew, and earlier in the year a nineteen-year-old had been shot dead in what police said was an escalating 'postcode war' between the rivals.

As I'd already established from Cody, this growing friction over territory in London was in part the explanation for why county lines drug dealing was developing. London gangs have sought out softer markets in the provinces. These are towns where drugs are already being sold, so there is an established market, but it's been catered for by local small-time dealers who can easily be usurped by a bigger and more brutal operation. But to get a sense of this push factor on the London gangs, I wanted to meet some of the young people at the centre of the postcode wars. The gang populates a four-storey housing block in north London, which, if it weren't for taller blocks surrounding it, would have a good view down to the city.

When we arrived on the estate, a group of young lads came up to the car along with the obligatory pit-bull terrier snuffling the ground on the end of a heavy-duty chain and choker. These youngsters that Cody says are being exploited and brutalised by their elders didn't look that intimidating, partly because they were so young. But they definitely fitted the profile I was looking for: young, gang affiliated, from a rundown estate in north London. In a quiet corner, six of them, aged between fourteen and sixteen, agreed to talk to me about what was going on – and why they thought violence between them and others was on the rise.

'It's like a territory thing. It's all about the money, innit,' says a mixed-race boy with shaved sides and a curly flat-top. 'You'll see a lot of men do their thing, trying to get money out there. Do their shotting thing. But we step on each other's toes, you know what I mean. So, people are clubbing together.'

Next to flat-top is a white kid, and actually I'm struck that this is the first gang I've interviewed where the kids are a mixture of black and white. Of course, they all talk like they're in *Top Boy*, whatever the colour of their skin. The white kid says: 'I think that people are trying to show them. People are fighting for the territories, ganging up on each other, innit. Stabbing each other. But most of all, people are trying to make money. Shotting. Selling weed, class A, white and crack.'

Another kid, wearing a bandana, kicks in. 'As he said, it's about the money – nothing else. It's about money and territory.'

'So, that's all it is?' I ask. 'But why do you want a larger territory? Why can't everyone just stick to their own areas?'

At this point, gang elder Rocco steps in. 'There's not

enough bread for all of us to eat. You know? Imagine an area where there's about thirty shotters. How are we gonna get money, if thirty people are eating off the same amount of people? It doesn't make sense. So, it's a thing whereby some people have to get taken off the map. Do you see what I'm trying to say?'

'When you say, "taken off the map", are they scared off by stabbings? There's been quite a few killings recently in north London. Is it getting to that stage now in this area?'

'That's something I don't wanna talk about.'

'Okay. Fair enough.' I turn to a tall skinny kid. 'Do you feel safe? Do you feel safe in your own area?'

'I'm telling you, I was born here. I was raised here. If somebody touches me here, my whole gang is going to come to you. Your whole family's getting killed. If you touch me, I'm touching your whole family. If you touch my breddrin, and if you touch him, him, him [he points to the rest of the group], I'm coming after you. Yeah, your whole family, your whole area is getting burnt down for my breddrin. I'll kill you for them. You understand?'

I understand – but actually, I don't believe him. I don't reckon this sixteen-year-old kid would go on a killing rampage of an entire family. I do imagine, however, that he might get into some pointless tit-for-tat stabbing feud. I turn to the smallest in the group – a slightly chubby kid with ginger hair, who is fourteen years old. 'How about you?'

'I stay here,' he says. 'And if I go out, I keep myself tooled. It's like that. If I'm in my area around the block, I've got my shit. I got my stuff. [He means places where he can stash his weapon close by.] Obviously, I don't want to talk about that, but if I go off from my area, I keep it on my waist and nobody's touching me. If somebody does, they get done. It's like that.'

'How old were you when you first started carrying a weapon?'

'Eleven. When I carried the weapon, I… I felt safe. I went to a different area when I had the weapon on me, and I was like, yeah, nobody is touching me now. And then when I stay around here, I'm clean. But yeah, when I go somewhere, either way I keep it next to me, so nobody can touch me.'

'Was there an incident?' I ask. 'Was there something that happened that made you think, right, I'm gonna have to start carrying?'

'It happened one time when I walked to another area. I saw a lot of people and I was like, no, I should have it on me. And next time I walk through, they didn't do nothin'. They saw me. They asked me where I'm from.'

'Did they know you had a knife?'

'They knew. I showed them. I showed them what I got. And they knew they had to back off – but they wouldn't do anything to me. They knew from that day.'

One of the gang then tells me that he didn't carry a knife, but only because he never left the area. 'I feel safer. It's a way of surviving, I guess. I don't feel safe if I leave the area. If someone wants to, like, meet up, then I say, "Yeah, come, but I'm not leaving this area."'

Again, Rocco, the gang elder, chips in: 'I'd say it's like a close-knit family. Everybody knows each other from way back. So, obviously, all our families live here. So, if I have people coming from wherever trying to set territory around … you know what I'm trying to say? We need to make sure that everything is alright. It's not just about the drug war and *rat-ta-ta*. We might get in trouble and people might get involved and our families might be involved. So, we gotta make sure everything's all right for our people.'

'So, if you got stabbed tomorrow, how many people would be after that person?'

'How many people? Untold amounts, untold amounts.'

'Would you describe yourselves as a gang?'

'It depends what you would describe as a gang. That's just a definition. It's a group of people who are looking out for each other. A group of old people could be a gang. A family could be a gang. Brothers and sisters could be a gang.'

'But you are all from different families.'

'Yeah, yeah, but we've all grown up together. We all know where we've come from. We're trying to just get further in life. So, whatever that means, that we have to do. We do what we have to do.'

I don't point out that Rocco has a job, and that he can't possibly argue that he's doing this out of necessity. He doesn't even live in this area any more, and it seems to me his only attachment to the estate is to maintain his control over these young people. I'm assuming they have ambitions of their own. I ask one of the younger ones what he wants to do in later life – and drug dealer isn't it.

'I plan to do engineering and stuff. I'm selling drugs and stuff now. But people are dying out here over nothing. I'm trying to turn my life around. I'm not trying to ruin it. I don't know if I can. I can die anytime, innit.'

It is this fear that means this would-be engineer carries a knife. 'If I go somewhere else, then if I don't have my tool on me, obviously, something is going to happen to me. Obviously, I'm still trying to change my life and stuff, innit.'

'So, if you want to be an engineer, are you going to college? Where are you up to with that?'

'Yeah, that's what I'm talking about. I'm trying to go college.'

'Are you trying to get the money together to do that?'

'Yeah, I'm trying to get it in a legal way, innit. I'm not trying to do it an illegal way. It's a waste, people are dying over nothing. Stabbing each other just for the money and stuff.'

'When you say, "just for the money", and everyone keeps saying, "it's just for the money", what do you mean exactly? If you're stabbing someone, where do you get the money from?'

Everyone chuckles, but I think it's a fair question. I'm not sure they have an answer. It's quite clear these stabbings are not robberies. So how exactly do they benefit financially? Territory? Really? Cody seemed to suggest that a lot of the violence is over trivial stuff – just feuding and 'Mad Max'-inspired senseless anger, and maybe these kids are inaccurately monetising their actions. There is a calm casualness in the way they talk about violence. They have that teenage advantage of knowing that the only person who really matters in the world is them – everyone else is a cardboard cut-out. I continue to press.

'Are you saying, "Right, I'm going to take over that person's territory and their clients"? Otherwise, where are you going to get the money from if you stab someone?'

Once again it's Rocco who has the answer: 'To be honest, I've got people that will call me and say they want someone hurt. So if they want someone hurt, they make a phone call and we get it done. You know what I'm trying to say. Certain people don't want to say it, yeah, but these things do happen and I'm not afraid to put it out there, that that's the life I live. I don't give a fuck.'

'What? Somebody you don't even know yourself, but your mate has told you to get them?'

'Even better,' says Rocco 'because they don't know who I am. So, if I hit them up nothing is going to come back to me. Simple.'

Cardboard cut-outs; people don't matter. They don't have grieving mothers and brothers and sisters, and lives they could have led, cut short because someone made a phone call and Rocco doesn't give a fuck?

'So, let me get this right,' I ask. 'You actively try and find someone who's not associated with that person, so there's no comeback – and they don't see you coming?'

'I don't care if I know them or if I don't know them. They can get it either way.'

'So, how many people are there that you would do that for?'

'I don't want to speak about that.'

'No, just numbers. I'm not asking for names.'

'I've got my little people that I'll do that for.'

'Is there hierarchy? Are there young kids who do certain things and older kids who do other stuff?'

'I'd say so, yeah,' says Rocco. 'I guess we'll all go through things in our lives – as an older and as a younger. I mean, we've all gone through things. You wouldn't expect a "big man" to go out and do certain things for money, whereas the youngers they're more … hungry. I mean, they got things like my man [he points to the would-be engineer] that he wants to strive towards. To try and get. So, I'm not looking at whether he wants to go legal or he wants to do the wrong thing. Whatever your angle is, whatever your point is, wherever you're trying to get to, we will get there regardless.'

Rocco is now styling himself a career facilitator – here to help these young men get to where they want to go. The starting point, I'm guessing, is that they sell drugs for him. These kids clearly don't have a decent role model telling them that there are other ways to strive to better themselves, so Rocco is manipulating their hopes and dreams for his own purpose

– his own little side industry as a financial top-up for his PAYE job. Cody was right: this is 'devilish'.

'So, I'm just trying to get an idea of how the hierarchy works.' I ask, 'What age would you come into the system?'

'I come into this thing from the age of ten,' says Rocco.

'What were you doing?'

'Deception, just fooling people, trickery, just mucking around – a lot of robberies, street robberies, low-level stuff.'

'And then as you get older?'

'Obviously, you know not everybody's on the same stuff. Eventually we'll see who's who, and who's on what. And they get passed through to go to different missions. It really is like a mission, and when you accomplish that mission there are rewards.'

'Are these missions getting more violent? Kids today seem to be getting more violent.'

Flat-top interjects. 'The elders are a bit more chilled. You see me, I'm a young man. That's my older. He tells me what to do, innit. I keep him chilled. I tell him, "Relax, I'll deal with it." Let him sit down and enjoy it. I'll go do it. I'll get my bread up. He'll give me money. I've got my bread off of him. Right?'

'So, you kind of work for him?'

'Yeah.'

'Like a little business?'

Rocco replies, 'It's a business. I call it entrepreneurial. I don't like to feel like I'm a boss. I wouldn't say I'm a boss. I like to look at these like my little brothers and I look after them to make sure they're good. But at the same time, if other people try to step on their toes, they know that their man has got them.'

I turn to the chubby ginger boy. Is he part of the business? Is it dangerous?

He says: 'Right, I'm not going to speak about what happened to me, but I know that I didn't want this but I had to do it. Because if I didn't do it I would die in a couple of days. I don't want that for my family and I don't want that to happen. I want my family to be safe.'

'What do you mean, you would have died in a couple of days? Can you elaborate a little bit?'

Rocco interrupts: 'Please, please. He doesn't wanna talk about it.'

Of all the moments with this gang, I found this the most chilling. What was it this kid felt he had to do to stay alive? Why wouldn't Rocco let him explain? There has been much in the media about gang initiations, where kids are asked to carry out a stabbing to earn their stripes. I wondered whether this was the case with Ginger. Whatever it was, he didn't want to do it but felt he had to.

When I later spoke to former Head of Drugs Threat at the National Crime Agency, Tony Saggers about these 'missions', he explained how gang leaders manipulated the children to feel like everything was being done for them. 'The gangs say, "We're giving young people an opportunity." What's actually happening is young people are providing an opportunity to drug dealers. That's the reality of it.'

In the first instance, the youngsters might just remain within a property on the estate, and not be sent anywhere, but the 'mission' could be to sit all day long bagging up small wraps of heroin and crack cocaine. That's where the phrase 'trap house' comes from: the workers and the drug-takers can become bonded into it. They may even get paid in drugs, and work then pays for their addiction, providing cheap labour for the dealer. After that, missions could extend into small tasks across town, such as drug deliveries, or holding onto something for somebody, like drugs, money or weapons. That could soon escalate, once they're trusted and seen to be efficient and reliable, to bigger, more dangerous tasks. They could be sent to do drug deals, or even, as Rocco suggests, stabbings for people higher up the chain – and if it's a county lines operation, they may end up on long journeys, sometimes for days at a time, sometimes for weeks, heading off by train, bus or dropped off in convoys or by taxis to other towns. And on some 'missions' they might be confined to a property far away from home and they'll just sit in that house all day, anonymously dealing drugs; not going on the street and not being seen by the police. Or they may graduate to street selling within a new market, or fighting for turf.

'I think they can expect to be around knives as the norm,' says Tony. 'You know, there's a big issue around "I carried a knife because he was carrying a knife." And I think it's very difficult for a fourteen- or fifteen-year-old around eighteen-, nineteen-, twenty-year-olds, who have all got knives, not to feel the need to possess one themself. Also, addictive drug use involves syringes, if it's heroin. It's not unusual for these young people to be found in houses where there is dangerous waste from drug use, like syringes. It very quickly spirals from a so-called 'opportunity' and something that seems exciting, to a life of exploitation. And they're being worked hard in a rough, dangerous environment and being paid less money than they thought they would get, while being exposed to high risk.'

Rocco was puppet-master in this gang. However, despite the increased pressure on his territory, it seems he hadn't yet made the leap towards a county lines operation. He still thinks the good money is in London. 'We go to architects, people that do doctoring, that take drugs. Because I think personally they do their nine to five, they work Monday to Friday, and they're glad to have a little release.'

'Do you think, though, that those people who are taking those drugs have any idea what's going on?' I ask.

'I don't really care, but obviously somebody's got to do it.'

'Yeah. But does it bother you?

'No, not at all.'

'Do you feel like there's one rule for them [the drug-takers] and one for you? You know if you get caught, you go to prison. That's not going to happen to them.'

'They're not going to go to prison, but they may have to go to rehab.'

Rocco has an answer for everything. He's smart and quick thinking. If he turned his mind to it, maybe he could be part of the solution rather than part of the problem, although there's not much of a living in that. Still, I'm interested in what he thinks could change things.

'Do you think gang crime would be reduced if there were more police on the streets?'

'I don't want more police.'

'I'm sure you don't but, if there *were* more police, would that make you think twice?

'My experience is the police come around and harass people that are trying to just better their life. From my experience, I was just trying to do my thing – make life better for my people and me. And they were coming around, stop-and-searching. A few years back, stop and search was predominant. Yeah, you know what I'm trying to say. They were really onto us for no reason. People would call up saying, "These guys are selling drugs."'

'I wonder, if you were able to sit down with the prime minister for few minutes and say, "I want to explain to you why I'm involved in this life", what would you say?'

'I'd tell the prime minister this: I didn't choose this life. This life chose me. You know what I'm trying to say? I didn't know. I didn't know what was involved in this life. What exactly was involved. But I grew to know it, and grew to end up loving it, because when that's all you know, that's all you know. I didn't know anything better. So, if they could come with something, some sort of opportunity, I would push the youths towards it. But they've got nothing to do. What they gonna do, sit on the streets, wasting their life? They try to go to college and they get kicked out. There's no other opportunities from there. So, what are they supposed to do? I mean, they got to think of a means to survive. So, I'd tell the prime minister to put some money into the youth. We've never had no youth club.'

'Would that help?'

'Yeah, it would help – it would take their minds off the rubbish. Nobody wants to do this, but we have to do this in order to survive. What you gonna do, just beg for money?'

'But there have been people living in poverty on rough estates for decades,' I say. 'Why now are we seeing an increase in knife violence?'

'That one's a bit of a mystery to me. It's a bit of a mystery because I don't think it's so much about the money [contradicting what everyone else has just said]. I think that, as the generations go, with the youth now it is more of an image thing.'

'An image thing?' I ask. 'You know, when politicians look for what's causing knife crime, they sometimes say it's things like drill music, rap music.'

'I would say it's not about the music. The music is the life they're seeing – what they are living and what they see is what they're talking and singing about. If they were seeing other things, going into work ... but they're not seeing that – there's no opportunity. What can they do? There's nowhere else for them to go. If they get more jobs for the youngest, then maybe they'll stop doing stuff like selling drugs, and they'll make money in a legal way, so the knife crime will stop or go down. I could try to get a job for a little younger, so he can make the money in a legal way instead of selling drugs and risking their lives, but it's a dog-eat-dog world. It's evil – that's how we survive.'

Except, of course, he has a job. He could survive perfectly well if he turned his back on gang life. I wonder if his gang members would be safer too – if Rocco left them to it. It feels to me like Rocco is the personification of what Cody was complaining about – elders not looking after the youth but instead putting them at risk. But Rocco is at least keeping his gang within their territory, and you could argue they have a sense of brotherhood. They are not involved in county lines dealing, and that, as we shall discover, is a whole different ball game. Indeed, Rocco is practically saint-like in comparison to the man I'm going to meet next.

I say goodbye to the gang and we leave things on good terms. For all his faults, I actually found Rocco disarmingly good company and open about his life. I think he'd warmed to me, too. 'Next time I'll bring my machete to show you,' he says, as a parting goodbye.

But it won't be long before someone else is showing me a knife – in a less charming fashion. After much negotiation, my fixer has got me access to a crack house, which is at the centre of a county lines operation from north London.

6.

UNCLE'S CRACK HOUSE

'You step on my toes, you're fucked.'

Uncle picks up a small white cube and hands it to a man in his mid-forties in return for £10. The purchase looks like a miniature sugar lump wrapped in toilet paper, and it's the first time I have ever seen crack cocaine. It seems absurd somehow that this is what it's all about – a small granular lump that you set fire to and absorb the fumes of; a multi-million-pound business that has never brought any of its customers any good.

We have arrived in the crack house in north London. I take in the room. Quite normal. Bedroom, kitchenette, living space all in one. In the bedsit are two drug dealers, one Turkish the other Somali (who refers to himself as Uncle), both in their mid-thirties, and one addict, white, in his mid-forties, his face ravaged by a twenty-year habit. There's a roll of money on the table, probably for show, and a large Rambo knife in a sheath, hopefully for show.

I'm with Sky News cameraman Hedley Trigge and with

us, too, is the person who will help smooth the cracks in this unnatural situation – my fixer. She knows one of the dealers and has arranged the interview. Just to be clear, no money exchanged hands. My fixer is someone totally trusted in this world and this meeting has come though long negotiations based on trust and agreement. Part of that negotiation is a guarantee to protect the identity of the dealers. Of course, things can go wrong at any moment, and we have a safety phrase if anyone feels uncomfortable. The phrase is 'Matt Barbet', the name of a rather handsome, former Channel 5 news presenter. If anyone says that, we just walk out. That plan is scuppered, though, when one of the dealers locks the door behind us. They have immediately taken control of the situation.

We are here to talk about a county lines operation that these two men are running from north London to smaller towns and cities. They have agreed to explain how it works, and I don't blame them for being cautious. I'm guessing they won't let us out with our footage without a lot of reassurance. The addict starts to load up a small metal tube with his purchase, while the dealers put black masks over their faces, so we can film and talk openly.

After pleasantries, we start rolling the camera. I decide to go straight in and interview the client, who is happy to be identified. He is called Mark, aged forty-two and he lives in this flat. As we mentioned earlier, drug addicts can sometimes get their homes taken over by dealers 'cuckooing' them, something I'll explore in more detail later. It's hard to tell whether Mark is in this situation, but he is clearly highly dependent on getting his fix. He takes out a lighter and burns the crack. It is rested on the top of the wire tube, which is about an inch long. He then takes a long draw at the other end and smoke pours dragon-like from his nostrils in two long plumes.

'Yeah, that's nice,' he says.

'How often do you do it?' I ask.

'Three times a week maybe. I spend about £100 a week.'

'How does that make you feel?'

'High.'

Stupid question. His eyes are turning to black discs as his pupils dilate. It's almost hypnotic, watching him go under. A film of sweat covers his brow and I'm drawn to the thick bags under his red-rimmed eyes in a saggy face that seems too loose for his skull.

'How long have you been doing it for?'

'Twenty years. After I've smoked … I can't talk.'

I realise I've started this interview a few minutes too late, but despite his stuttering, Mark seems up for further conversation. He continues: 'I started smoking it with friends… I started smoking it… I took LSD, Es, and then I started on crack and heroin.'

'Has it got cheaper?'

'The crack isn't the same, I can't talk … it isn't the same as what it was, it's got weaker.'

I'm feeling bad. He's paid good money for this. 'Am I ruining the experience for you?'

'No… it's okay.'

'Do you wish you could give it up?'

'No. I like it. I'm not on it all the time. Yes, I like it. Yes, it's nice.

It's not surprising Mark doesn't want to give it up. Crack cocaine is one of the most addictive drugs you can take. It is made by heating up normal powder cocaine, often using a microwave and cutting agents (usually anaesthetics). Although all cocaine is imported, all of this much more deadly and addictive crack cocaine is produced from the raw material here in the UK.

'Should it be legal?' I ask.

'No … yes. It would be nice if it was.'

'What's been the impact on your life?'

'Money. The cost. Once I start smoking, I can't stop … until the money's gone.' He nods at this. I can see some regret. Mark is unemployed and single. This is his life. He'd be happy with it, but for the dent in his wallet.

'So, all your spare money goes towards it?'

'Yeah. Yeah, all of it.'

The dealers sit silently in their masks. They look like faceless *Doctor Who* monsters. The Somali sits in a chair with his money and drugs on an adjacent table. He's wearing a tight black stocking that flattens all his features. The Turkish guy sits on the bed next to the addict. He has weird black goggle-eyes on his mask, like a giant ant-face.

'How does the metal tube thing work?'

'This is m-m-m-my metal tube,' says Mark. He holds it up. 'It used to be a Martell brandy bottle, but they stopped selling them. They changed the bottles, so now there's other ways of smoking. I use that.' I check this later, and it turns out Martell bottles were indeed used by crack addicts until they changed the shape.

Next to Mark is a filthy rag and a pack of rolling tobacco, but everything in this flat is fairly normal for a forty-two-year-old man living on the breadline. I've been in worse-kept homes. The dealer's phone rings: 'Hello… hello… lost him.' I realise it's time to talk to the key players here.

'So, what can people buy from you?' I ask the Somali with the stockinged, featureless face.

'We sell everything. It's like a pharmacy. You can get crack, you can get coke, you can get weed. You can get anything you want. As long as there is demand there will always be a supply.' He is flipping through his roll of fifties and twenties.

'And is there a good demand?'

'Yes always. Anywhere, everywhere.'

'How does it work?'

'For instance, crack – you buy a fat rock. You break that rock down into smaller pieces. Those smaller pieces go at a higher price than the whole.' He holds up another miniature sugar cube. 'You sell this one for a tenner. The more you buy in bulk, the cheaper it gets. That's how you make your money.'

He lets me handle the crack and embarrassingly it starts to break up in my fingertips, so I try to coax it back into the wrap before replacing it on the table. Then he begins to explain his county lines operation.

'I sell in the area here, but most of it is sold outside of London. Me and my buddy over there – we will go somewhere, find a crackhead, give them some crack, get them to give us some numbers. You get a whole page of numbers for some crack. Then you'll have a new line in no time. So, I'll give them some rocks for their numbers – for users, for their friends.'

'Then what?'

'Once the area is established, and I know I'm making a nice amount, I'll go out. I'll leave the area and I'll get kids to go out there for me. I pay them three or four hundred pounds a week.'

'What age?'

'Younger the better – twelve to fifteen, sixteen.'

'How do you find them?'

'It's good money for them. They have no money and it's the holidays, and they will come to Uncle I_____ [at this point he says his real name.]'

'You might not want me to use that name,' I tell him.

'Oh yeah – cut that out.' The dealer puts his head in his hands. 'Don't use that.' This is awkward but hopefully I've earned some trust by pointing it out. He shifts the giant knife on his desk. I notice, next to the blade, he has a porcelain ashtray and matching miniature pipe, which I assume is another method for consuming crack. I'd rather he wasn't playing with the knife. A friend once told me a trick for getting people to put weapons away, especially guns – which he used quite a lot in the Middle East when travelling with gunmen. He used to tell them, 'My brother was shot and killed by a gun that misfired so, if you don't mind, I'd rather you put that away.' It's quite clever, because it's both polite and a compelling personal reason for being nervous. At this stage, I just decide to move on.

'Let's go back to the last question. How do you find these kids?'

'It's the holidays. They need some money. Mummy ain't got no money. So they come to Uncle (this time not his name, just *Uncle*). Uncle will send them out there and let them have a week or two in boot camp. See what money they get.'

'What is boot camp?'

'Outside of London. Train them up. I will go with them once. Show them how it works. Once they get the hang of it, let them be.'

So, like Rocco, Uncle has kids doing his dirty work. But this isn't dabbling in the local drug market to supplement a wage packet – this is a much bigger criminal enterprise. I'm looking at a modern-day Fagin. Rather than 'pick a pocket or two', his underlings are selling his drugs in out-of-town marketplaces. He's admitting to exploiting a team of children. It's something that has become recognised as exploitation under the modern slavery act, and it's a new method the police are using to prosecute the people like Uncle who are further up the chain.

'Do they go to people's houses? Are they selling on the streets? Where do they go?'

'Everywhere. You'll find us in clubs. We sell to everyone. School teachers, people who work in nurseries, anyone and everyone.'

'How far do you travel?'

'A couple of hundred miles.'

At this point, the guy in the goggle-mask decides it's his turn to speak. He cuts in: 'Anything that's one or two hours away, places like Reading. In Reading, there's a bunch of crackheads who all take it. You get one, two – then you get five [clients]. Get some more people to try it. They take it once or twice – then they don't want to stop.'

'You are building a community of addicts?'

'Yeah. Of course.'

'In how many places?'

'We are currently dealing with two or three areas.'

So far, everything chimes with what police and other experts have told me about the operation. These people are, for the most part, trying to tap into existing markets that may in the past have been run by local dealers. Tony Saggers puts it like this: 'County lines has become the expansion of London in all respects – in terms of the violence, the knife crime, the young people involved.'

In London there is high demand, enough to keep Rocco and his gang going, but they are getting frustrated, confined to their small surface area within their borough, and because of the postcode element of it, if they deal drugs somewhere else, it creates agitation, violence and potentially killings. Travel out of London, as Uncle has, and there's a whole new opportunity but also a problem, because you need to expand your workforce. You're expanding the geography of your operation, so you need more people involved. It's not like a London borough, which you can dominate with half a dozen people. If you're ambitious, you could soon be covering six counties and a dozen towns, and so you need to recruit more and more young people. And they have to be coaxed, coerced and eventually kept in check through fear.

Detective Saggers says: 'I think the first thing to recognise with county lines is it is opportunist. What I mean is that the networks exist. People know each other through prison, through young offender institutions, through families and just through general social media interactions. So, quite often knowledge that a town has a marketplace pre-exists before you even visit it, but there's a bit of a scouting exercise certainly in the early days of county lines, where a couple of members of the gang would be sent out to that town. They would spend a few days there assessing the scale of the demand. People know where the unemployed will be; people that have sort of fallen out of society. It's not difficult in most towns to find stereotypically where the drug users congregate.

This sort of assessment will be done quite quickly, he says, adding, 'The reputation of county lines is to supply good quality deals at the right quantity. An opportunity for a county line would be where people are complaining about the quality of their crack and heroin. A county line will remedy that through the efficiency and the volume of supply, and they establish the market on that basis. They go out, they scout, they establish, they go back and they start supplying.'

Part of the county lines dynamic is to go into an existing market, rather than rally a new one, and take control of a supply that was previously in the hands of someone else. This is exactly what Uncle is doing. But that means there is instant competition and potential for a feud.

Tim Champion, the silver commander at the National County Lines Coordination Centre – a Home Office-funded unit set up in 2018 with a £3.6 million investment to tackle organised gangs – told me: 'If it was a business environment, you would call it a hostile takeover. In the world of finance it's done through buying shares in a company – in the criminal world they use what is available to them and that is violence. But it's all about money and profit – for the dealers and the children who are coerced into it. If you have no qualifications and an opportunity arises for you to bring money back into a home, then you take it.'

With the background and reputation of London gangs – their emphasis on violence and exploitation and carrying knives – they are highly intimidating to the local drug dealers, and some of them may decide to work for the new boss as their only option to maintain a position in the supply chain. But what happens when those dealers push back, or a different group from London wants to get in on the action? In the crack house, I put this to goggle-face, and my question brings the inevitable machismo response.

'There's always problems with other dealers,' he says.

'And what happens?'

'You've got to sort out your problem. You give it to the kids to sort. You go up there, give them a little weapon and they will do it. Get them happy. Tell them you'll give them extra money. They'll go and do it and the job's done.'

'So, what do they do?'

'They'll hurt the other person, yeah.'

'What, a warning stabbing, something like that?

'Yeah, of course. If it gets deeper than that, then what happens happens.'

'Guns as well?'

'Yeah, of course.'

'And how big a problem is that for you and your business? What is the impact?'

'Once you've sorted one or two problems, then that's that. They tend not to come to you again. And if they do, you do what you have to do—'

At this point Uncle interjects. But now he is standing up. Now he is coming from behind me and he is holding the knife.

'Let me take this…'

'Yeah, sure.'

'Anyone can get it, yeah. Anyone can get it.' He walks past me, knife in hand, and we are facing each other. His featureless mask is moving slightly where the mouth isn't. 'It doesn't matter who you are. If you come and violate and step on my toes and you're fucking up our business, you'll get shanked up, you will get shot, you'll get shot in your face, you'll get stabbed in the neck.'

Could be time to say something like *Matt Barbet*. Nobody does. He's tapping the knife against the palm of his hand. I imagine how terrified of him I would be if I was one of his runners.

He carries on: 'It doesn't matter who you are. If you're a little boy or if you are a grown man – anyone can get it. You step on my toes, you're fucked. You are signing a contract to an early grave. It's that simple. It's that simple.'

He is buzzing around the small room like a wasp trapped in a jar, seething under the gauze of his face mask. The mere suggestion of a threat to his business has rankled him. It's time for me to bring things down a bit.

'You don't have any worries that that is going to happen to *you*?' My mouth is dry. Tongue sticking to the top of my throat. It's an Oprah Winfrey-style question – I'm putting myself on his side and deflecting the mirror back at him. 'Has it happened to you?'

'A few times. Nearly.' He sits down. I prefer him in the chair. 'I've avoided death so many times.' This consideration for his own peril has released the softening I was going for, but only for a moment. After he's given it some consideration he reverts to type. 'The day it happens, if I don't die, if they are coming to get me, they had better kill me. If they don't kill me, I'm coming back to kill them. That's how it works.'

'That's how it works, isn't it?' I'm in full Oprah-mode now. Just repeating what he's saying. I can hear myself doing it. I'm agreeing with him because, effectively, he has threatened me with a knife and that's not what usually happens in interviews.

'It's normal,' he says.

'Is it getting more violent?' I ask.

'Yeah, of course,' says Uncle.

'Why?'

'Because more people want money. If they want money, where do they go? There's a lot of people coming out of jail. Where are they going to go to get money? People can't survive living off their nine-to-five all their life.'

People do. Lots of people do. Most people do that. But I'm letting him off the hook this time.

'This is reality for some people. This is my reality. Seeing people die – seeing people get shot, seeing people get stabbed. Seeing pregnant women smoke crack. This is my reality. This is normal. It is just normal to me. It don't affect me. It's nothing.

'You guys might think, yeah…' and for a moment he catches himself. This is getting to him. It's actually getting to him. I can't see behind the mask, but, just for a second, I think he might be upset with the world he has just described. As if maybe all the misery and pain he's witnessed doesn't just bounce off him in the way he says it does.

'Hey, don't worry, I understand,' I say, to the kid-exploiting drug dealer. 'It's a tough life, right?'

'Yeah,' he sighs. 'What's the word?' I don't know the word. 'It's a hard-knock life – that's what it is.' He is quoting *Annie* – the faceless drug dealer who threatened me with a knife a minute ago is now quoting a kid's musical.

I carry on. 'Do you feel like you're on edge the whole time?'

'On edge, no, I wouldn't call it being on edge. I'd call it being alert. You've got to be alert. It's the jungle.'

'And… [I may as well acknowledge it now we've connected] you've got a knife right there?'

'This?' As if he's only just noticed it. He unsheathes the 12-inch blade and holds it to his face. 'This is nothing, man. This is what I give to the people, the little kids who go out for me. This is a *little Rambo*.'

I ask if he has it ready because someone might come in and cause problems.

'Yeah. I mean, me, I don't start problems. But if people start problems with me, that knife there will go right inside their throat. And that's a fact.'

'And have you had to do that?'

'I've had to.'

Ant-face decides it's his turn again.

'Sure.'

But I'm still focused on faceless man. 'Do you have any regrets about going into this kind of business?'

'Regrets? Nope. No regrets.'

'Then what needs to happen?'

'To stop this from happening – to stop this from rising?'

I nod.

'The best way, in my opinion, is to target the little kids while they are young. When they are young their minds are vulnerable and they can be corrupted. There are no youth centres. There is nothing for them to do. What can they do? Kids have got nothing to do nowadays. And this is what we do. There needs to be more jobs and more everything. It's micro-business.'

This leads me to ask whether he is in a gang. It hadn't occurred to me until this point to ask.

'All this gang shit, it's bullshit. There is no gang – it's just a group of friends. There's no such thing as gangs.'

Ant-face adds: 'It's poor kids from the block. They go out and do what they have to do to survive.'

'That's all it is,' agrees Uncle. 'It all starts from poverty. You know. The police, they will never stop this. They need things like this to happen. If there was nobody to arrest, who is going to pay them? There would be no need for police. Shit like this is always going to go on. You are always going to have violence and drug dealing and shootings. It will always be there. Always.'

He's probably right. But it's one thing it always being there – another if it's getting worse. Those studying this phenomenon say it's not just the perennial problem of drug dealing: things have evolved – in a bad way. As Tony Saggers puts it: 'Drug dealing used to be a team effort and now I don't think it's a team effort in the same way. I think it's about having lots of people at your disposal. And to run them ruthlessly and efficiently. And I think when you've got those people around you, in the confines of a London borough, they're far easier to control and find and potentially punish. What county lines has done is put these young people out on their own, conducting tasks for these very ruthless people that are staying in the crack houses back in London organising all of this. And those organisers have to make the kids fearful, fearful of breaking the rules and being less efficient. So, there's a lot of pressure. It's high, high-pressure sales.

'And because you are sending people further away, the ruthlessness and the threats and the potential for violence is greater, because it's all about maintaining that control. It's about making sure your young person goes out with the drugs, sells them quickly and gets a lot of money back to you in the central hub.'

Uncle keeps himself at arm's length from the coalface. And that makes him harder to implicate. In the next chapter, we will see what it takes for the police to catch someone like Uncle. It's time to leave him and the Turk. As we are packing up to leave, Mark, the addict, makes a noise. I'd forgotten he was there. He is standing at the kitchenette now, which has no food on the worktop, just an ashtray full of fag ends, some small scissors and a battery. He is working a screwdriver to clean out his metal pipe. Then he pushes in some wire wool, presumably to act as some kind of filter. This done, he cranks back his head so the pipe is vertical in his mouth. He balances another lump of crack on the top and lights up. Just as he'd said earlier, he won't stop now till the money's gone.

7.

THE CASTRO LINE

'My mission was to dismantle the Castro line.'

Zakaria Mohammed saw the blue lights in his wing mirror as he pulled off the M6. The good news was he didn't have any drugs in the car and nor was he ferrying kids. But still, as he pulled over, the twenty-year-old drug dealer couldn't be sure there wasn't something. Why were they stopping him? He wasn't speeding. The police officers asked him to step out of the vehicle and then came the questions: 'Where's your driver's licence, sir? Where is the car registered? Do you realise this car is uninsured?' Most people would be worried about this sort of encounter, but for Mohammed it was just a relief – this was nothing but a routine stop by traffic officers. His car wasn't insured. They must have done a number-plate check. He was in a bit of trouble, sure, but the inconvenience of having his car impounded was nothing compared to what they'd have done if they'd known what he was using it for. However, what Mohammed didn't realise was that this was what police call 'a bit of theatre'. His car wasn't going to the pound – it was going to forensics.

Operation Arkle began in January 2018, when two drug users in Lincoln got more than they bargained for. They'd bought some smack off a couple of kids and then decided to steal their money back, along with a few extra wraps. These new dealers in town looked like they were barely out of primary school. They were scrawny and undernourished – easy to overpower. But things didn't quite work out as the addicts planned. The kids had weapons. They retaliated in a flash. An hour later, the two users were in hospital with serious stab wounds and major blood loss.

Police assigned to investigate the stabbings couldn't get anything out of the addicts. The wounds were close to being fatal, but the victims refused to give up information about who had stabbed them. Further investigations indicated that there had been a number of new young drug dealers in town and, what's more, the drugs they were selling were associated with a phone line. This line had a constantly changing number. Drug users would get texts every time it changed, but the 'brand' of the line would stay the same. In other words, callers knew it had a reputation for a certain level of quality, and it had rapidly become the first point of call for at least 100 addicts in Lincoln. It was called the Castro line.

The Castro line began as a mystery, but it would end in a landmark case that would change the way the law regarded young people caught up in county lines. This was the first time Lincoln police had come across a county line in their town. When considering places with drug problems, Lincoln isn't the first place that springs to mind. The city in the West Midlands has a population just below 100,000 and is known for its historic buildings, including Lincoln Cathedral, a piece of gothic magnificence that towers over the city. Built in 1072, it was the tallest building in the world for over 200 years. If that's not enough, there's also the eleventh-century Norman castle, which holds one of the last four remaining copies of the Magna Carta. So, Lincoln attracts tourists from around the world, but, like any other English town, it also has a drug problem. And in 2018 police were becoming increasingly concerned that the Castro line was about to make things a lot worse.

For example, a county lines number could be part of a larger business enterprise working in several towns, meaning a big player was moving in on their market. That could have all sorts of ramifications. It was likely that dedicated 'phone builders' had already been deployed to build up contacts of addicts in the area, giving out the number and free drug tasters. This could lead to a worsening of Lincoln's drug habit – it could create more committed users and new addicts. The addicts could become indebted to brutal but more remote gang-masters. This would create more drug-related crime and it could bring an increase of gang activity to the city. And all of this might be orchestrated by people outside of Lincoln; the person running Castro was no local dealer, and their route in, nothing more than a phone number.

'County lines is all about the phone,' says Tim Champion at the National County Lines Coordination Centre. 'We used to have overt markets. The drug users would congregate around a telephone box. When the car pulls up, the police can be waiting. The person inside the car is arrested. But now you can contact your users by mobile phone and they can come to meet your dealers. You are running the market; the market isn't running you. So, it goes underground. Therefore, you need more police resources to deal with it.

'And the whole point is that you have a brand. Branding is important. And, just like a supermarket brand, they will loss lead. They might cut prices to outprice the competition. They want you to know they are there and offering deals. Two for one this weekend, for example, just like a supermarket. The whole thing is about building up the address book.

'Part of this is like anything where the retail model has flipped from the high street to online delivery. It's come from simple advances in technology, bulk-texting for example, that makes things so much easier for the dealer.'

Each line could be worth thousands of pounds once established – and that means dangerous, organised criminals were taking a stake in Lincoln, feeding on the local drug market. That would generally lead to more crime and violence, as evidenced by the recent stabbings of the addicts. So there was a lot to be concerned about. Lincoln police needed all the information they could get to stop this developing.

Officers never reveal where they get their intelligence from, it could be a mouthy drug user or a local prostitute, but someone from that community directed investigators to a property that appeared to be housing some of these new arrivals who were dealing the drugs. In the dawn raid on the flat in late January 2018 they discovered two fifteen-year-old boys. Both, they would later learn, had been reported missing from their homes in Birmingham, ninety miles away. One had been gone for a week, the other three weeks. The children were dirty and unkempt, as was the flat. Searching the property, police also found a large bloodstained knife wrapped in a plastic bag, a bundle of cash and two other hunting-style knives. There were no drugs but officers were quite sure the place was being used as a supply base for local addicts.

Lincoln police got in contact with West Midlands head office based in Birmingham and they set up Operation Arkle, its objective to close down and arrest those responsible for the Castro line. But they weren't getting any help from the children they'd found at the flat. Both refused to say a single word in police interviews. Without help from the wounded addicts, it would be impossible to get to the bottom of whether these two were responsible for the stabbings. They were passed on to children's services and eventually returned to their families.

And herein lies the problem with investigating county lines – often this is where the investigation comes to a crashing end. There may be a metropolitan street gang, or an international cartel running the drug supply, but the furthest you will ever get up the chain is questioning young boys and girls at the very bottom of it, who have been coerced into the business. It's one reason why it has become such a successful model for the dealers. For the police, the easy thing to do is to simply prosecute the children. But in this instance, the Lincoln force decided they couldn't leave it there. If they didn't nip this in the bud, the problem would only grow.

The other difficulty is that while police know a phone line exists, those lines are not easy to trace. The handset is always anonymously obtained. The children won't have the county line themselves – they will be remotely controlled elsewhere – by what's called a 'burner phone'. A burner can be easily disposed of and regularly swapped, and even if police were able to identify the device, that won't necessarily lead them directly to the user. A gang member, or one of their child runners, will purchase a pay-as-you-go device from a high-street shop. The buyer is rarely the person who will ultimately use the device. Paying over the counter, and buying a non-contract mobile, leaves very little audit trail or record-keeping by the mobile-phone companies. So, while the police may have been able to obtain some phone records from mobiles used by the kids – these phone lines are fluid and hard to trace.

It is well known that police rely on principles of triangulation to track phones. Cellular networks allow a phone to communicate with a number of nearby cell towers, and for each cell to evaluate the signal strength of the phone. Network analysis software can estimate the distance of the phone from each tower, by using the phone's signal strength from each location to estimate the geographic position of the phone. But this is not an exact science, and while it's often used in investigations once a phone has been collected – to confirm whether an individual has been in a certain location where a crime is committed – it is quite another thing to use it to track down a phone in real time. And even if you could, it's difficult to prove who has been controlling that phone.

With no other line of inquiry, a twenty-four-hour sur-veillance was placed on the raided flat. Who knew whether anyone would come back to it? But here is where the police had their first breakthrough. Maybe through the expectation that no one would bother putting in resources to watch a flat that had just been raided, the supplier made his first mistake. Officers watched as the property was visited by someone driving a Seat Leon. A number plate check showed the car was registered to a Zakaria Mohammed. Further checks showed it had been making regular trips from Birmingham to various addresses in Lincoln.

Over the next two weeks, they kept a close eye on the vehicle and found it sometimes had teenagers inside. Police also paid particular attention to any reports of missing children in Birmingham, and in the course of two weeks, three more vanished from their homes in unusual circumstances. In an interview for this book, senior investigating officer Detective Inspector Tom Hadley tells me: 'All of these children were living with families. The majority were in full-time education and not known to the authorities and had not been recorded missing from their homes before.'

These weren't vulnerable children taken from care homes, for example. The parents tended to be from poor backgrounds and were all Somali in origin, but none of the children had a history of truancy and they were not members of gangs. The families were racked with concern and had no idea why their children had vanished.

'The parents certainly didn't want kids to go missing,' says Inspector Hadley. 'They were worried sick, but clearly struggling to protect them and control them.'

Based on the movements of the Seat Leon, the suspicion was that two of the missing children had been taken to Hartlepool and one to Lincoln. Mohammed seemed to be operating a triangular drug line using the children as dealers. His wholesalers were in Birmingham and his clients were in Lincoln and Hartlepool – but police didn't have the evidence yet, and were not sure who else he might be working with.

So, in February 2018, Inspector Hadley decided on a plan to take a closer look at Mohammed without giving away that they were on to him. From background checks they knew the twenty-year-old was also Somali, born in Mogadishu and raised most of his life in the UK, but he had no previous convictions. However, it turns out he had insured his car to a fictitious address, and his insurance company had recently got wind of this and cancelled his policy. It was time for the police 'theatre'.

A road traffic team was assigned to intercept the uninsured car just as it was coming off the M6 in Birmingham. Mohammed was driving and had already travelled that day from Hartlepool via Lincoln. They hauled him out, seized his car for being uninsured and took it back to the station for a forensic examination.

There were no drugs inside the vehicle, but the search uncovered a bigger prize. Inside a glove compartment was a phone. The SIM had been removed, but with the handset alone, police were able to find 100 contacts of drug addicts in Lincoln. It became clear from cross-checks that this phone carcass had previously been used to run Castro. The car also contained a pair of black school trousers, a white shirt and school tie, which the forensic team would later be able to show belonged to one of the missing children from Birmingham. A Mountain Dew drink bottle and a Ribena carton were also found on the seat. Police decided to run forensic tests on these too. The DNA found matched two of the fifteen-year-old boys who'd recently disappeared from Birmingham.

The absence of a drugs find was a disappointment, but perhaps it gave Mohammed confidence to think that the police had simply stopped him for being uninsured, because he continued to operate. With his car impounded, he booked regular taxis, with fares at more than £100 per trip, to ferry himself and children to the Lincoln drug dens. 'He'd lost his wheels – but he couldn't afford to lose his lines,' says DI Hadley.

Of course, officers continued to monitor him. Lincolnshire Police recorded videos of children passing drugs to punters on back streets and around the backs of garages, completing deals every ten or fifteen minutes. The videos showed that they had pre-arranged deals, which would have been set up through the Castro line, but they also managed a bit of passing trade on the street.

'He was using "clean skins" to sell the drugs – children who had no previous convictions,' says DI Hadley. 'His deliveries were always in small batches so, if anyone got stopped, there wasn't a lot of gear. The Castro phone number was outside Lincoln, so he'd take the order and relay it to the children. But that number would often change. So, he would port all the contacts and send out a bulk text for the new number for Castro to his clients.'

With regards to the children who were being monitored, DI Hadley observed that they were 'doing nothing you'd expect children to do'. They were never seen playing games or hanging around with mates – they were simply selling drugs. In every respect, they were behaving like adult dealers.

Another West Midlands Police investigating officer, Detective Constable Max Gebhard, said: 'Mohammed was a very busy man, living the life of a travelling salesman, sleeping in service stations and out on the road for many hours each day taking drugs and phones to children in the cuckooed addresses in Lincoln whilst taking away the money that had been made.'

Investigators built up a picture of what was happening and where the drugs were being stored. Mohammed was quite accomplished at cuckooing. He would find addresses of drug users and move the kids to these properties, but rotate them on regular occasions. That meant the police needed to be quick getting their warrants to do property raids. Indeed, on the day before they were planning to raid one property, the children were moved to another. Even so, under what's called the Police Criminal Evidence Act (PACE) warrants can be acquired quickly if children are considered at risk. So, the day the children were moved the police were able to swap the address of the warrant and conduct a dawn raid.

On 12 February 2018, detectives bust down the door to a flat in Foster Street in the city. Again, uniformed local officers were used to give the sense that this was just a routine drug raid. Three fifteen-year-old boys, all from Birmingham, were found inside the one-bed flat, along with two adult class A drug users. A total of twenty-five wraps of heroin and crack cocaine were found and the room was littered with syringes. There were bundles of cash, and this time the weapons discovered were two Zombie knives.

One disturbing thing found at the property was a jar of Vaseline, which it was thought was used by the children to help them store drugs inside their bodies – an activity known as 'plugging'. They are encouraged to do it to protect themselves from being robbed out on the street or caught by the police. With a child, police can't conduct the same internal searches as they can with an adult. But the suppliers know they are putting the child's health at risk.

The other health hazard was of course the flat itself and the company the children were keeping. A police camera of the raid shows a chaotic environment with toilet roll, syringes and cardboard boxes strewn across the floor. The washing machine is full of damp clothes interspersed with rolled-up packages containing drugs.

Superintendent Richard Agar, West Midlands Police's lead for county lines inquiries, said of the children: 'They had gone through a significant ordeal. They were found in a flat that was dishevelled, it was unhygienic, and it was covered in drug paraphernalia. There was no heating in the flat and there was no food. The children appeared to be disorientated; they were dishevelled themselves. It was unclear when they had last eaten.'

DI Hadley describes the flat as, 'filthy, cold and there was no food in the kitchen.' He added: 'There was no heating, even though it was February. It was just a one-bed flat with five people living in it. There was barely room to swing a cat. There were just a couple of mattresses propped against the wall, so some of them must have been sleeping on the floor. The two adults – the man and a woman who lived there – were heroin addicts, and the man was wanted for robbery. The children looked drawn, tired and hungry. They were dirty and they stunk to high heaven. Among them were two of the kids that we knew had gone missing from Birmingham, but the third we didn't know. He'd been missing for two weeks but his mother hadn't reported him missing.'

It would turn out that this child's mother had mental health problems. Even so, through Birmingham children's services, he would eventually be returned to her. DI Hadley maintained his ethos of treating the children as victims, but he says: 'The children never uttered a word to us. They were completely silent. I don't know if they'd been conditioned not to talk, or they were frightened. Mohammed was still out there. Or it could be mistrust in the police. But I never really understood how they got recruited. They all knew each other, and I think one would call the other, and they would in effect turn into facilitators themselves, getting their friends involved. They had a shared socio-economic background. They came from low-income families. So, there wasn't much money going around. My hypothesis was that it was false promises. They were being told that this could be a good life. But it was a lie. Children are often groomed to deal drugs with promises of money and the allure of leading an exciting lifestyle. But there was no evidence that they were getting any financial reward. They didn't have anything to show for it.

'Can you imagine what a fifteen-year-old boy would do with 400 pounds a week in their hands? They'd buy the best trainers or the best phones. But there was no indication they'd got anything. What's more, their personal phone activity dropped off a cliff. I suspect they were being told not to use them. That's quite unusual for a teenager, to stop using their phone, so there must have been a level of control. Culturally, Mohammed is an adult, they were kids, and so he commanded a natural level of respect. But I'm sure he was also saying, "You will be rewarded."'

A single county line phone can be worth up to £20,000 a week, and the Castro line was certainly earning thousands a week, but police were never able to find any evidence that the children were getting any of it. DI Hadley concludes: 'They were not making money – they were having their childhood stolen from them by Mohammed, who considered them expendable "workhorses". That's the reality for children lured into this world through false promises. There was no recognition of their humanity. They were just seen as a commodity. In essence, they were slaves.'

DI Hadley was clear what he needed to do. He'd set it in his head that the children, despite their lack of cooperation, were being manipulated. They were the victims in all of this – and there was a master villain at the top pulling the strings. He says: 'My mission was to dismantle the Castro line and protect the children of Birmingham.'

Meanwhile, after this second raid, Mohammed knew he had a problem with the Castro line. He'd lost another two of his dealers. He was still fairly confident he'd managed to keep his personal footprint out of the equation. There was nothing to connect him to the property and he was fairly sure the kids would stay quiet. The last two had. But maybe it was time to set up shop somewhere else. The next day he went out and bought another car, a VW Passat, and he went on a trip.

Using Automatic Number Plate Recognition (ANPR) police tracked Mohammed's car to Skegness, Barnsley, Scarborough and other towns up the east coast. It seemed almost certain he was trying to set up a new location for his line. But it can't have been easy; perhaps there were other lines in place and too much competition, or not enough of an obvious market, but ultimately, after about two weeks, he came back to Lincoln. It was probably just too much money to turn his back on. He needed to maintain his existing clients and his established brand before it was lost to someone else.

West Midlands police now had a constant dialogue with missing children's services, and they kept a close track on Mohammed's car. Then, in late March, two children went missing and a few days later there were intelligence reports that the Castro line was up and running again. But Mohammed hadn't been out in his car – in fact, his vehicle had just run into another insurance problem, so maybe he didn't want to risk getting it impounded again.

Perhaps he'd gone back to using taxis – but would he risk that? DI Hadley asked CCTV operators to go back to the day the children disappeared and check the cameras at Birmingham bus and rail stations – especially along routes going to Lincoln.

It was a best guess that he had resorted to using public transport, and it turned out to be spot on. In grainy footage an operator spotted Mohammed walking into the concourse at Birmingham New Street; behind him were two smaller figures. Then, he's picked up buying rail tickets for two children, going down escalators ahead of them, at times trying to keep himself separate, but clearly not separate enough, as he ferries the teenagers from Birmingham to Lincoln on the train.

From the images, police identified the boy aged fifteen and a fourteen-year-old girl as children who'd been reported missing. A week later, in early April, Lincolnshire and West Midlands Police raided another property and they found the two missing children, again living in squalid conditions. More drugs were discovered. This time the cash amounted to £1,400 – and, yes, you guessed it, more knives were at the property, in this instance of the hunting variety.

It was the first time Mohammed had used a girl in his operation. DI Hadley says of the fourteen-year-old: 'She of all of the children had the biggest red flag. She'd been in trouble before and had previous arrests for carrying weapons and drugs.'

As for the fifteen-year-old boy, he was one of the same children who had been recovered from a property in Lincoln in the raid in February. And this was perhaps the most depressing thing for officers in the investigation: learning that rescuing a child from county lines once is no guarantee that you won't discover them in the same position a few weeks later.

This time, the raid was conducted simultaneously with the arrest of Mohammed. His Passat, now reinsured, was stopped as he was driving, as you might expect, from Birmingham to Lincoln. He was taken into custody.

Now came the interesting bit. West Midlands police had evidence to prosecute Mohammed as a drug trafficker, and several of the children had been caught on covert cameras selling drugs, so they could be prosecuted in the youth courts for supply. That would be the easy way of doing things. Or they could break with convention – treat the child street-dealers as victims and effectively accuse Mohammed of being involved in modern slavery. DI Hadley chose the latter. It had never been done before.

It has taken a while for the law to catch up with the idea that drug-dealing children could be victims rather than criminals. In many ways, you could argue they are no different to sex slaves, who are recognised under anti-trafficking laws. These laws have been in place for some time.

The internationally recognised definition of human trafficking is called 'The Palermo Protocol'. Adopted by the United Nations in 2000, it states: 'Trafficking in persons shall mean the recruitment, transportation, transfer, harbouring or receipt of persons, by means of the threat or use of force or other forms of coercion, of abduction, of fraud, of deception, of abuse of power or of a position of vulnerability or of the giving or receiving of payments or benefits to achieve the consent of a person having control of another person, for the purpose of exploitation.'

But, for a long time, no one really applied this to children in drug-dealing gangs. After all, they were involved in criminality themselves. However, things started to change in the last decade. There were a number of legal precursors to the modern slavery act of 2015, which were used by police to try to prosecute emerging county lines gangs for exploiting children. Some, based on immigration laws, demonstrated how you could build a case against a ringleader.

For example, Section 4 of the Asylum and Immigration Act of 2004 deals with how immigrants are treated by their traffickers. But those laws applied only to immigrants. In some ways, prior to the modern slavery act, people trafficked from abroad had more protection than a child trafficked from Birmingham to Lincoln. The legal system simply hadn't imagined the workings of county lines.

In 2009 the Coroners and Justice Act created the offence of 'holding another person in slavery or servitude or requiring another person to perform forced or compulsory labour'. And under the 1999 Youth Justice and Criminal Evidence Act the law assumed that a victim trafficked for sex was deemed to have been 'intimidated'. But it wasn't until the Modern Slavery act of 2015 that those rules of intimidation were applied to other forms of exploitation. Even so, when it finally arrived, many regarded the Modern Slavery Act as something that could be used in mitigation for a child who was committing a crime, rather than a lever to prosecute an adult for exploitation. The Castro line case was about to venture into new legal territory.

'I had to write up a big policy decision,' says DI Hadley, 'and it went against twenty-two years of culture and experience I'd had in the force. But I looked at the kids and thought about what their background was, what would be their defence. Section 45 would be available to them.'

Section 45 of the Modern Slavery Act 2015 came into force

on 31 July 2015 and introduces a defence for victims who are compelled to commit criminal offences. This comes into force if a child's crime is a direct consequence of having been a victim of slavery or trafficking. DI Hadley was convinced that, in this case, it would make a compelling defence. But could it also be used to make a compelling prosecution against Zakaria Mohammed?

'Sometimes Section 45 is used when it's unwarranted. But in this instance, I did believe they'd been exploited. I thought about the state of them when we found them. You couldn't imagine anyone genuinely wanting to live in those conditions. When they were returned to their homes they smelled, they'd lost weight. I didn't make the decision lightly, and it was not until right after the arrest of Mohammed, I said, "This is what I'm thinking. This is what I truly believe." And the thing is, during the proceedings, at no point did the defence council or the judge ask me to justify that decision.'

And so, rather than just accept that Modern Slavery laws could be used in mitigation by the children as defendants, West Midlands Police decided to test the theory that it could actually be used to present further charges against the ringleader, Mohammed, thus increasing the severity of his crime and his time in jail.

Initially, Mohammed refused to cooperate under questioning. Then his defence became clear – he tried to claim that he was just a driver, just another external player, not the organiser, and that he didn't know they were children.

So many things stacked up against this. Not least the school uniform found in his car. He certainly ought to have known they were children. But also, forensics showed that he handled the drugs and the phone line. Evidence from his journeys to and forth painted a picture of Mohammed as the man at the centre of the Castro line who was trafficking children to facilitate his business. Those children had clearly been coerced because he held a level of control over them – for example, them not using their personal phones and being prepared to live in dreadful conditions.

At the eleventh hour, Mohammed offered a plea. Realising the weight of evidence against him, he had to accept that he played a significant role – an operational and management roll – and he had a degree of control over the children.

He pleaded guilty to five counts of supplying drugs and, in October 2018, he was given six years in jail for this. But crucially, on top of this he admitted to five indictments for trafficking. For this he was given an additional eight years in jail – to serve consecutively. Now twenty-one years old, a man with no previous convictions who was given credit for his guilty plea, faced fourteen years behind bars.

West Midlands Police had produced the first example of how to successfully convict under the Modern Slavery Act for county lines. It was the first time anywhere in the UK that police treated child drug dealers as victims. Operation Arkle was a landmark case and it sent out a clear message to those involved in child trafficking.

In court there were questions raised over the role played by Mohammed. His defence barrister, Emma Stuart-Smith, told Birmingham Crown Court that he was a university business management student and had become 'quickly embroiled' in the drug world after falling into the debt of 'more senior' players within the operation. She added that while he had been a 'trusted cog' he was 'not at the top of chain'.

DC Max Gebhard said after the case: 'Mohammed claimed

to be playing the role of a trusted and informed lieutenant, and that there were drug bosses further up the chain, but I believe he was very much in charge. This was a hugely significant conviction for West Midlands Police and law enforcement as a whole across the UK. It showed that we could go after county lines offenders not just for drug supply but also under trafficking legislation due to them exploiting children. And that means stiffer custodial sentences for offenders.'

There were also arguments after the ruling over whether this type of prosecution would open the door for genuine young criminals to claim that they had been exploited. Facing this concern, a Crown Prosecution Service spokeswoman said it judges each case on its merit and the prosecution would not 'open the floodgates' for criminals to claim they were trafficked. She pointed to the case of Marsela Kreka from August 2018, who was found with 1 kg of cocaine in her car but claimed she had been a victim of human trafficking.

'Despite her claim the CPS was able to demonstrate she had not been forced into committing the offences.' She added: 'The CPS works in close partnership with police, the National Crime Agency and other partners to ensure we identify those who falsely claim to be trafficked so they can be prosecuted while ensuring the genuine victims of human trafficking receive protection under the law. Kreka's conviction should not deter genuine victims of modern slavery from coming forward.'

Criminal defence solicitor Joseph Kotrie-Monson, of Mary Monson Solicitors, told HuffPost in October 2018 that he welcomed the prosecution. He said: 'This sort of prosecution has been a long time coming. Generations of crooks have used kids to commit crimes and even in fiction we've had characters like Fagin and his band of child thieves. These kids were clearly in a vulnerable position and criminals will take advantage of that. You see it with cannabis farms in the UK where a drug dealer will use immigrants to look after the grow and they are the ones who get picked up by police when they raid it.'

It's believed that as many as ten children were exploited as part of the Castro line, but Mohammed's prosecution only related to two of the boys who were found in one of the flats and the girl who he was seen buying the train ticket for at Birmingham New Street Station.

Passing sentence at Birmingham Crown Court, Judge Nicholas Webb described him as a 'trusted lieutenant and driver' who had made trips from Birmingham to Lincoln, Durham, Grimsby and Skegness. He accepted that Mohammed was acting on instructions from those 'higher in the chain' but said his role was 'pivotal'.

Wearing a grey tracksuit, Mohammed sat in the dock, as Judge Webb continued: 'You even hired a taxi to take you to Lincoln at a cost of £170. This was a lucrative enterprise in which you played a significant role.'

The judge said CCTV showed how the trafficked children would secrete drugs in their mouths before passing them to customers. In summing up, he told Mohammed: 'The essence of this case is that all these children were very vulnerable and you enhanced that vulnerability …You took them hundreds of miles from home to a property that was squalid, stinking of mould and urine and it was cold …You were delivering them into a situation fraught with danger … The fact is the children were being taken away for days or weeks, exposed to potential danger in a squalid environment.'

The case was a success, but even with careful tracking of Mohammed West Midlands Police hadn't necessarily got to the people at the top of the chain. Also, it was becoming clear from children's charities and research by the Children's Commissioner that many children were involved in this kind of activity. Lots of them were vulnerable, scared and very unlikely to go to the authorities themselves. The challenges facing future police forces wanting to replicate this case will not be easy.

The verdict immediately placed more responsibility on the intelligence services and police to rescue children caught up in county lines, highlighting how behind closed doors, even in twenty-first-century Britain, young people were being exploited and treated like slaves, and that even once found, they might return to the perpetrator. They might be too afraid to do anything else, and ultimately the mental scarring of the nightmare they've lived could have a lasting impact.

Tony Saggers was NCA anti-drugs boss at the time of the investigation, and describes the Castro case as 'a fabulous success'. But he also recognises huge challenges ahead for police in similar cases. 'Convincing a drug runner that they are a victim is sometimes difficult,' he says. 'Either because they've been intimidated, or because through grooming or their peer environment they'd rather be considered a drug dealer than a slave. But equally, convicting these drug dealers of slavery is a game changer. Because sometimes a drug supply conviction is a badge of honour for some people, and if they go into prison as someone who has successfully dealt drugs for a long period of time, that's a notch on their success sheet, in a perverse sort of way. But for people convicted of slavery, with the connotations of that word, it could be very damaging to their reputation, and I think it's a good thing that that legislation is being used where it can be proven.' But, conversely, he adds, 'It shouldn't be used every time, because sometimes we can't prove the key elements. So, it's better to go down the drug-trafficking route.'

DI Hadley admits it took a lot of resources over several months to put together a case that would prove Mohammed was the key player of a child-trafficking drug line. Throughout the gathering of evidence, none of the children offered to help. DI Hadley concludes: 'Could we do this with every case – no.'

As for the children, they were referred via the human trafficking National Referral Mechanism (NRM), where they and their families received support from Birmingham child services and would hopefully be steered towards better futures. It doesn't always work.

Some of the children went into temporary foster care, notably the one who hadn't even been reported missing by his mother. But eventually they all ended up back with their families. At least three of them are now back in school and engaged with social services. However, here's the worst of it: two of them have since been linked to other county lines.

This throws up the final and the most difficult question of all. At what point do these children turn from victims into criminals? Some of them may even be recruiting children themselves. And it is not just the dealing, but also the other crimes being committed while in a situation of exploitation that blur any black and whites into a fuzzier grey: the violence, the carrying and the use of knives...

What would have happened, for example, if the two addicts at the beginning of the story had died of their stab wounds? Would the children involved be victims then? You could still argue, yes. The problem is the county lines phenomenon is warping the norms of society. Children placed in this very adult and dangerous world are ill-equipped to cope. They are actually more likely to make irrational and dangerous decisions, because they don't have the maturity to deal with the stark and sometimes deadly dilemmas they face. When it comes to gang life, in particular, it sometimes seems that these children learn about violence in the way children learn about other things – through play. The whole thing is a game. Even if that game is life or death.

8.

THE SCOREBOARD

*'Their reality becomes a game where you
score points by killing people.'*

DCI Brown watched the lily pads sway on the water,
wondering whether this could really come to anything. A
fingertip search is hard enough, but more so when you're doing
it underwater in the darkness of a riverbed. It had been his
decision to make a formal request for the Met Police specialist
dive team to come all the way to Suffolk. They'd rocked up
in the early hours, in an impressive HGV lorry containing
vast amounts of kit, which made DCI Brown think of Arab
racehorse owners turning up with giant horse boxes. But no
torches, apparently. The frogmen told him that's not how they
worked. 'Everything is done by touch and feel, Detective Chief
Inspector.'

How on earth were they going to find it? he wondered. It was
a needle in a haystack.

'You don't need to worry,' the men in the wetsuits reassured
him. 'If it's in there, we'll find it.' Then Brown told them about

the white van, which was alleged to have taken the gang of youths to the scene of the murder. It was later spotted at this location next to the river. It's a small town; people notice things. A witness reported seeing a group of youngsters walking down the towpath. One of them had lifted up his shirt and taken something from his waistband – 'A shiny object which glinted in the light of the sun,' the witness had said. It was thrown into the middle of the river. But here was the best bit: it had landed right next to some lily pads, and they just happened to be the only lilies on the river that were currently flowering.

So the frogmen had a fantastic point of reference, as they pushed through the low undergrowth on the riverbank and sunk down into the water. DCI Brown stood in his suit on the towpath and watched. He listened to the radio coms with the dive-control unit as the men reported reaching the bottom. The Met team hadn't asked for anything to be cordoned off, so members of the public wandered past, wondering what was happening, and were asked to quickly move along. The local media must have been asleep, thank God, because no journalists turned up.

For hours they watched the water and waited. 'Shopping trolleys,' DCI Brown said to himself. 'That's what they'll find.' The normal rhythm and buzz of Ipswich continued in the background, but this was a relatively quiet spot, tucked away from the nearby bustle. A good place to sink a secret.

It was getting towards lunchtime when, beneath the surface of the water, in the pitch-black murk, a police frogman sifting through the grime felt something solid. His gloved hand clutched what felt like a handle to something. It was long, thin and sharp. At this, he uttered the code – the phrase over the radio link above: 'Nine Bells,' it crackled. The radio operator gave a thumbs-up. It indicated a significant find. Was this the moment they had been waiting for? It came again: 'Nine Bells.'

A shiver of expectation flushed through the detective, which sharpened as the diver came to the surface. In his fist was a black handle, from which came a glistening 8-inch blade. DCI Brown breathed out a sigh of relief. This had to be it – the knife that just over a week earlier had been used to stab a teenager to death. It was a major breakthrough in his case against the killers.

We are back where we began: in the Gipping River, where the shrimp tested positive for cocaine. Two hundred metres away, 'Snipes' was dossing in a flat on Great Gipping Street. He came to Ipswich to sell drugs; he didn't come here to kill anyone. But that is what he had done. Whether he admitted it to himself or not, he'd read the news. He knew the kid was dead. In just a matter of weeks of arriving in town, he'd been involved in a murder.

His real name was Adebayo Amusa, and he'd been in Ipswich for just two months before becoming part of a group who smashed a bottle over a young man's head and plunged a knife into his heart and throat. Only he and a few others knew exactly who did what in that moment of pure red, brutal madness. But as far as he knew, nothing linked him to what had happened. He'd just carry on. Some of the others had been arrested already. But they were obvious suspects. Everyone would be okay as long as no one snitched. They knew to stay quiet.

The knife recovered from the Gipping had been used to kill a seventeen-year-old trainee mechanic called Tavis Spencer-Aitkens. The chain of events that led to his horrific murder is utterly depressing. It is one of the many acts described in the newspapers these days as 'gang-related'. At the centre of it are young men who are high on bravado and short on opportunity. Selling drugs and hanging out with friends and feuding with kids from a rival location was just part of life. But in this case, one thing led to another, resulting in five young men savagely killing a teenager. The most disturbing part of it was something that has also been imported from London, along with the drugs – it's called the scoreboard.

Just like Uncle and the Postcode Gang, Snipes found that his local drug market in Barking, east London, had become overcrowded. He'd been a dealer since the age of thirteen, and didn't know any other way to make a living, but sales were lower than he would have liked. Talk of going 'OT' to sell crack and heroin sounded alluring. It could be more lucrative than his home market, and so, aged nineteen, in April 2018, he travelled to Ipswich to form an out-of-town business. He started out as any new dealer might – sleeping in the homes of drug users and offering them a few wraps in return for a sofa.

His arrival in Ipswich came with a reputation afforded to any London drug dealer. He was a big man from the city, but he needed to make his mark. He learned there were two street gangs in town. The first was called J-Block and the other Neno, and there was a bitter rivalry between the two. There were already county lines routes running into Ipswich, but these two local gangs appeared to have their own markets, on their own estates, so they were worth getting to know. He would choose one as an ally.

The new dealer in town decided to team up with members of J-Block. His initial contact was a kid called Kyreis Davies, who was sixteen but already had a wild reputation and, like Snipes, had sold drugs since the age of thirteen. The dreadlocked teenager had a certain confidence. He was into fashion, confident around girls, walked into places like he owned them. He had worked his way up the ranks and had his own sub-line, running narcotics from Ipswich to a trap house he'd set up in Colchester, near to his mother's home address. His mother was none the wiser, even though Davies was making thousands of pounds from his deals.

Another member was Aristote Yenge, known as Gio, an elder in the J-Block gang in his early twenties. He was more like Snipes. He'd also originated from London, but had been in Ipswich for a while. He had convictions for robbery and possession of heroin and crack cocaine with intent to supply. He'd also been jailed for eight months in a young offenders' institution after being involved in a fight with members of Neno in 2016. On that occasion, J-Block had turned up in their rivals' territory armed with baseball bats and machetes. Yenge had armed himself with a bottle from a shop and, caught on CCTV, was charged with violent disorder.

Ipswich, with its population of just over 130,000, is not a large town. The J-Block members from Jubilee Park would regularly stumble across Neno members from Nacton Road, as their two territories bordered on one another. Whenever they met, there would be fights and aggravation. That was just the way things were.

The third player was an eighteen-year-old called Isaac Calver, known as 'Flex'. He also had previous convictions for supplying class A drugs. A tall, skinny lad, he had an Afro haircut that sprung out in wild directions.

Rather than seeing these three established players as a threat, Snipes decided to team up with them. A year on he would regret that decision, as he stood alongside all three of them in the dock, being sent down for murder.

It turned out that his three new acquaintances weren't just dealers but were also known locally for their 'trap' music, and particularly their highly produced videos, which had gained quite a following. Davies would write the music and create the beats, and they would rap together about street life and post crafted creations on YouTube.

The videos were extremely popular locally, and the J-Block trio sometimes performed in a local pub. In this generation, enamoured by social media, there was a sense that these three rap artists could become stars, influencers, respected musicians. Social media was democratic, so anyone could make it big. You could come from a rundown estate and suddenly break through. But this form of celebrity relied on an infusion of ill repute. You had to be bad to do drill music. In one video, Davies alludes to his personal stardom along with his notoriety for carrying drugs. Calling himself 'Youngz', he sings: 'That is Youngz, can I have a picture please? Course you can, but can you be quick? I've got a pack on me, and I've just seen CID.'

The language of the music is sometimes hard to follow. Their earliest track, 'I Founda Plug', refers to finding someone to ingest packaged drugs for them to act as a mule. In the video, the gang wear expensive Giuseppe Zanotti designer trainers. In other films, they can also be seen apparently making crack cocaine, drinking alcohol ('juice') and flaunting their money. The thousands of local kids watching the videos probably didn't understand all the references – but J-Block looked cool, slick, really bad, and they sang about things that many young people in Ipswich connected to –

in particular, escaping poverty. One song is actually called 'Poverty', and in it they sing: 'I just want to leave the hood and all the poverty'. In another, they warn – 'look at what you've created'. It's undeniable that their music embodies something we established as a key driver of county lines in the second chapter of this book – *a lethal absence of hope*.

The beats are not particularly angry or angst-filled. It is blunt, matter-of-fact – this is how life is and this is how we survive it, by selling drugs and being violent to rivals. The videos often showed the three gang members directing insults at Neno – who were also called 'the three', in reference to their IP3 postcode. In one of the films, Davies and Calver make a number 3 with one hand, and gun signs with the other, in an apparent threat to shoot their rivals. In another they rap about 'scoring points like 23'.

It was this video that first alerted me to the Ipswich case. I had been speaking to social workers in London who had expressed concerns about so-called 'point-scoring' – where gangs were totting up marks for stab wounds to certain parts of the body. A youth worker called Jennifer Blake, a former gang-member and a prominent force working with young people in Peckham, south London, told me: 'The scoreboard goes like this: fifty points for a wound to the head; thirty points for the chest; twenty for the stomach; ten for the leg and five for the arm.' She described it as 'a taboo that needs to be talked about'.

I then spoke to the parent of a victim in south London, who said his siblings had received texts describing his murder as points scored by a certain gang. Another anti-knife campaigner, Elaine Donnelly from Rise Against Violence, based in Camden, said several members of her group had also come across the points game, and a mother from her group believed her son's murder had been deemed as gaining points for a rival gang.

Then there was the case of Rhyhiem Barton, seventeen, who was gunned down in May 2018 in south London. Prior to his murder he rapped about 'the scoreboard' in a drill video, which has had over 300,000 views. Rhyhiem was a member of the Camberwell gang, Moscow17, which had been engaged in a vicious feud with nearby Zone 2 from Peckham. By 2018 the rivalry had led to an explosion of violence not dissimilar to the 'ultra-violence' seen in the classic dystopian novel and film, *A Clockwork Orange* – but in the case of Moscow17 and Zone 2 it was glamorised in drill-music videos.

Their faces covered with hoods, masks and scarves, they rap about 'cheffing' (stabbing with a long knife), 'splashing' (stabbing an enemy repeatedly until they pour with blood) and 'capping' (shooting someone). On one track, Moscow17 urges members of rival Zone 2 to 'check the scoreboard' and asks, 'How you gonna make it even?'

The answer to that question appeared to be the shooting of seventeen-year-old Rhyhiem. His youth worker and friend, Sayce Holmes-Lewis, told me: 'Is there a literal scoreboard? Yes. People are keeping count of the attacks that each organisation is carrying out.'

He added: 'You stab a person in the head or the chest, you get a certain number of points. You get varying points for the severity of the violent act. Young people's reality seems to be very warped when it comes to violence. They think it's a game. Taking somebody out and killing somebody is now fun.'

Mr Holmes-Lewis runs a mentoring programme for young people in gangs on the Brandon Estate in south London where Rhyhiem was killed, and was with him on the day he was murdered. He told me that within hours the rival gang was boasting about the murder on social media.

He said: 'I saw the videos bragging about Rhyhiem's death, and the Instagram accounts, and Snapchat. It was sickening, and it made me extremely upset. These videos are not being taken down quickly enough and they should be screened before they go on. I know it's very difficult, with the high volume of traffic on social media, but these are young people – young people are dying as a result of some of these things that are being released on YouTube, on Instagram and Snapchat, and more needs to be done.'

A few months later, in August 2018, the two gangs engaged in a mass knife fight involving up to thirty teenagers, next to a children's play area. The Mail Online reported, '…scenes rarely witnessed outside a terrorist atrocity or motorway pile-up. A virtual field hospital was set up to treat the wounded.' The most badly hurt were hooked up to drips and oxygen masks, before being wheeled away on stretchers. And so, more points had been scored by both sides – and although nobody died this time, several were left with life-changing injuries.

The scoreboard came up in a conversation I was having with a former police officer, who mentioned the videos that the two gangs were making in Suffolk. He remembered that the one by J-Block made reference to scoring points.

When my Sky News producer Andy Hughes showed the video to his contacts, they concluded the phrase 'scoring points like number 23' was a clear reference to high-scoring basketball player Michael Jordan, who wore the number 23 shirt. Police officers working on the Tavis murder case wondered if the video was a poke at 'Section 23' – the power to stop and search, as much of the track was also about dealing drugs and carrying weapons. But they also considered the Michael Jordan reference – the player who never misses.

At the time we first watched it, in spring 2019, the J-Block video had more than 112,000 views on YouTube – and three of the stars of the song were in the dock for murder. Curious about the lyrics, I asked Chris Preddie to look at it. Chris grew up on the fringes of south London gangs. His cousins were infamous, convicted of killing ten-year-old Damilola Taylor. Chris now works with young people and has been awarded an OBE for his efforts in turning people away from gangs.

He sits down in an edit suite with me to help translate the video. He says: 'They are always "scoring points like 23" means they always get their target. The more violent the attack, the more points. You get a lot of points for the face and the head, because it's visible. They sing about "riding dirty, never clean". It means they've always got drugs or knives or guns.'

He also found references in the videos to preparing drugs in trap houses and cuckooing people to take over their flats. Chris was one of the first youth workers to notice the scoreboard, and his take on it is that the whole thing has come out of video games such as *Call of Duty*. 'They've been playing these games and now they're making them a reality,' he says. 'So their reality becomes a game where you score points by killing people.' There's a level of surprise in his voice as he says it, as if it can't really be true, and yet he's met young people who have bragged to him about the scoreboard and he knows it's happening – it's not just the bravado of drill or trap music: it's being translated into stabbings and murders.

But Chris also believes a lot of young people feel pressured to put on a persona. He adds: 'They look tough in their videos, but a lot of these kids are thirteen or fourteen. They're still watching Cartoon Network. They've still got Power Rangers bed sheets and are asking their mums to iron their shirts. We need to start pulling the reins in. Parents always say "not my kid", but they should start at home. I say to parents, "When did you last stop and search your kid to see if he was carrying a knife?"'

The victim in the Ipswich attack also got involved in making drill videos that were posted on YouTube. Tavis Spencer-Aitkens was known by his friends as 'Bigz' because he was over six foot, with a size 13 shoe. His parents split when he was little and he lived with his mother, Sharon, until he was fifteen. But after being excluded from school for fighting, he went to live with his father, Neville, and his step-mother, Helen Forbes. Not long after he was kicked out of mainstream education, they got him into a pupil referral unit, the Lindbergh Campus, and teachers say he was engaged in lessons and rarely missed school. He started getting tutoring and took up an interest in mechanics.

Tavis told his parents he wasn't in a gang; the Neno bunch were just a group of friends he'd known from school, and that was true enough. There weren't any strangers infiltrating the group, and they all went back a long time. But his parents asked him about the drill music, because sometimes he'd skip his mechanics training to go and make a video, and it seemed like nothing was more important to him.

'He enjoyed it,' says step-mum Helen. 'It's not bad for everybody. But it's how far it goes, isn't it? He'd say there was nothing wrong with them songs, and a lot of it was okay – but there were lyrics about trap houses, and I'd say to Tavis, "Why are you singing about something so negative? You're talented… you could say something positive." But Tavis said,

"Just because we sing about it doesn't mean we do it." He'd talk about video games and say people say *Call of Duty* is a bad game – but it's only bad if you do those things in real life. You can get grade-A students who are playing those games for fun. He'd say to me, "I wouldn't go and act out something off *Call of Duty*, would I?"'

Tavis's group used the name DaRealSideOfIpps on YouTube, and in videos they can be seen spraying their tag in rival J-Block territory. They even film a rival gang member looking out of his window, in an obvious statement that they were not afraid to visit their opponents' turf. In one video, they sing, 'Don't fuck with the three', many of them wearing black masks and smoking weed.

The rivalry between these two gangs was set to music and played out on social media in a small town where the two parties shared the same high street, visited the same shops and cinema – there was a certain inevitability to what came next.

As DCI Mike Brown puts it: 'They were trying to up their reputation through music, through videos and the "culture", and I'm careful when I use the word. And not to blame drill music, and not to say this is responsible, because it's not, and okay, some of the stuff is of quite a high standard. But within it you had that threat and intimidation, and videos of them coming on to each other's patches spray-painting.'

'The music played a part,' says Helen. 'I don't care what anyone says, that music is not good for the youths. For whatever reason these boys didn't like each other. But Tavis, he was a gentle giant. His foot went down the wrong path for a little while, but we've never seen him with knives. In the end, he just happened to be in the wrong place at the wrong time.'

So, we come to the day of the murder – 2 June 2018. Tavis had breakfast at around 8.30am, prepared by Helen, and rather than go to his uncle's garage – where he was doing an apprenticeship – he had a project nearby with a friend, Bradley. They were installing a car engine. They spent the morning preparing the chassis, and around mid-afternoon he came back to pick up an engine hoist from his father's house. Helen watched as he pushed the hoist down the road. No one could imagine that his fate had already been sealed by events that had happened earlier that morning, in Ipswich town centre.

Around mid-morning, J-Block members Aristote Yenge and Kyreis Davies had been walking down the high street when they spotted two members of Neno – the very kids they'd been threatening to kill in their videos. The Neno members immediately came at them, and Yenge and Davies decided to run for it – the nearest point of safety was a branch of Lush. The pair, who'd looked so cool in their video, suddenly found themselves hiding in a soap shop. The so-called 'gangstas' ducked behind products with names like *'Honey, I Washed the Kids'* and slogans offering to *'pamper and cleanse from top to toe'*. This was the polar opposite to scoring points like Michael Jordan.

Neno members came into the shop shouting, 'IP3! IP3!' at the top of their voices. Staff and shoppers had no idea what was happening. It was a policeman who came to the rescue. A plain-clothes officer happened to be nearby, and quickly stepped in, getting the Neno (IP3) members to leave the store. In scenes no different to the scuffle I witnessed in Southend, the situation was talked down, and the rivals separated. The two J-Block members, Yenge and Davies, made a run for it while the plain-clothes officer conducted a search on the two apparent aggressors from Neno.

This was total humiliation for the two rappers. Davies and Yenge had failed to stand their ground. The town centre was considered their home turf. Worse, they had run screaming into a soap shop frequented by little girls attracted by the cute cloud-shaped soaps and make-your-own bath bombs.

'It sounds almost silly,' says DCI Mike Brown, 'almost childish, and, because they were then rescued by a plain-clothed police officer who took the aggressors out of the shop to search them, it allowed Yenge and Davies to flee, and they did flee – we saw them on CCTV running through town. And the town is closer to their area than it is to Neno's. And it's a small town, and there's always going to be a crossover, there's always going to be a rub, but J-Block thought the town was theirs. Yet, here they are, the high-profile members, the front men on the videos, effectively being made to look silly.'

As far as the two J-Block members were concerned, there was only one way to avenge this total loss of face – they had to strike back on Neno turf. DCI Brown says: 'Almost immediately they were making phone calls to bring everyone together, to seek retribution for this loss of face.'

Two hours later, the pair had rounded up their friends with a plan to get their revenge. Snipes said he could get hold of a van. He knew a local drug user, Leon Glasgow, who was pliable and could bring a vehicle. 'The driver was simply a user who'd scored off them in the past,' says DCI Brown. 'He wasn't associated with the gang, other than he had driven them to a few places before. He was offered drugs to drive the vehicle around the town. He later told the court that if he had known what the gang was up to, he wouldn't have done it. And we have to go with that, because that's what the jury believed.'

Snipes arranged the meet point at Alderman Park, and when they got there he gave Leon his payment: £30 cash and £20 worth of cocaine. Yenge, the eldest gang member, got in the front seat – a mistake he would regret. Then, into the back of the van jumped Snipes and Davies, along with fellow rapper Isaac Calver, aka Flex. As they drove into IP3 territory, looking for members of Neno, CCTV captured a cyclist following them in convoy. On the bike was a nineteen-year-old called Callum Plaats, also known as Chico. He had been brought along as a spotter for the J-Block gang. His job was to look out for anyone who might be associated with Neno – anyone at all, it didn't matter who.

As they got in the van, Leon, the driver, stashed his drugs payment and cash into his sock. Yenge sat in the passenger seat and gave directions. For quite a while J-Block drove around central Ipswich but there was no one about, so they decided to go into Neno territory, intent on picking out the first person they recognised who had an association with the IP3 postcode gang. It could have been anybody. Tavis really did pick a bad moment to walk home.

'It didn't matter who it was,' says his step-mum, Helen. 'It could have been any one of his friends. The people who killed Tavis – they didn't know him.'

Tavis had just finished for the day, working on the car at his friend's house, and was walking past a parade of shops in Queen's Way when the van pulled up. The gang inside may not have known him personally, but they recognised him. Indeed Yenge, who'd been convicted of fighting with a bottle outside this very parade of shops two years previously, might have recognised Tavis as one of the people he'd attacked back then. Tavis had been arrested that day too, along with six others, but back in 2016 police released him, as CCTV images showed he'd only been defending himself from the J-Block members, who'd come armed with machetes and baseball bats.

As for now, it didn't matter that Tavis had not been involved in the incident in the soap shop. He was a Neno associate – he'd appeared in some of their videos – so he would do. The moment they saw him, the gang piled out of the van and set upon him. The seventeen-year-old mechanic just about had time to see what was coming, but barely. He managed to reach the bottom of his home road of Packland Avenue, when they closed in.

A witness who also lived in the avenue saw Tavis run past the driveway and slip over. Tavis tried to crawl back onto his feet, but four of the gang with their hoods up jumped on him and pushed him back into the concrete pathway. Then they lay on him to keep him down. Now the witness could see the young man on the floor turning on his side and being punched multiple times by members of the gang. What the witness couldn't see was that at least one of those punching fists was holding a knife.

Tavis couldn't hold back the blows. He couldn't fight back. He was pinned down. The punches struck him everywhere. The frenzied attack lasted less than a minute, but in that short time he was stabbed fifteen times, including a wound to the throat and his heart. Then the attackers scattered.

The unnamed witness described seeing the gang getting up and running off. Tavis was trying to get to his feet, but then one of them turned back. As if the savagery of the last minute hadn't been enough, this attacker needed one more parting act of brutality. He raised a wine bottle and brought it crashing down on Tavis's head. The glass exploded on contact. Tavis staggered backwards, and this last member of the gang made his escape.

Incredibly, Tavis collected himself and staggered onwards, up the road towards home. Despite the ferocity of what had happened, this big lumbering boy still had strength in his bleeding legs to haul himself 250 yards.

The witness walked outside and watched Tavis 'swaying' up the road. He says he didn't realise he had been stabbed until he noticed some blood on the ground, and next to it a trainer.

Helen was near the front of the house when she saw her stepson's friend running up the garden path. She opened the door and he fell through screaming. Then she saw Tavis, hanging off the fence with blood pouring down his face. She called her daughter, Candice. 'Tavis has been stabbed,' she yelled. They ran out as he collapsed on the floor. Helen called 999 and ran to get towels to help stop the bleeding. Candice ran out onto the road and Tavis slumped to the ground. She held him in her arms. His face and clothes were covered in blood and he was only wearing one trainer. 'What happened?' she asked. 'Who did it?'

'J-Block, man,' replied Tavis. She could see the deep cut to his throat. As she lifted up his shirt, she saw injuries to his back. Her mother came out with towels and together they tried to apply pressure to stem the blood. All the while they kept talking to him. But his breathing was shallow. His once-white T-shirt was soaked red.

'Who was there?' asked Candice.

Tavis looked up at his stepmother. 'Don't let me die,' he said. 'Please, Helen, don't let me die.'

He was gasping. Candice was willing him to breathe. 'Breathe, Tavis, breathe.' She started doing breaths with him.

'Who done it, Tavis?' she asked again.

'It was them J-Block Mandem,' he replied.

'Who? Who?'

'There were too many of them,' he said. And then he started to slip. 'There were too many of them,' he said again. He didn't name anyone. He probably didn't even know them that well. Kyreis Davies had been in his class at primary school. But really, that, and a music rivalry on YouTube, was all that connected them. Tavis turned to his stepsister and pleaded, 'Don't let go of my hand.' The blood loss was severe and he was drifting in and out of consciousness.

Helen recalls: 'We're trying to put compressions on the stab wounds, but every time we compressed one, there was another one, and it was just bleeding from everywhere. He'd been stabbed in the back, and in the chest, the heart, the throat, the legs, the arms; smashed in the head by a bottle right across the forehead. That was all hanging open. You can imagine how frantic we were getting towels, trying to compress. And I'm on the phone to the ambulance operator, who was saying, "Compress this", and I'm saying, "I can't, I can't. There are too many!" And when the police came they were shocked. I'll never forget the police officer's face – the first one on the scene. His face just dropped. And he said to me, "You've done all you can, let us take over."'

A helicopter came and ambulance arrived and paramedics put a sheet up to perform open-heart surgery. And now the family couldn't see him, as the area around him was cordoned off. All Helen could think of was the words Tavis had repeated until losing consciousness: 'Please don't let me die, Helen.' He'd begged her to keep him alive.

In this time, the gang had fled. Aristote Yenge, aka Gio, got back into the front of the van, his top now covered in blood. The victim's blood would later be found on the seatbelt Yenge used. The group of killers made their way from the scene to do what they could to distance themselves from the crime: get rid of clothes, throw the murder weapon into the middle of a deep river, get out of town.

But police were quick to identify the van, recover it, conduct forensic tests and collect footage of its journey across town. The images showed that one of the gang members was wearing a distinctive white and black hoodie as he sat by the passenger seat window. It was captured in nearly every CCTV and vehicle dashcam video that was recovered. Knowing that J-Block were prime suspects, it didn't take long to identify who that young man was. He was already known to the police – Aristote Yenge.

Two days later, Yenge, Davies and Calver were arrested at an address in Colchester. Plaats, the cyclist, was arrested on 6 June. It wasn't until 24 July that 'Snipes', real name Adebayo Amusa, the dealer from Barking, was tracked down and arrested in his trap house, just a few hundred yards from where the knife had been discovered. It was the bottle smashed on the victim's head that connected him to the murder. His, and only his, DNA was found on the glass.

While the investigators didn't have CCTV of any of them getting in the van, nor images of the actual attack, nor any shots of the gang abandoning the van later, they were building up a picture of what happened with the help of witness testimony, forensics and phone records.

There was no DNA on the knife; it had washed away from languishing for eight days at the bottom of the river. But it was still an important find. Forensic teams could prove from its length and shape that the blade recovered from the Gipping was capable of causing all the injuries found on the victim. And it was part of a matching set of knives that was recovered from the property of one of the gang members, along with the box the knives came in.

During the trial, which began in November 2018, all the suspects denied being in the van at the moment the vehicle pulled over for the attack. But in evidence, the van driver, Leon Glasgow, didn't help. He said he arranged to meet Snipes at a place called Alderman Park, and he'd wanted the £30 cash and £20 of cocaine for his time. Snipes had agreed. He'd done a few drug runs for Snipes and the others before, and that was the usual price for his wheels and time.

But Glasgow didn't bring his usual van. He'd been staying with a work colleague and decided to borrow his delivery van rather than his own, because it was cleaner and closer to get to. He said he got the keys from inside the house, and it was the first time he had driven his colleague's van without asking. That meant that the gang couldn't claim they'd been in it on a previous occasion. It was new to everyone, so any forensic evidence could only come from the day of the murder.

Glasgow had known the van had a tracking device since he started working for the delivery company that employed him and his colleague. When he got to Alderman Park, Snipes, a man he knew as 'M', and twenty-year-old Aristote Yenge, who he hadn't met before, walked over to the van.

'M' is a mystery in this case. He was never named. He was either involved in the murder but never caught, or he was a fictitious character that the gang created to blame for the murder – and they convinced the driver to go along with the deception. The only thing is, the driver didn't exactly protect everybody – certainly not Yenge.

The driver was clear that Yenge and 'M' got into the front of the van and Snipes gave him some drugs. He said Snipes had then gone to the back of the van and he'd then heard the side door of the van open. He hadn't paid any attention to who the others were, as he was concentrating on putting the drugs into his sock.

During the journey, he heard two or three voices in the back of the van but couldn't hear what was being said. Again, when he stopped the van at Packard Avenue, some people, but he couldn't say who, had got out of the back, but the only people he recognised during the attack on Tavis were Yenge and the mysterious 'M'. Yenge, he said, had got back in the front seat with a blood-splattered top.

Following the attack, he was worried because he realised he could be in trouble for what had happened, and had 'got rid' of his passengers as soon as he could.

Now, Yenge must have been really regretting sitting in the front – because not only did the driver identify him as an attacker, but, as we've established, his white and black 'West Coast' top was picked up on CCTV all across town through the window of the van. His own blood was found in the van, and blood from Tavis had transferred from his distinctive top to the seatbelt. He would have to claim that someone else was wearing it. So he told the jury it was all a 'terrible mistake'. He had only been implicated in Tavis's murder because someone else had borrowed his jumper.

He claimed he'd only gone in the van as far as Iris Close, and had got out there leaving his jumper behind, because he'd taken it off to cover his face as he didn't like the smell of crack cocaine smoked by the driver. So, then what had happened, in Yenge's imagination, is the man called 'M', who'd remained in the van, had put his jumper on before going to Packard Avenue. Yenge, meanwhile, claimed he was actually in Constantine Road in Ipswich at about the time Tavis was killed.

If only CCTV could back that up. But as Oliver Glasgow QC, prosecuting, pointed out during cross-examination, it didn't. Yenge had to admit that when police showed him CCTV footage of people walking along Constantine Road at the time and location he placed himself, he didn't appear to be among them.

It also didn't quite match with the idea that having been publicly humiliated in the soap shop, he would get a group together, get Snipes to organise the van, and then leave them all to it. The rest of the gang soon realised that Yenge had a terrible defence. He was most visible on CCTV, most in the frame from the driver's statement. So they tried to land all the blame on him. The only problem with this was that it was clear from all the witness statements that someone had to be in the back – so the remaining gang members turned on each other.

Snipes said he'd just organised the van, but didn't come for the trip into Neno territory, even though police found a palm print to suggest he'd been in the back at some point. It didn't help that his DNA was also on the neck of the bottle used to deliver the final blow to the victim's head. Then, in evidence, his co-defendant, Davies, contradicted Snipes. Davies couldn't deny being in the van himself because his blood was found there, so he could, at best, try to raise doubt by claiming that at some point he'd got out before the attack. He insisted he'd also only gone as far as Iris Close, where he said he'd needed to collect crack cocaine from his supplier. Then he'd spent around ninety minutes in the trap house dividing the drugs into shots. So, like Yenge, he wanted the jury to believe that having been humiliated in the soap shop, he too decided to leave the others to exact revenge. But if he'd been in the van as far as Iris Close, he'd have known who else was in the back. He decided Snipes had been there. He told the court that as he'd closed the van door, Snipes was in the back.

What about his long-standing friend, Isaac Calver? No, he hadn't been in the delivery van at all. That matched with what Calver claimed – and no doubt they'd discussed their alibis in the two days before they were arrested after the killing.

Calver decided not to take the stand. He just let it be known that he'd not at any point been a part of the venture. But the idea of Calver not being there was contradicted by a fingerprint found on a plastic bag in the back of the van – Calver's fingerprint. And it also contradicted what Snipes had said. So everything turned in. To save his own skin, each had to tell a different story and place someone else in the van.

The gang 'sold each other down the river in a cut-throat defence', according to DCI Brown. 'There's a group of individuals who know exactly what happened on that day. But if they are not prepared to talk about it, for whatever reason, then we can only present the evidence we have and ask the jury to make their decision.'

'But in effect they all convicted each other?' I suggested to the detective.

'They did. And this is where it all comes down to acting as a group. It's one of our biggest warnings to people in gangs. You might think the part you play is not directly responsible for the death of that individual. But what you have to recognise is that you might be convicted as part of a group acting together with knowledge of what was going to happen. If you are found guilty of that, you are found guilty of the murder.'

'The way they acted in court was disgusting,' says Helen. 'It's one thing not admitting what they'd done. But I'll never forget when Gio got up in the stand – and he looked up at Neville in the gallery, and he said, "I know your son's been murdered but I didn't do it." And Neville just got up and walked out of court. Because we knew they'd done it. It was just a show for the jury's benefit.'

She added: 'There's this idea that, as gang members, they might stick to some kind of brotherly code. Well, none of them stuck to the code. They were snitching on each other. In trying to get themselves off, they snitched each other up. They don't care that their friends are up for murder – they want to get themselves off. So you have one saying something like, "I wasn't in the van", and the other would say, "Well, you were in it. Because when I got out the van, I shut the door, and he was still in it." So the code went out the window.'

At one point Yenge and Callum Plaats even attacked each other in the dock. Everyone had to leave the court while the two were separated. Helen says she wishes she could have videoed the way the gang members behaved – to show it to young kids, some of whom still idolise J-Block, who need to see what they were really like.

Music videos aside, Helen believes the drug dealing and violent mentality imported from London ultimately led to her stepson's murder.

'There were two who weren't from Ipswich. Yenge [aka Gio] and Amusa [aka Snipes] were both from London. They both claimed they didn't know Tavis. And they didn't, because they were down from London and setting up county lines down here, with a crew that had already built up a county line. We know that because they were saying it all in court. All their county lines were read out in court. You had one kid, sitting in court, aged sixteen, and he's telling the court he's been dealing drugs from the age of thirteen and living in trap houses. He was talking about his drug activity to try to dismiss himself from being convicted of murder. I think their reputation – it goes to their heads. We are in real trouble, big, big trouble, with county lines and knife crime. It's so easy to get into it – but you try coming out of it. They are trapped.'

DCI Brown agrees that it was unusual how the defendants would think by being honest about their lives as drug dealers that they would somehow swerve the more serious murder charge. 'In court, they took the route of talking about how they were only class A drug dealers, and they'd set up their trap houses and were trying to get on, making thousands of pounds selling class A drugs to addicts. It's not the best defence in the world. They didn't take the route of saying, "I was scared for myself or my family, if I don't go along with this."

'Is it about image?' he asks himself. 'Because if you are so ingrained into that group or gang or culture that all you want to do is think about how you're going to be perceived and try to gain respect, then what better way to do it than to stand in front of a judge and tell him all about your criminality and what a bad person you are?'

'Do you think they were expecting to get off the murder charge?' I ask.

'Yes, I do,' he replies. 'There was a real confidence. And we do see it with other trials too, this real confidence that you're not going to convict them – that they are going to get away with it.'

'Maybe they were deluded by their own perceived untouchability,' I suggest.

'I think that's a good way to put it. Untouchability in how they viewed their own persona. How they perceived themselves on social media. Because on social media you can be untouchable because you're behind a keyboard and you're putting a video up.'

DCI Brown says Ipswich does have a problem with county lines, but it wasn't his job to investigate who was selling what, and whether there was some kind of connection to other gangs elsewhere. His focus was on convicting the killers. His gut feeling is that the two rival gangs in Ipswich were for the most part locals, dealing in their own areas, and the actual killing had no connection to any sort of drug turf war.

He says: 'If you look at county lines – a county line will come up, the runner will have a nickname, and that will sometimes be the name of the line: "Snowy", for example. And that is fed from London or Manchester, say. But what we had in this case were local gangs also dealing drugs. Now, depending on where they are in the town, and how big their business model is, they don't always rub up against each other. But when you have a county line, the local gangs can either get picked up and integrated, or squashed.'

J-Block and IP3 were on opposite sides of town from each other, and police say they were not necessarily competing in a drugs turf war; that the initial dispute may have been sparked over a group of girls who'd gone out with people from both gangs. DCI Brown adds: 'The antagonism built up from there. It's that loss of face transported into a deliberate antagonism, because that's what they're seeing in London, and that's what they want to emulate. So the rivalry, it's about trainers, clothes, watches, jewellery. What's the fastest way to make money and get this stuff?'

But it's clear that Amusa (Snipes) was what one would categorise as someone looking to generate an OT business, expanding his operation into a smaller town, which he thought would be more profitable and easier. In some ways, his co-defendant Davies was the next step down. Davies had decided that even Ipswich was getting too saturated, so he'd set up a sub-line from Ipswich to Colchester.

The trail ran for four months. In his closing speech, prosecution counsel Oliver Glasgow QC said the case centred around two rival gangs that would stop at nothing to 'get one over each other'. He told the jury: 'Few of you could have imagined that a summons for jury service would have seen you immersed in a world of young men who see drug dealing as a way of bettering themselves, who run with gangs because they seem to have nothing better to do, who make music that glorifies crime and who fight with their rivals simply because they live in different postcodes.

'The scourge of knife crime that has blighted so many towns and cities across the UK, the stories of gang violence and postcode killings that we have all read about, are it seems in fact much closer to home than we might like to think. Tragically, Ipswich is no different to anywhere else.'

He said the whole feud came out of mutual hatred, and that the eventual killing 'was perhaps inevitable' because neither gang wanted to back down. 'Thus, it was that they taunted each other, insulted each other and fought with each other until, eventually, someone was murdered.'

He added: 'The cowardly nature of their violence, where an armed group launch a surprise attack on a defenceless individual, is made we suggest all the more shocking when you realise that his attackers must have assumed that no one would want to speak out against them – why else would they feel confident of doing what they did in the middle of the day and on a residential street? These defendants acted like a pack. They hunted their prey and they showed no mercy.'

In March 2019, four of the gang were found guilty of murder. Callum Plaats, the cyclist, was found guilty of manslaughter. His barrister told the jury that his client had been diagnosed with ADHD (attention deficit hyperactivity disorder), autistic spectrum disorder, poor concentration and an IQ in the lower end of the average range. He also had much less association with the gang, so it's possible he hadn't been fully aware of how brutal the day would turn out. Plaats was given fourteen years in jail.

Isaac Calver (Flex), 19, Aristote Yenge (Gio), 23, Adebayo Amusa (Snipes), 20, and Kyreis Davies, 17, were found to be equally involved in the murder. The last to be convicted, Isaac Calver, was in court on his own when the verdict was passed down. As it was read out he collapsed in his chair. 'He started crying like a baby,' says Helen. 'And this is supposedly some big old gangster who came up here and stabbed Tavis to death. And you're crying now?'

But she says there was no remorse. When Tavis's parents Neville and Sharon read out the impact statement, Neville told the gang, 'You didn't just murder my son – you murdered me as well.'

Helen says, 'They just looked at him [Neville] like they were gangsters. They looked right through the family.'

As they were sentenced, the defendants were somehow able to laugh and joke with each other in the dock. The youngest of them, sixteen-year-old Kyreis Davies, smirked as he was told he would serve a minimum of twenty-one years – his last chance to show the world his cool image. But, in the gallery, Tavis's mum was furious, and some shouted 'coward' and 'scumbag', while his father Neville simply watched it all unfold, heartbroken that this thing called justice would never bring back his son.

Judge Martyn Levett said the attack was a 'grim demonstration' of how knife crime has 'blighted towns and cities across the UK.'

A minimum of 21 years was also given to Isaac Calver. Adebayo Amusa was handed 23 years, and the oldest in the gang, Aristote Yenge, 25 years. So, the average number of years for the four murderers came to '23'. Finally, the mystery was solved as to what they might have been singing about – '23' wasted years in prison.

So, with a gang of high-profile dealers off the street, did anything change for Ipswich's drug market? Not really. Perhaps drug dealers keep across local news, because within a few weeks of the J-Block arrests, a new line called 'Rico and Frank' emerged. Like Kyreis Davies, it also appeared to have a connection to Colchester. Young people from Essex and other towns in Suffolk were brought in to serve the line. A drug user on Wherstead Road had his flat taken over, and quickly found himself in debt to the gang. Two teenagers were installed to help prepare and distribute drugs.

But they too found that selling drugs in Ipswich came with problems. In a situation similar to the dealers of the Castro line in Lincoln, one of the runners came back one evening claiming that a user called Daniel Saunders had tried to rob him. So two of the young dealers went on a trip to Southend and bought themselves a machete and a large knife.

The next day, a Sunday afternoon in December 2018, one of the seventeen-year-old dealers was out on the streets selling drugs. Thirty-two-year-old Daniel Saunders was in the same area accompanied by a friend, Ben Wright. They saw the dealer and followed him into the alleyway to make a purchase.

Ben bought a wrap of heroin and crack cocaine. During the sale, the teenager told Ben that his friend Daniel had been involved in an attempted robbery. Ben told him he'd got that wrong, and he then turned to walk away, but then Ben heard Daniel cry out. He didn't see exactly what happened but the next moment his friend was running away with blood pouring from his stomach. Ben looked back to see the seventeen-year-old runner holding a large knife, and he ran for his life. Daniel suffered catastrophic blood loss from a blade, thought to measure 30 cm. Paramedics found a victim with serious damage to his internal organs and blood vessels. He died at the scene.

The murder investigation that followed found that after the attack on Daniel Saunders, his killer, who was not named in court because of his age, returned to the flat he was operating from and called a taxi to take him and a friend to the Premier Inn in Colchester. Here they met up with another teenager and two older men.

The gang had been using a room at the Premier Inn as a temporary base for the 'Rico and Frank' line, and here two men and the two teenage boys helped the killer dispose of his clothing and commence a clean-up operation in the room. Then they went back to the cuckooed flat to collect some money. The occupant later told police that one of the men joked about the stabbing by falling to his knees, clutching his stomach and saying, 'Give me half a gram.'

In a matter of days detectives traced the group to a caravan park. Armed officers stopped a taxi where Daniel's killer was found with a sword down his trouser leg. Another seventeen-year-old had a machete down his trousers.

In interviews the killer told police that Mr Saunders and Mr Wright had tried to rob him in the alleyway, and that he had grabbed a knife being carried by Mr Wright and stabbed Mr Saunders in self-defence.

But after a six-week trial, the teenager, originally from Bury St Edmunds, was unanimously convicted by a jury at Ipswich Crown Court. Five other defendants were found guilty of assisting an offender by disposing of his clothing and harbouring him at a caravan park. Yet again more dangerous drug dealers were taken off the streets of Ipswich and put behind bars.

But more will come. As DCI Brown puts it: 'A county line has the ability to reset – if a runner is taken off the street, they have an ability to replace them. They have an ability to influence people who may be vulnerable through poverty or perhaps abuse. And by using these people you have an almost endless employment trail.'

Suffolk Police and Crime Commissioner Tim Passmore described county lines as the 'biggest threat facing Suffolk'. And added: 'Our message to the evil, barbaric leaders of these cartels is that they will be hounded out by rigorous enforcement. They are the scum of the earth.'

Forty-three children aged sixteen or under were arrested on drug-dealing charges in Suffolk between 2016 to 2018. Some were as young as thirteen. Several were in the care system or had been groomed in London estates and transported to Suffolk. In total, 1,455 people were charged with drug offences in Suffolk in that time.

In 2018 the Suffolk Safeguarding Children board summed up the situation in Ipswich in a report that stated: 'Local concerns consist of two main elements interacting with each other: the emergence of at least two recognisable urban street gangs based in Ipswich and the arrival of drug dealers travelling from drug export hubs to establish local drug-dealing networks (county lines). In Suffolk these networks tend to be run from London. Over time these two elements have connected and interacted together, resulting in some individuals including children and young people linked with urban street gangs also being associated with county lines. County lines are a major conduit for illicit drug distribution across England and Wales, and have also helped to spread the violent culture of some metropolitan gangs into new locations, and this has been the case in Suffolk.'

The report paints a familiar picture of what we have seen in Ipswich and elsewhere – children established in trap houses, often the homes of vulnerable adults, and an increase in the movement of children around the county to sell drugs. Those most at risk were young men aged between twelve and eighteen, although younger children, girls and young women were also being recruited.

But Suffolk police claim the tide is turning. They say that in 2019, while other areas saw an increase in county lines, the number of lines running into Suffolk had halved from forty to twenty. There is a pro-activity in Ipswich that I will come back to when we look at the solution to this problem in the final chapter. But there is no silver bullet. I asked DCI Mike Brown if he could put his finger on a solution.

'Whoever finds that has got the answer to the million-dollar question,' he replied. 'I can talk about partnership working, early intervention of families, parents knowing their kids, and asking questions, and being probing. I can talk about schools and support, volunteers and charities, and it's all really important, and it all has to work together, and everybody is trying to find that fix.

'We have to find the support for those who need it so we can stop this constant accessibility to these young vulnerable people who are being used and abused by these gangs. We are passionate about this. You have to put yourself in the shoes, or the trainers, of these young men. For them, what they are being offered seems like the opportunity of a lifetime, because the choice is set against poverty, or maybe abuse and isolation, and if you are young and impressionable – what are you going to do? And once you're in it, if you've got nothing to go back to – why go back?'

To really understand the backgrounds these children are fleeing and the dangers they are walking into, it's time to meet a child runner.

9.

THE RUNNER

'He just took out a knife and stabbed me in my arse.'

Lucy is sixteen years old and has the face of an angel. She's 4 feet 9 inches, blonde with blue, pool-sized eyes and is about as far removed from my image of a drug dealer as anyone I have ever met. But she is – or at least she is part of the process. She carries drugs from London to Southampton for a gang, so it's perhaps more accurate to describe her as a mule. So far, we've focused on young men involved in county lines. But as we saw with the Castro line, girls get sucked into this, too. As DCI Brown said, it's worth putting ourselves in these young people's shoes – to see how it happens.

'My mum is a heroin addict and my dad's a gambler,' begins Lucy. 'My brothers are all in prison. And my sister, actually, she's okay.' She surprises herself, as if she'd forgotten, and suddenly remembers that by some miracle one family member was dragged through the thorn bush of childhood and came out unscathed. This is not the case with Lucy.

A common feature in county lines drug supply is the

exploitation of young and vulnerable people. As we've already learned, dealers like Uncle target children, or adults with addiction problems, to act as drug runners or to move cash or even carry out violence against rivals. The reason is obvious. It means that Uncle can stay under the radar while the children take all the risks. What's more, a girl who looks like she's going to the sweet shop is less likely to get stopped by police. The innocence that allows children to avoid detection is also exploitable, and it's quite clear that even if they've got involved voluntarily, they are at risk from people like Uncle. County lines runners are often attracted by the promise of easy money but are exposed to threats and physical or sexual abuse. In some instances they might be trafficked to areas a long way from home as part of the network's drug dealing business – or what Uncle calls 'boot camp'.

There are some similarities to gangs who groom children for sexual exploitation. Often the children don't see themselves as victims, sometimes the authorities don't see them as victims either, but the police and government are now beginning to recognise them as such – and if the runners are victims that means the people exploiting them are breaking even more laws. As a result, county lines drug dealers are now beginning to face additional charges, under modern slavery laws – as evidenced in chapter 7, The Castro Line.

Like many children involved in this business, Lucy was targeted while living in care. She'd lived with her heroin-addict mother and gambling-addicted father until her early teens. Her parents, when together, were always fighting. She says home life became ever more unstable, but especially when, aged thirteen, Lucy became pregnant. Her boyfriend, the child's father, was fifteen and was a violent gang member. He got Lucy running errands. Aged thirteen and pregnant, she was carrying parcels she suspected contained drugs or weapons to meeting points – sometimes to hub stations in London. Her boyfriend's gang was involved in robberies and Lucy would be asked to hide stolen goods. But her boyfriend was often violent. As well as a lot of verbal abuse, Lucy was beaten up, left bruised or given black eyes.

'I was often black and blue when I was pregnant,' she says.

No one at home seemed to take much notice, but after Lucy gave birth to a little boy, her drug-addled mother found that looking after a battered daughter and a screaming baby grandson was all a bit much – so, aged fourteen, with a six-month-old baby, Lucy was 'kicked out' of the family home.

Homeless and with a child, she was high on the list for social services to house and in the short run they found her a place on the Isle of Wight, where she had no family or support network. After a short while she was rehomed with her baby in Bournemouth, where she was closer to family, but after a year, she was considered too young and unstable to care for her child. They were separated. The baby went to live with the abusive boyfriend's grandmother and Lucy went into care in Worthing. At this point she had given up on the boyfriend.

'I just couldn't take the shouting. He never hit me in front my baby. But I knew that when he got older, maybe the baby would have seen it.'

Worthing is a seaside town on the south coast of England, situated between Brighton and Portsmouth. Like any English town it has its smarter and its rougher areas. It has a high street, parks, a marine parade, and it has drug addicts and dealers. In 2018, at an annual meeting with residents in the Assembly Hall, Mary D'Arcy, director of communities for the local council, said: 'Adur and Worthing do remain some of the safest places to live in the UK, so we do not want to frighten you. However, we cannot pretend we are immune to rising national trends: young people are involved in organised drug supply chains.'

Residents were told about cuckooing and how the gangs had infiltrated 'all levels of education'. But Lucy discovered they had also infiltrated the youth care system. And it was at the care home where Lucy says she began to 'get involved with the wrong people'. Although, it's hard to think of any 'right' people that had been involved in her life thus far. 'I was fifteen years old and living in a care home, and I met some wrong older guys. They got me involved in drug running,' she says. 'When you're in care, when you live with them and you know them and they are in care as well, they would, you know, they would, like, get me to do stuff.'

'Presumably there is some kind of curfew at the care home?' I ask. We are sat in a park in south London having this conversation – again, I'm protecting Lucy's identity. It's not her real name but I can't emphasise how innocent she looks – she has the face of a primary-school girl. Nothing coming out of her mouth matches the face that is saying it.

'Yeah, but people in care do go missing. Because, often it's about drugs and earning money.'

'Okay, so you're fifteen, living in care, and you're being asked to do what exactly?'

'Sell drugs. Sell heroin. Crack. Cocaine. Everything.'

'And where are you going to do this?

'Southampton.'

It becomes clear then that the older teenagers in care with Lucy are also part of a county lines drug-running gang. They fall into the age bracket most likely to be exploited by gang masters (fourteen to seventeen) and are being directed by an 'Uncle' type character who only one or two of them has contact with – and who Lucy never meets.

'It's always confidential who the main person is with the money and the drugs. There are other people who get the drugs to me, so I don't know who the main guy is.'

Lucy gets the train from Victoria to do drop-offs along the line to Southampton. Then she brings the money back. It's become more common now that child runners get sent instructions on Snapchat, and are observed by geo-tracking devices on their phone while doing the run – even though they may never meet the people at the top controlling the operation. Lucy says she's never had any contact with 'the main guy', but she got to know the regular customers and she also had contact with 'the dealer' in Southampton – not always a pleasant man.

She would travel down once a day. The best clients would pay a few hundred pounds a day, and Lucy says she could 'do quite well' for herself, making £200–300 in a day. But early on Lucy got robbed of her drugs, and that's where things started to go badly wrong.

'I'd gone to do a usual drop-off and I got robbed for the drugs. I go back and say, "I'm this much short."'

The dealer in Southampton was furious and decided Lucy needed to be punished. They needed to make an example of her. Nobody loses money or drugs without facing consequences.

'I got stabbed,' says Lucy. 'He just took out a knife and stabbed me in my arse.'

'And that was a punishment?'

'Yeah, it was.'

A stab wound to the bottom is a common punishment in these circles, as it is considered an area of the body where a deep cut is unlikely to be fatal. It's also a humiliating area of the body, as it's a while before the victim can sit comfortably again. Some gang members think it's safe to plant a knife in the upper thigh – not realising that severing an artery in the leg can cause a victim to bleed out in minutes, as happened with ten-year-old Damilola Taylor in November 2000.

The attack in Peckham by well-known criminals Danny and Ricky Preddie left the little boy bleeding to death in a stairwell, and it shocked the country. However, it was thought his injuries were caused either by being stabbed with, or by being pushed onto, a broken bottle, which gashed his left thigh. It ended in convictions of manslaughter. The courts accepted that the attackers hadn't intended to kill.

A note on this: Damilola's murder was probably the most high-profile killing in London that decade. If nothing else, one thing that should have come from it is that people who carry knives and intend to use them should now know that a stab to the leg can be just as dangerous as a knife in the heart or neck. Yet leg-stabbing does seem to have become a 'thing'. I recently met a mother, Christel Stainfield-Bruce, who was stabbed in the leg while pushing her three-year-old son in his pram in north London. She believes, as there was no other motive for the attack, that it must have been a gang initiation process; that the perpetrator was trying to prove himself.

It seems appropriate to quote Patrick Ness from the novel *The Knife of Never Letting Go*. In his fictional dystopia, the people of one particular town become initiated into manhood by stabbing and killing another person. His main character, Todd, makes the observation: 'But a knife ain't just a thing, is it? It's a choice, it is something you *do*. A knife says yes or no, cut or not, die or don't. A knife takes a decision out of your hand and puts it in the world and it never goes back in again.'

I now quote this to every gang member I meet. The casualness in which young people now use knives is deeply worrying. But with Lucy it wasn't completely casual – there was probably calculation in the decision to stab her.

In a sense she was lucky: the wound was deep but not fatal. She went to hospital and got stitched up. As you would expect, the hospital staff enquired about the injury and the police were called in. But Lucy kept quiet about what had happened. Of course she did. She was scared to death. When the police interviewed her, she refused to open up. 'I just said nothing. They tried to get me to make a statement, but I just disagreed. Yeah … there was nothing they could do. The hospital had treated me.'

But the hard reality is that Lucy was probably set up. The dealer who stabbed her as a punishment was almost certainly behind the initial robbery of the drugs. This is a way of debt-bonding the children to the gang. 'Now you owe us,' they are told. 'You lost our drugs – you lost us money. You'll have to work it back.' It's a cruel trick. Plus, the child now knows what will happen if they make mistakes again, or try to leave.

As Lucy recounts her story, I think of Uncle with his Rambo knife. It's exactly the sort of thing he would do. It's a cold-hearted, inhuman ploy to control the widening supply routes. Children's Commissioner Anne Longfield tells me she has come across numerous examples of this and describes it as 'part of the grooming process'. She says: 'The runners are robbed by members of the gang whom they don't know, then punished and scorned for letting that happen, but then they are let back in with the understanding that they will have to work back the money they've lost.'

A report in July 2019 from The Children's Society also identified this method of ensuring compliance by putting a child into 'bondage'. The report says: 'When on the periphery of the criminal group, they may be asked to carry or hold something of value, as a sign of trust. At this point, the young person will be robbed or jumped and unable to pay or give the item back, placing them in debt with the perpetrator. Unbeknownst to the young person these robberies are often contrived by the criminal groups as a way of bondage.'

Things like 'punishment stabbings' are also not uncommon, and health workers in small trauma clinics are seeing an increase in the number of shallow stabbings, especially in the buttocks. This is extremely painful and horrific for the victim and, as has already been explained, can be very dangerous. It is done to discourage runners like Lucy from considering an exit strategy, because if that person tries to flee, they're not just leaving the chance to make money, they're also walking away from a debt and a threat, and both of those things are going to come after them. Criminals that are running county lines realise that young people won't want to stay for ever. It grinds you down. So, even after a very short time, they employ ruthless tactics to bind them to the work by the creation of artificial debt. What is shocking in Lucy's case is that she was not only debt-bonded but was also stabbed for something that the punisher knew wasn't her fault.

This practice of ritual humiliation first came to light in a groundbreaking county lines court case in 2019. Five years earlier, Hampshire Police had arrested six teenagers as part of

a drug-dealing gang in Portsmouth. They soon established the group of youngsters were all originally from London. And so they began investigating the county lines link.

In May 2019 three men were convicted of trafficking children. What makes this different from the Castro line case, is that their crimes preceded the Modern Slavery Act (the arrests happened in September 2014) – indeed it was this case that helped push through the new legislation.

Like the Castro line in Lincoln, or Uncle's operation in Reading, the London gang had established a network of addicts in Portsmouth and used a mobile called the 'fly line' to make deals. They texted clients with what was available, and buyers would call back to place orders – up to 300 a day. The gangsters were making £2,000 a day on this line and using children to oil the operation.

Like Lucy, the teenagers were plucked from care homes and were used to restock the drug supplies and arrange the deals. They would often stay overnight in squalid drug users' homes, dealing late into the night, and later bringing cash from the sales back to London.

The three men from the London gang – two in Lewisham and one from Tottenham – were successfully prosecuted under drugs charges in 2016. But the care-home teenagers were treated as victims, so it was hoped that in a second trial they would give evidence about their experience of being trafficked – and this would lead to more charges for the men running the line.

The police operation was known as Pibera, and Tim Champion, from the National County Lines Coordination Centre, was involved in the case. Just like officers involved in the Castro case, they wanted to send out a message. He tells me: 'I said we needed to get these dealers for something else. Being arrested for drug supply is an occupational hazard. We have to protect the youngsters from themselves.'

But without the Modern Slavery Act as an option, they decided to use the Asylum and Immigration Act. With this legislation, if you are under eighteen you don't have to prove coercion in order to prove you've been enslaved.

But a judge at Woolwich Crown Court threw it out. Tim says the view was that it wasn't modern slavery because it fit neither the category of domestic servitude or sexual slavery. However, the police won their case on appeal and the trial went to the Crown Court in 2019.

Then came a familiar problem: the victims would not testify against the dealers. In the end, only one victim gave evidence. The oldest one, nineteen years of age, suffered from autism and spoke from behind a screen. He told of all forms of humiliation and intimidation, including being subjected to a mock execution by other gang members after a user stole £100 in cash and £100 of drugs from him. He was stripped naked and had a gun placed in his mouth. As with Lucy, it is more likely than not that the London gang themselves arranged for the drugs to be stolen.

In this age of always-available technology, one can easily imagine that the mock execution was filmed to show to the others. Although there's no evidence of that in this particular case, it seems highly likely that the perpetrators would have filmed it on their mobiles. No wonder the other victims were too scared to even give statements to police. But officers pieced together the case using DNA evidence and mobile phone data. The men were convicted of trafficking three girls aged fourteen, fifteen and sixteen, and three boys aged fifteen, sixteen and nineteen. Already serving time for the drug offences, the three ringleaders had additional years added to their sentences.

'The issue was having to do it victimless,' says Tim Champion. 'But the purpose is to change behaviours. And it has worked. Gang members and drug networks are starting to ask people how old they are. That is a behavioural change. We have evidence that that is starting to happen. These people don't want the stigma of being involved in modern slavery or being shown that they are exploiting children.'

But the success of the Lincoln and Portsmouth cases has raised concerns that recent modern slavery legislation is being used as an incentive to coerce children. The gang members can now tell youngsters that they won't face prosecution if they get caught – so even more reason to get involved. But this is a high-risk strategy by dealers, and children too have to be careful with this – there are still plenty of circumstances in which they could end up being prosecuted.

'It's never black or white,' says Tim, 'but each case has to be considered on its merits. That's why we use the National Referral Mechanism [a framework for identifying and protecting victims of human trafficking], which has processes in place. But it has to be a balance between how far the exploitation might outweigh the crime. You could have a seventeen-year-old running five county lines – now, it's clear that that young person isn't being exploited.'

County lines-style enslavement is on the rise. The Children's Society found that criminal exploitation was the primary type of slavery uncovered in 370 police operations in April 2019 – an increase of 1,956 per cent from 18 operations in April 2017.

The number of children affected is believed to run into the tens of thousands. Many police forces believe this form of exploitation has developed over the last five years, and because it is relatively new it is still evolving. For example, the criminals have learned that police forces are more savvy about identifying exploited children by the length of time they go missing, and have begun to develop a shift system, so that the kids go missing for shorter periods of time.

There are reports of children deliberately behaving badly at school so that they are temporarily excluded to be able to attend a shift. The Children's Society report, published 5 July 2019, said: 'The fear of repercussion for not complying with their exploiter [was] greater than that within their school.'

One example was a young girl who would deliberately turn up in clothes that broke the school uniform code, so she would be sent home to get changed without the school informing her parents. But instead of going home, the gang would pick her up for her run.

Some gangs refer to their youngsters as 'Bics' because of how disposable they are. There have even been reports that children can sometimes be 'rented' or 'bought' from other gangs to work on a line.

The Pilion Trust runs a shelter for young people who have been in county lines gangs. Its chief executive, Savvas Panas, said most could not go home for fear of reprisal. He said they were groomed 'quietly' by groups over a long period of time, often in apparently innocuous public spaces. 'They target loners and autistics and children from troubled backgrounds,' he said. 'They'll be alone, sitting in a park, playing ball, and someone comes along and says, "Do you want to kick a ball around with me?" Just like that, throwing a ball or going to the shop.'

The Children's Society also identified a trend towards

using younger children in what they called a 'web of exploitation' that filtered down through age groups, and especially through siblings. A Manchester head teacher told researchers how teenagers were starting to groom primary-school children. Fourteen-year-olds were picking up ten-year-olds from school. They might start by getting them to do smaller tasks such as stealing from shops before coercing them into the main operation. One respondent to a police survey said an eight-year-old had been suspected of being groomed to carry drugs; another told of a seven-year-old who was receiving support.

Interestingly, their study showed that in London the number of ten- to seventeen-year-olds getting involved in drug dealing had dipped slightly, while those arrested for intent to supply drugs outside of London had gone up 49 per cent in three years, from 338 in 2015–16 to 505 in 2017–18.

This complies with our theory that the London market has stagnated and is looking for places to grow. A correlating statistic shows the number of children being trafficked to sell drugs outside their home area has nearly doubled over three years. That said, these figures are based on data from only eleven police forces. The report's authors were critical that two-thirds of councils didn't have a strategy in place for tackling child criminal exploitation and that many councils and police forces simply didn't have enough data on what was happening in their area.

Nick Roseveare, former chief executive at The Children's Society, said: 'This shocking report reveals how cowardly criminals are stooping to new lows in grooming young people to do their dirty work and in casting their net wider to reel in younger children. Yet the response from statutory agencies is too often haphazard and comes too late and a national strategy is needed to help improve responses to child criminal exploitation.'

He recommended better early help for children and training for professionals, access to an advocate to ensure all children are supported as victims, and a greater focus on disrupting and bringing to justice the perpetrators who are exploiting them.

The response to the report by Councillor Anntoinette Bramble, chair of the Local Government Association's children and young people board, was frank and revealing. She admitted they were overwhelmed. Why? Because they didn't have enough money. She put it like this: 'Councils' youth offending teams have an exceptional record of reducing youth crime and making a real difference to young people's lives, but they are under huge pressure after seeing their government funding halved over the last decade.'[5]

Her point was that children's services are now starting more than 500 child protection investigations every day, but are also facing a £3.1 billion funding gap by 2025. In Councillor Bramble's words, it was 'forcing councils to divert funding away from preventative services.' Councils everywhere had already cut local youth services, youth offending teams and public health budgets. All they could afford to do now was firefight the emerging problems by creating services to protect children who are at immediate risk of harm.

Even that is getting more difficult, because of the pressure being applied to the children. The Children's Society concluded that young people had been 'groomed, been told not to trust professionals, been told not to talk, will be silenced through

---

5   www.local.gov.uk, 4th July 2014

threats of violence'. They talked of them being raped or forced to commit sexual acts.

Although boys are understood to be most at risk of child criminal exploitation, the report finds nearly one in six children referred to the National Referral Mechanism as suspected victims of child criminal exploitation are girls. And when it comes to female drug mules there are clearly greater dangers around sexual exploitation. Unfortunately, Lucy has also experienced this.

As we sit in the park, Lucy tells me: 'I know a lot of girls get involved with the boys because they think about the money or the thought of having a bad boy. Yeah, and they'll end up meeting with them and the boys get them completely drunk. Rape them and everything and just leave them in a park or on a bench.'

'This happened to friends of yours?'

'Yeah, and it happened to me after I lost my baby and was selling drugs. I was drinking quite a lot and I thought I was actually being really, really careful. This one boy that I felt I trusted, he just got me completely drunk, paralysed. Then he had sex with me ... yeah.'

'How old were you?'

'I was fifteen.'

As I'm looking at her, and she is just so small and sweet natured, her features betray nothing of what she's been through. She's trying to be quite casual about it, but I'm sure it still hurts. I ask, 'Do you recognise that if you are having sex with someone when you are that age, not just because you're drunk, but also underage, that is rape. They are effectively raping you?'

'Yeah?'

'You are not of the age of consent. Do you look back now and accept you have been sexually exploited?'

'Yeah, it's horrible. I don't … it's something I try to keep to myself and just block it out.'

'Is that the right thing to do?'

'I don't know.'

'Have you spoken to people?'

'I'm going to get therapy. This is just another one of them boys. Who are all, like, the same. Yeah.'

'But you think some young girls see this life as glamorous?'

'I think some girls are easily tricked.'

'Is it the money? These guys have got their cash…'

'It's not always just the money. Sometimes these guys act seriously genuine. And it's just scary. They seem so genuine. So, it's a lesson, really – just don't mix with older boys.'

The sexual abuse of girls has become infused into gang culture; drill music videos posted on YouTube by young men in gangs glamorises disrespect for girls, making it almost fashionable to treat them like possessions. This is nothing new. The hyper-realised lifestyles adopted from American rap videos, and even from games like *Grand Theft Auto*, have long been consumed as a skewed aspirational culture, where working for a living is seen as being for mugs. Men are judged on the bragging rights of their sexual prowess and wealth, and a woman's only currency lies in how she measures up to an impossibly proportioned sexualised physique. But real life isn't like that. And the reality of 'shotting' on the streets of Southampton is a very long way from the glossy 'lux life' of fictional fun-lovin' criminals in West Coast USA.

Lucy's experience echoes what professionals are observing across the UK. A youth worker quoted in The Children's Society

July 2019 report talks about battling against the odds to help children: 'You work behind the tide every single day. As soon as you think you've understood something, it has changed. And because of the level of violence that's perpetrated towards our children, the fear and the threat that they live with makes it almost impossible for them to accept [support].'

It is terrifying to think that Lucy's experience is just one of thousands happening across the country. Peer grooming into county lines often takes place in schools, via social media, and in the local community. The methods used can lead a child to believe they have made an active choice to become involved. At the same time, the situation leaves them feeling frightened, unable to see a way out, and unable to refuse to do what they're told.

Although they may fall into it casually, they can soon become hyper-vigilant and may carry a weapon for protection. This all-pervasive fear of retribution makes for a high level of stress that will ultimately impact on their mental health. They are at increased risk of anti-social personality disorder, anxiety, psychosis and substance misuse compared to other young people. And, of course, long-term exposure to the fear of violence is a risk factor for depression and post-traumatic stress disorder.

I ask Lucy for her observations about the world she's been living in, and she starts talking about what she feels are growing levels of violence.

'I've lived everywhere. I think I could say that Southampton has more knife crime. London is definitely more gun crime. It varies quite a bit, but they are upgrading. The gangs are upgrading to everything now. They have things like tasers and acid. A friend of mine was tasered by a gang member. And there's a lot of acid. I've seen people carrying acid around. I know of many people who have it.'

'Do you feel you've been exploited? Or do you feel guilty?'

'I definitely feel like I was exploited. I've done programmes, obviously. People have told me that it's definitely not okay, what's happened to me. I've done a drugs programme and, yeah, I've done domestic violence courses.'

'What's the ambition now?'

'My ambition is to get my baby back. Go to college. Not mix with anyone, just being completely on the straight and narrow. Things are much better. Like, I started dating someone who is decent. They take me out all the time and there's no shouting and I'm not, like, being pushed to do things I don't want to do.'

Lucy told me then she'd given up the drug running, but friends of hers told me she hadn't. Perhaps she does it less often, but she was still running drugs to Southampton. She was also still smoking a lot of weed.

About six months after our interview, I'm sorry to report that Lucy was committed to a psychiatric ward in a mental-health hospital. I hope and pray she gets out the other side. I've never met anyone so damaged, so young.

That said, it turns out there is a whole group of young people in our society who are being raised ready for incarceration. As we're about to find out, the conditions that propel a young person into gang membership and a mental-health unit are almost exactly the same.

10.

THE PSYCHOLOGIST

*'An abnormal reaction to an abnormal
situation is normal.'*

Carlotta was frustrated. A clinical psychologist and psycho-
therapist, she was working for a London street therapy project
in 2012. A walk-in clinic had been set up for young people in or
at risk of joining gangs, to help with their mental-health needs.
But shortly after joining the project, she realised they were
struggling to deal with the complexity of the challenges they
faced. Young people were presenting with all sorts of problems,
and the local authority didn't seem to have the systems in
place to deal with them. Housing services, welfare and mental-
health provisions were all available, but were so disjointed and
unnavigable that cases were getting log-jammed. So, one day,
Carlotta said to the team that they should suspend everything
else they were working on. The next person who walked
through the door would get the help of all staff members –
working flat out – in order to see how long it would take to
solve that one individual's problem.

A seventeen-year-old walked in. Let's call him Mike. Mike hadn't been able to change his clothes for several days, or wash. He hadn't slept for two nights and hadn't eaten that day. He was exhausted. It turned out he had left home due to extreme difficulties with his parents. He'd been involved in a local gang in the past, and, without a roof over his head, he was under increased pressure to go back to them. But he'd found a way of avoiding being out on the streets. The local hospital had an A&E waiting room, which didn't ask people to leave as long as they didn't cause trouble or fall asleep. So, that is what Mike had been doing. Night after night he camped out with the walking wounded, watching the clock tick by, trying to stay awake in the plastic chairs and under the strip lighting of Accident & Emergency. He was having some unusual experiences, such as hearing voices. It may have been that he was becoming unwell, but also might have been a result of sleep deprivation. In addition to this, he had started having suicidal thoughts. The first thing he needed was some temporary accommodation so he could sleep. 'I'd been full of optimism at that point,' said Carlotta. 'I thought we wouldn't stop until we'd got this young man somewhere to live. I thought it would take us 24 hours max, maybe two days at the worst.'

Staff got in touch with the housing department and, when things seemed to be dragging, quickly actioned processes up to manager level. They spoke to local councillors and the MP to add some pressure. The priority was to find the youngster a bed in a safe place. But the local authority housing department said the individual's mental-health problems were not severe enough. He was not considered vulnerable enough for urgent housing assistance.

Carlotta had time and again encountered housing decisions

based on seemingly arbitrary factors such as the dose of a client's medication. She was once told, with a client present, that 'the way they tried to take their life was not serious enough.' Perhaps then she could get this seventeen-year-old seen by mental-health services. But it turned out they couldn't help Mike either, not until he had housing in place, because he needed a foundation of safety before he could get treatment. Without housing, Mike couldn't register with a GP either, or get employment support. It was an infuriating catch-22. One form of assistance could not take place without the other happening first, which in turn needed the other to happen first. A full team of experts and charity workers couldn't solve the problem.

After five days of persistence, it was clear there was nowhere in the borough that Mike could go. He would have to move away – possibly outside of London. 'There was just no plan,' says Carlotta. 'Even after herculean efforts, and personal gestures such as staff cooking food themselves to bring him and letting him sleep on a sofa in the reception area for a while, what shocked me at the end of five days, is that more than a dozen of us hadn't managed anything – other than to be told he'd have to go to another borough. I asked myself, would I send my own potentially mentally unwell child to a completely different place, with no money or support network, and just cross my fingers and hope they were okay? No, of course I wouldn't.'

Carlotta then had a heartbreaking moment that consequently motivated her into years of researching a solution to the UK's gang problems. She sat on the steps with the teenager and simply said: 'I'm sorry that despite our best efforts we haven't been able to meet your needs.'

Mike responded: 'Now do you see why it's easier to stay in the gang?'

Carlotta thought to herself: You are absolutely right. If I was in your position, I'd have given up before now. She refrained from saying this, and marvelled at his willpower. The team continued to try to meet his multiple needs.

Several weeks later, housing was found, but it was where gang members from the group Mike was trying to avoid had also been placed. Carlotta fought for him to go somewhere else but failed. Mike ended up rejoining the gang. Carlotta felt she had failed him.

Carlotta is an experienced clinical psychologist. In the mid-1990s she worked with children who'd been excluded from school in the UK who had also come from traumatic backgrounds. At that time, it was thought children couldn't suffer from post-traumatic stress disorder (PTSD) or any other form of complex trauma. But Carlotta set out to show they could, and that it was treatable through a process she developed called Children's Accelerated Trauma Technique (CATT). This therapy model helped children transfer memories into an area of the brain where they could put them in the past. The technique would later be adopted by practitioners around the world, with one of the first countries to introduce it being Rwanda, where people were still struggling to deal with the mass genocide of the civil war in 1994. Carlotta worked within that country, training staff, and then founded Action for Child Trauma International, which helped introduce the technique to hundreds of clinicians globally, in countries such as Uganda, South Africa, Turkey, and Pakistan (to name just a few).

It was much later in her career, after the 2011 riots, that she became involved in exploring the mental-health needs of children who'd got involved in gangs in London. The riots had been accompanied by an increase in gang violence, and money had been made available to try to fix the problems. That's when Carlotta was drafted in to work with a small charity (which she won't name or locate, due to confidentiality agreements), which aimed to create the street therapy project. What she witnessed in this role was that many symptoms displayed by gang-involved young people were no different to those she'd seen in children traumatised by war. And it was the frustration of not being able to help vulnerable clients like Mike that led Carlotta to embark on what she described as 'one of the most emotionally challenging tasks' she had ever faced.

She wanted to understand why so many children were falling into gangs in the first place. Her investigation began by talking to young people, and not just those who came to the centre, but, rather, hundreds of young people. She tells me: 'In talking to lots of young people who were gang involved, I found their journey into gangs started very early on. A lot of them had been exposed to domestic violence, for example. Many had symptoms of post-traumatic stress.'

The most obvious symptom of PTSD displayed was hypervigilance. This is where the person feels a heightened sense of threat. Carlotta's participants would often sit in corner seats in a café facing out so they could see the whole room. When walking down the street they'd look right and left and check in the wing-mirrors of cars parked next to the pavement to surreptitiously check if they were being followed.

Some gang members would get flashbacks and nightmares. Others had a sense of a foreshortened future, meaning they could live in the here and now, but couldn't foresee a future for themselves. They could be impulsive, defensive and unable to regulate stress.

Many externalised their symptoms by 'acting out' and trying not to let on that they were suffering, 'because that would be a sign of weakness,' says Carlotta. 'But essentially they were trying to survive.' She said she met many young people who would have benefitted from treatment, but for a variety of reasons were not getting any help, and were left to survive alone.

During her research, Carlotta mapped some of the young people's histories, from birth to present. She found that for some there were multiple examples of young people with histories that included exposure to violence at home, or abuses (physical, sexual or emotional). Some had been stabbed, and even if it was a case of mistaken identity, they could have been left feeling that they weren't safe unless they were in a gang. They might have been neglected, or their family hadn't had the money to meet their needs. Often, they'd tried to tell someone and nobody had done anything to protect them. These were clear, evidence-based narratives of their background histories, and they would say things like, 'Once I'd asked for help eleven times, I gave up, so joining a gang seemed like the best way to protect myself.'

What Carlotta discovered was a failure to safeguard young people earlier in their lives. Hypervigilance wasn't being identified as a problem by youth services, yet this sense of threat was a key motivation for young people joining gangs, under the misguided perception that gangs offered safety.

She says: 'The main narrative that came from this, was a failure to safeguard young people earlier in their lives, and that due to fear and anxiety, hypervigilance and a heightened sense of threat, one main route into gangs was the seeking of protection and perceived safeguarding they may provide.

'Some gang recruiters spoke to me. They explained that they sought highly vulnerable young people to join the gangs. Some recruiters might have thought they were helping the youngster by offering protection and money, but obviously it was exploitative higher up. Once they were in a gang they were exposed to more violence, and that could exacerbate the hypervigilance and post-traumatic symptoms.'

So, the children Carlotta met had become involved in gangs in a misguided attempt to deal with their problems, but actually gang life had made their mental-health issues worse – and once in, for various reasons they weren't able to get out.

At this point Carlotta became frustrated at seeing how the post-riot funding aimed at fixing the problems was not being spent on evidence-based interventions. She says that money often went to 'people on the fringes of gang involvement but who may not have been directly gang involved and didn't necessarily focus on early intervention that could have stopped young people joining gangs in the first place.'

Having met teenagers like Mike, and interviewed other gang members, Carlotta was so moved that she started trying to get some support from central Government to undertake rigorous research looking at the actual risk factors that caused young people to join gangs. She believed that if she could pinpoint causes, be they social, economic or psychological, then she could create a screening measure – a preventative tool to reach young people much earlier and get them help before they joined gangs. Services were stretched, that was obvious, but if they could be targeted, she believed they'd be more effective.

'I did a deep dive and helped in the way I felt I was able to, because it bothered me so much; because a lot of the people I was working with at the time had friends who had ended up with serious injuries or had been killed because of gang membership. These were very live and serious issues, and there was a lot of money available to tackle the issues. I thought that if I could help to identify the main reasons that people became gang involved, the money could be targeted in the right ways, to the right people, and potentially make a sustainable difference.'

The research became an all-consuming passion. Government agencies couldn't necessarily financially support the research, but they assisted in whatever way they could, says Carlotta. 'I started doing a clinical doctorate, which meant that I could work clinically with the NHS and be funded to do research one day a week, but I would often be working every evening, all weekend and be up until the early hours of the morning trying to work out the answers! I felt I owed it to the young Mikes out there.'

Early on, Carlotta found there wasn't much research in the UK on why children and young people joined gangs. So she spent the next two years looking at international papers on the subject as part of her doctorate. 'I did a systematic review on what were the "predictive risk factors" of young people joining gangs.'

Carlotta submitted the findings to the Home Office in the summer of 2016. Both papers were published in 2017. I ask her if she had a response from the Government to her work. 'No,' she replied, 'not specifically. I did a small talk, to share the findings, which was well received in 2016 after doing the research. I haven't heard from anyone since about if/how the findings could be used. To be totally honest, I got to the end of it and was exhausted. I felt I had reached the end of what I could offer: an answer to the question of what risks predicted gang violence, which could allow for preventative interventions to be better targeted. Then I returned to full time clinical work, where I felt I belonged!'

There's no evidence that they have done anything with it. Searching online, I couldn't find any mention from the Home Office of the reports, but staff told me the first paper was used as part of the government's Serious Violence Strategy, published in 2018. But having looked into it, they seem to have sidestepped the main conclusion of the two studies. Perhaps the home truths within it were a bit too hard to stomach. So, let's explore what Carlotta found. What are the *predictive risk variables* likely to lead a child into a gang and, by extension, county lines drug dealing?

FAMILY. The data she gathered suggested, as you might expect, that low parental supervision was a predictive risk variable. There was also an association with familial gang involvement (an older sibling, not necessarily a parent) or difficult family dynamics such as abuse (sexual, physical, emotional and neglect), and running away from home. For those lacking the right attention at home, Carlotta's study found that 'gangs acted as an alternative socialisation process by providing acceptance and belonging'.

SCHOOL. Another predictive risk is low academic performance. Again, you might expect that someone with low commitment to education would be more open to gang affiliation. Difficulties in struggling children were often more pronounced during the transfer from primary school to secondary school. Lack of academic achievement can of course stem from neglect at home. But if children are not performing, the chances are they are not going to fit in as well in the classroom and get on with teachers. Sometimes, this can feel like another rejection by positive role models, which leaves them vulnerable to more antisocial friends.

PERSONAL DEVELOPMENT. When it came to individual traits, the study found children involved in gangs had difficulties getting things into perspective, along with a lack of responsibility. She found these individuals had developed problems in early childhood such as 'reduced self-control, hyperactivity, inattention, low morality, angry ruminations and poor interpersonal skills'. Anyone demonstrating antisocial behaviour had an added predictive risk variable – once in a gang this behaviour rapidly worsened, becoming more violent.

DRUGS. So far you might have been unsurprised by the above findings, but here it gets more interesting. Drug use doesn't necessarily correlate with gang affiliation. However, someone who has been in a gang was more likely to end up a drug user. So here is a longer-term impact that is rarely considered: gang membership can lead to a lifetime of substance use, especially with marijuana, which itself can lead to increased mental-health problems.

ETHNICITY. Carlotta couldn't draw conclusions about ethnicity. Her report states: 'It appeared that being BAME [Black, Asian and minority ethnic] was a predictive risk; however, this was confounded by a myriad additional factors (such as historic relationships with the police, stop-and-search experiences and higher arrest rates, which were more closely related to ethnicity than they were to gang affiliation).' The literature also suggested that 'the ethnicity of gang-affiliated individuals merely reflected the demographics of the area in which the research was conducted, and was not a unique risk indicator.'

ECONOMIC DISADVANTAGE. This is a straight-up, undeniable predictive risk factor. Aspiration to escape poverty was a driving force. Someone with limited opportunities is much more easily lured by the belief that gang membership can lead to wealth. But the study found the reverse was true. It states: 'Being a gang member impacted negatively on the individual's ability to secure employment, creating a vicious cycle.'

COMMUNITY. Being raised in an urban, antisocial or economically deprived environment increased the predictive risk, but more so if gang presence was highly visible and threatening in the area. That just made young people more inclined to be a member, presumably under the ethos that if you don't want to feel intimidated by them – join them.

MENTAL HEALTH. And here is the big issue. Along with disturbed families, poor school records, antisocial behaviour and poverty, the factor most associated with gang affiliation was mental-health problems, both as a cause and as a result of gang membership. According to Carlotta's report: 'The analysis unanimously demonstrated high psychological distress in this cohort. Low self-esteem was a predictive risk in this area, but high-quality cross-sectional studies showed additional associations between gang affiliation and PTSD, anxiety and depression.'

The systematic review of different studies found that there were differing opinions about suicide rates. Some found gang members were less likely to take their own lives than those from the same backgrounds who stayed out of gangs. However, what is worrying with regards to county lines is that this risk changed if someone had run away from home to join a gang, or if they had been subject to sexual abuse. While we can't say that everything related to gang membership will also apply to children in county lines, it seems highly likely that the conditions they are subjected to by this exploitative model would only make matters worse. In other words, the county lines problem is creating a cohort of children with serious mental-health problems.

Carlota concluded: 'The strongest line of narrative from the higher quality papers in this section appears to be that gang-affiliated individuals had difficulties with interpersonal skills and had low self-esteem. Although mental-health symptoms were suggested, whether these were intrinsic, consequential to gang affiliation, or both intrinsic and exacerbated by gang affiliation, was unclear. However, it appeared evident that gang affiliation created obstacles to future employment and facilitated further violence, exposure to violence and drug use.'[6]

Having completed her review, Carlotta was convinced that potential gang members could indeed be identified at a young age, and therefore targeted for early intervention. There were a number of factors which, when lumped together, created a cumulative risk. The report describes 'a toxic web' during crucial developmental stages of a child that ultimately traps the child into the gang. The sticky strands of this spider's web include low parental supervision, poverty, neglect, abuse and

---

6 Extracts from: 'Identifying risks for male street gang affiliation: a systematic review and narrative synthesis', The *Journal of Forensic Psychiatry & Psychology*, Carlotta Raby & Fergal Jones (2016).

school suspension. The children hope that by joining a gang they will get a sense of belonging, increase their social status, secure financial independence and be protected. Sadly, in most cases, none of these things actually happen.

Having gleaned all this material from international reports spanning five continents, with the majority being from the US, Carlotta sought to clarify whether her findings applied to gangs in the UK. So she worked with the Home Office and the Met Police gangs unit to get access to and interview people on the gang matrix (established gang members known to the police).

She then picked one London borough and interviewed 100 young people who were gang involved and 100 who were not but shared the same demographics. She says: 'We were looking at which factors make people faced with the same problems join a gang versus those who don't join a gang. Then we created a measure based on that. So, in the end, we could say what risk factors there are – and say with some certainty that if young people faced these kind of things, they were likely to join a gang. Then, finally, the question is – based on all that, can we do anything about it?'

Carlotta created what is called a Gang Affiliation Risk Measure (GARM), which found fifteen key factors, and concluded that once a child reaches over seven of those cumulative risks then they are highly likely to join a gang. And you can tell by the age of ten.

The questions are as follows:

1. Do you usually tell your family where you are going, when you go out?
2. Is your biological father living at home with you?

3. Have you been kicked out of school at any point?

4. Have you witnessed violence in your area?

5. Do you think it is easier to make money through gang involvement rather than getting a job?

6. Have you been badly beaten up?

7. Have you been in trouble for fighting or hurting other people?

8. Do you have the sense that life will be short?

9. In your area, do you feel that you have to look over your shoulder all the time, to stay safe?

10. When you get home from school, does anyone ask you how your day has been?

11. Have you witnessed violence at home?

12. Do you *often* have aggressive thoughts?

13. Do the people who you live with sort out problems using violence?

14. Have you regularly heard about people being shot, stabbed or killed in your area?

15. Are you aware of post code gangs in your area?

Answering 'yes' to seven or more of these fifteen questions would indicate a future risk of gang affiliation, and would suggest early intervention support is required in these areas.

The report concluded that: 'Robust age-appropriate screening measures and evidence-based treatment should be employed to identify and treat those in need of mental-health support, and reduce ongoing offending behaviour.'[7]

The report conceded that this process of identification and

---

7 Extracts from: 'Design, development and validity testing of the gang affiliation risk measure (GARM)', The *Journal of Forensic Psychiatry & Psychology*, Raby, C., Jones, F. W., Hulbert, S., & Stout, J. (2017).

provision could still be fraught with difficulties, warning that: 'Postcode territories, the stigma of mental-health difficulties, the risk of being perceived as weak and an inherent lack of trust in authority could make accessing help challenging.'

Carlotta's attempted solution to gang violence is essentially what is called an 'epidemiological core infection model', which she described as 'rather than fishing people out of the water downstream, you look upstream at why they are falling into the water and you try to fix that problem.'

In this case, the rickety old bridge upriver appears to be our lack of safeguarding and targeted care provision for young people. The research found that most boys in this at-risk cohort showed symptoms of hypervigilance by nursery school age – many by the age of five. Carlotta believes screening of these children should start at Year Six and that a questionnaire could be given to children and used to work out whether they are at risk. A pilot project could possibly see whether this had any impact on future gang membership. But Carlotta says there's a problem.

'Even if you did identify young people at risk of gang affiliation, could you find a borough that can guarantee to have the resources to meet these children's needs in this current climate?' She adds: 'If you were to ask most, they would say "probably not". The other problem is that everyone works in silos – housing does housing; welfare does employment support; CAMHS does mental health.'

As we demonstrated with Mike at the beginning of this chapter, getting help isn't straightforward. Carlotta concludes: 'Many people have an overwhelming number of needs and there are services set up to help – but they are not designed to work holistically with young people.'

In 2018 the government published its Serious Violence Strategy, complete with a section on predictive risk variables and interventions, which was enhanced by Carlotta's work. The government's report mentions the Perry Preschool programme in the USA, which targeted three- and four-year-old African-American children living in poverty. It followed up participants at the age of forty, finding decreased levels of violence, including murder and robbery. When looking at the value of this intervention, they found: 'For each £1 spent on the programme there was £1.61 in benefits estimated.' This was split between increased earnings and reduced crime. But in this area the government strategy concludes that: 'We still do not really know the most important causal drivers of serious violence', and it calls for testing with larger samples.

It seems a shame, then, that they didn't look at Carlotta's second paper, as GARM appears to answer this question, and would allow them to get on with providing a solution rather than kicking the can down the road. That said, the Home Office media factsheet, updated in November 2019 for the general election, reminded me that the government announced investments of £220 million into early-intervention projects, and the first wave of this money, £16.2 million, was given in 2019 to 22 projects across the UK aimed at diverting young people from getting involved in serious violence.

I decided to discuss Carlotta's work with someone who has helped me a great deal with this book. Nevres Kemal is a social worker who famously blew the whistle on Haringey Council over their failing children's services just before the infamous death of Peter Connelly. Known at the time as Baby P, the seventeen-month-old Peter was failed by the council's child welfare authorities. Despite being on their radar, he suffered more than fifty injuries over an eight-month period while in the care of his mother, Tracy Connelly, her boyfriend, Steven Barker, and Barker's brother, Jason Owen. The three were later jailed for contributing to his death. Prior to Peter's death, Nevres twice wrote to authorities highlighting the failures of the borough's child protection system, but she was ignored.

Since the Baby P scandal, Nevres set up her own charity called Raising My Voice Foundation, which helps people in the community with an array of social problems from housing to probation. She and her daughter Azra have acted as fixers for me at Sky News, and have helped me gain access to some of the characters interviewed in this book. Nevres has her finger on the pulse of London's streets, and she agrees with Carlotta's conclusions.

She says: 'There is lack of intervention, one hundred per cent. But it's also the quality of the intervention. Because these people do pass through the system – they just don't get the right help. It goes back to councils saying, "We haven't got any money." A lot of boroughs have poorly qualified social workers and a general lack of resources, and they only kick in the resources when things are looking really bad. By then it's too late.'

Nevres gives an example that surprises me. She says she started noticing young people going missing from her local area around 2010, and she soon figured out these were kids joining county lines operations. One of them was a girl that her daughter Azra helped me get in touch with – Lucy, 'the runner' I interviewed in the previous chapter. It turns out Lucy has an eleven-year-old brother, and he has recently gone down the same path.

Nevres tells me this eleven-year-old stayed with his addict

mother after Lucy went into care, and was essentially neglected in the same way. He started roaming the streets and selling drugs. She describes him as 'streetwise and vulnerable at the same time'. It seems obvious, but as Lucy's problems came into focus, one might have expected social services to pay attention to her little brother as well, but they didn't. After going feral, he was eventually put into care, but like his sister he then met 'bad people' and joined a gang.

Nevres says: 'Care can be like prison – you meet people with contacts. They don't have to go out recruiting. They are living in the same place. So, this little boy, blonde, blue eyes, he's a smart kid. They offer him stuff. He gets a pair of trainers and, what's more, he now belongs somewhere. Anyway, he's on the streets – stealing, selling drugs – and sometimes he goes back to his dad's house. But social services tell the dad he mustn't take him in because that will only encourage him to run away from the care home. So, for two months the kid slept under the swings in a playground near his father's house. No one came to get him. Finally, it got to a point where he could drop dead – then they spent the money.'

This eleven-year-old was eventually sent to a residential care home in Wales, and is now under round-the-clock care. 'It is really, really messed up,' says Nevres. 'Now he is locked up under twenty-four-hour supervision, but the damage is done – they left him with the mum too long, and this is a mother who they knew used to smoke crack when he was a baby.'

Nevres observes that the education system didn't help either. Despite being a smart kid he wasn't getting on at school, probably because his home life was so disruptive. 'Right now, not only are a lot of these children traumatised at home, but then our education system kicks them in the nuts and tells them they're not good enough. We have resources in this country, but they are not targeted.' Nevres's charity is trying to get into primary schools to identify these children, much in the way Carlotta suggests, and create more clubs and sports facilities and holiday activities for them. 'Kids start to wander in the holidays,' says Nevres. 'They have no provision, unless they are part of social services. But you can't wait until they hit social services. By the time they are eleven or twelve they can be engaged in selling drugs; they may have had sex – effectively been sexually exploited. The young girls are being especially messed up. These are potential mothers. So then we have this next generation of women who think it's okay to be sexually violated. Traumatised people having traumatised babies, and they don't know how to parent. Everyone's smoking weed; it all becomes normalised. No one is doing anything. Society doesn't have a conscience and, to be honest, I think we've missed the boat.'

If early intervention is failing, it seems the system is equally neglectful in trying to get kids out once they fall into gangs or county lines. A report on county lines published by Jo Hudek in May 2018 for the St Giles Trust found: 'The overwhelming view of contributors to the scoping research was that there is a gap in the specialist services needed to support children involved in county lines activity.'

It went on to say: 'Specialist one-to-one casework and/or mentoring was most commonly cited by statutory agencies as the intervention they feel would be most effective in addressing the identified gap in expertise.' But added: 'Very few organisations seem to deliver the specialist services that seem able to meet the needs of children involved in county lines.'[8]

8 Extracts from: 'Scoping County Lines – a snapshot of challenges and emerging practice',
Jo Hudek, St Giles Trust (2018)

The St Giles Trust has launched pilot schemes in London, Kent and South Wales, designed to help children exit county lines activity. This includes helping them engage in education, get jobs and have better family relationships. The Trust specialises in helping people from disadvantaged backgrounds but, interestingly, its 2018 report found that children who get involved in county lines come from a variety of backgrounds, ranging from 'chaotic and risky home circumstances' to 'those from well-ordered and materially comfortable families'. It suggested that county line owners look to recruit children that blend in with the drug market that the line is intended to exploit, and these can vary both in ethnicity and affluence. It concedes, however, that the majority of children come from similar backgrounds to those described in Carlotta's report.

The St Giles Trust is one of only a small number of organisations providing specialist face-to-face services that help children in county lines. Others include Safer London and Catch 22, but many of these services are London focused. Provisions are still catching up with the spread of the problem to other parts of the country. In terms of national support services, Missing People has been setting up a phone-based national support service, SafeCall, for children and family members affected by county lines. Whilst there are other children's helplines – notably Childline, which offers advice for children in difficulty – we can't just expect these children to pick up the phone and call for help.

Redthread is perhaps the best example of a proactive approach. The charity has specialist youth workers embedded in A&E departments working alongside the doctors and nurses. They try to identify children who are being exploited by gangs. If a child is admitted with stab wounds, for example, they do all they can to offer support. There are many ways to spot an exploited child, be it stomach pains from concealing drugs internally, to noticing that they come from an area different to the hospital where they have admitted themselves. But again, Redthread is geographically limited – focused in London, Birmingham and Nottingham.

The St Giles Trust report refers to 'reachable moments' where interventions could enable a child to avoid getting further entrenched in these activities. It states: 'These include in the initial stages of grooming, exclusion from mainstream education, being returned from a missing episode, after violent assault (including admission to A&E), release after arrest, court appearance and serving community/custodial orders.'

These potential 'reachable moments' are clearly something charities and government services need to focus on. But perhaps even more so they need to look upstream. It's clear from Carlotta's extensive research that, for most people, joining a gang or getting involved in county lines is the end of a long line of things that have gone wrong in their lives – and the 'reachable moments' could indeed come at a much younger age and, if acted on, could be more effective.

When giving a presentation of her work in October 2019, Carlotta quoted the words of the famous psychologist and holocaust survivor, Viktor Frankl. He said: 'An abnormal reaction to an abnormal situation is normal.' An abnormal reaction to an abnormal *upbringing* is also normal.

We need to stop demonising these children and start accepting the fact that we are helping to create them. We are standing by and watching it happen. Reflecting on her work, Carlotta told me: 'I'm used to doing work around trauma in areas affected by conflict with children and young people, but

I was genuinely shocked at how serious this problem was. I hadn't expected it to be so hard to find solutions, or to be so affected by it. I couldn't just walk away and say, "Good luck with that, bye." I am glad I didn't. We have to do something about it. It was a really moving piece of work to be involved in, and all the young people who assisted in the project taught me a phenomenal amount, in a genuine attempt to help prevent other children and young people from becoming involved. In the beginning, here was a real split between people involved in policy development. Some people knew and acknowledged that there were serious social issues impacting on young people which led to gang involvement, and some others seemed to believe that some people were "born bad" and that nothing could change the pathways of these young people, but that's not been my experience; that's not what I saw. It's also not what young people told me, furthermore, it's not what the majority of evidence demonstrated. We need to take responsibility for the causes of this issue. A failure of preventative safeguarding and caregiving is what young people are saying, and it's what the research objectively backs up. So, let's do something about that.'

In light of Carlotta's work, you may think it is only children from broken homes who can get involved in this kind of thing. But think again. Next stop. Yorkshire.

11.

THE LAST-CHANCE SALOON

'You either pull together, or you end up falling apart.'

Helen sits in a stark recreation room with whitewashed brick walls. A table-tennis table dominates, and behind it a poster states the house rules. Bad behaviour, smacking bats, fighting, foul language or refusing to leave when asked, earns you an X. Get two Xs and it's a week-long ban from the table-tennis table. Clearly, the people who use this room have anger management issues. Helen is a dinner lady now but has worked in prisons before as a warden, so she's used to the minimalist décor and strict instructions on walls. But this isn't a prison; it's the school her son goes to.

We are in Grove Academy Pupil Referral Unit in Harrogate, which is a last-chance saloon for children who have been kicked out of mainstream education. Helen's son Callum has been a student here for two years, and he's also a former county lines drug runner. His story is a wake-up call to parents everywhere that, really, this can happen to almost any child.

Helen describes Callum as a typical boy, fun-loving, happy-go-lucky, but he did struggle with his education. At the end of primary school, he was diagnosed as having a learning difficulty, dyslexia. His diagnosis came late, as he was in a small village primary school, and his dyslexia wasn't really taken into account at secondary school, so he fell behind in class.

'He couldn't read simple things,' says Helen. She wears a white blouse. Her hair is pulled back into a ponytail and she speaks in a Yorkshire accent. 'He found it very hard to write, as well, so he was really struggling. You're talking of a book that's probably for a seven-year-old child, and he couldn't read it. So, I knew there were problems.

'They offered him a little bit of help, one-to-one, for a short period of time, but then they said there were children of greater need.' Helen looked for a different school and eventually found him a place where he could get some extra help, but things soon began to go downhill as he became more and more withdrawn. It would turn out, however, that there was more to this than his learning difficulties.

By the time he was twelve, like other children of his age, Callum wanted to spend time with his friends. The main hangout point was at a skate park, five miles from his mother's house, in a next-door town where his father lived. His parents had separated when he was eight. Callum would sometimes pop in on his father, but was less and less interested in spending time with his family. Before long, his behaviour started to deteriorate. He became aggressive, and despite previously being close to his mother and two older sisters, he began to shut out his parents and siblings completely. At first, no one made the connection between his personality shift and his visits to the skate park.

Helen tells me: 'He didn't want to mix with us. He didn't

want to really do anything. When he got in, he'd just go to his room. He became really, really distant. And when you asked him, there was just nothing. He didn't even talk to his sisters about what was going on. He just shut everybody out, which was really strange because previously he was very, very close to his family.

'So, we didn't know why. We couldn't put our finger on what it was. It was deteriorating to the point where the school was calling us in and saying he was getting suspended. We just didn't know what to do.'

One day, Callum's school rang again. He had turned up under the influence of drugs and this was the final straw. Aged fourteen, he was kicked out permanently. 'They said it was disruptive behaviour,' says Helen. All this was a complete shock to his mother. Callum grew up in a small village outside Harrogate, which Helen describes as, 'in the middle of nowhere.'

This sleepy environment was about as far from drugs, or the heaving metropolis of Tottenham, as you can imagine. The village, which Helen has asked me not to identify, has a single road running through it, a pub and a village shop that includes a post office. Residents are proud that a village this size has managed to maintain its post office, when others across the country have been closed down. In the latest parish newsletter, the most controversial story is about dog poo.

On the face of it at least, this is hardly 'drugs central'. For Callum's parents, news that he had been expelled for taking drugs was shocking enough. Where did he even get them from? He told his mother that two girls had given him some cannabis and it was the first time he'd ever tried it. Helen believed him. The idea that he might be more deeply involved in a sinister network of dealers was beyond anyone's imagination. No one in the village, least of all Helen, had ever heard of county lines drug dealing.

It was the drug offence that meant Callum ended up at Grove Academy Pupil Referral Unit in the nearby town of Harrogate. The table tennis room in this PRU is where Helen and I sat together for our first conversation. PRUs are often considered dumping grounds for children the mainstream system simply can't and never will deal with. A more positive outlook would be to regard PRUs as an educational repair centre for broken teenagers; a place where they get the attention they need to make a new start. Either way, there is no doubt that excluded children in PRUs are high on the target list for drug dealers.

In the story of county lines, these last-chance schools play a crucial role. It's why you'll read plenty of stuff in the papers about how PRUs are a breeding ground for gangs. How they help collate all the bad apples into one geographical basket, making them easy pickings for the gang-groomers. We will explore this issue later. What I can tell you is that Callum was already deep into dealing drugs when he was in mainstream education – and it was the pupil referral unit that saved him.

Like Helen, staff at Grove Academy had also never heard of county lines until Callum arrived at the school. They could tell quite early on that this newcomer to the PRU had a drug habit, but that was nothing unusual for a school that caters for excluded children. The art teacher at Grove Academy, Kate Kersey, told me that more than half of their students 'take drugs on a regular basis'. Many of them have mental-health problems and are highly disruptive, so the teachers are used to drugs and angry kids.

With Callum, 'Things came to light slowly,' says Colette Munro, head of pastoral care at Grove Academy. 'You begin to put two and two together and you think, hang on a minute, this is really serious. There was something particular about his behaviour – teachers began to work out that he was actually scared to death of something.'

In these instances, you can argue that a PRU is better equipped to deal with the complexities of drug issues than a mainstream school. For starters, they're not going to kick Callum out for turning up stoned. Rather they would talk to him about drugs. They would actually consider him not as a troublemaker – but more someone who was maybe *in* trouble. He comes from a good stable home. His mother and father had split up, but lived close to each other and clearly still loved him. He had a roof over his head and meals to come home to. But he was defensive, a closed book, and he was angry. He wasn't getting into fights with others so much, but there was an internal rage that could suddenly erupt. Callum was so incapable of controlling his emotions he was twice rushed to hospital after pumping his fists into the classroom walls and cutting open his knuckles.

His mum Helen says of the PRU: 'They helped by giving him a one-to-one, bespoke timetable and just being there. Letting him rant and listening to him and trying to understand why.'

Through this process, and having extra support, Callum finally opened up about what was going on. He admitted that on one occasion at the skate park he had been approached by older boys and offered some money to deliver cannabis to some customers. He was shown a big wad of cash. The dealer let him touch it. He'd get a share if he just helped out. When he did, he was actually paid with a bit of cannabis rather than the money. Before long he was also being offered harder drugs including MDMA and cocaine.

'They got him addicted,' says Helen. 'At first, I believe they sort of made it out to be a really good lifestyle. He could be what he wanted to be and make a lot of money out of it. But the reality of it is, you can't. No way. Then it was, "Here, just have a bit of stuff," and that was it. "Oh well, now you owe us. So, you've got to do that for me. You've got to pay it back."

'They used his addiction to get him to become a supplier. And this goes on everywhere. Older teens at the skate park were watching for the younger children. The ones they could exploit, the weak ones, I suppose. And that's where it all started, from being twelve years old. So, it is very, very widespread. In the area we're in, people don't think it happens, but it does.'

While Helen thought Callum was hanging out with friends in the skate park, he had actually started running drugs in the local area and was becoming an addict himself. He was at the bottom end of the supply chain that came through Leeds and may well have started in London, Liverpool or Manchester. Slowly, his market area expanded. He supplied the larger town of Harrogate and areas beyond. Often, he was driven around Yorkshire to drop off drugs, and several times he was trafficked to bigger cities.

On one occasion, he was taken to Leeds where his job that evening was as doorman to a drug dealer's house. He let in clients and other dealers. He watched as gang members arrived, leaving their guns and knives on the table while they discussed business. For Callum, this had been a frightening experience, and he decided he didn't want to be involved any more. But it was too late, the gang wasn't about to let him go.

When he told them that he didn't want to work for them any

more, they showed him a video. It was a recording of the gang members beating someone up. He was told, 'If you don't do as you're told, this is going to happen to you and your family.' At this point he was thirteen years old. He was trapped and scared to death. He couldn't get out – this was his life now and he was stuck with it.

'We needed to get him out of the area,' said Colette. Once Callum had opened up about what was going on – now aged fourteen – everyone realised there was only one course of action. Social services would have to find a way to relocate him for a while. 'We begged Children's Social Care to take him on,' says Collette. 'They were reluctant. They tried to say his mother was neglecting him and not taking on her parental responsibilities properly. But she couldn't safeguard him. She just couldn't.'

I spoke to Helen about this. How had she let things slip so much that her son was out of control at such a young age? She says that, at first, she simply hadn't realised what was going on, and by the time she did it was too late. She remembers going up to his room one day and discovering that he wasn't in his bed. He'd just snuck out in the middle of the night.

'He was being told to sell drugs and thought he had to or they would hurt his family,' says Helen. 'That was the thing. So he kept running away from home and I couldn't understand why because he had a good home. And it was definitely the thought that they would hurt his family that made him do it. But we didn't know this at first.'

Once Helen realised she had a problem, she started locking the front door and hiding the key. But Callum would slip out through his bedroom window.

'I used to wake up in the morning and go upstairs and his

bed would be empty. You wouldn't even know he'd gone. He'd get up in the middle of the night and, unless you were in the room watching over him all night, there was nothing you could do to stop him going because he was determined. Even if the police brought him back, an hour later he'd go again.

'We were out two, three, four in the morning, driving around looking for him, and I couldn't find him. His two sisters came along too because they were older. We all went out looking. My husband [Helen had remarried] would stay at home with a young one and we just didn't know what to do. You're just looking for him, and looking for him. And everyone's got to carry on as normal and go to work the next day. It takes its toll very much. You either pull together, or you end up falling apart.'

Callum's absences became a source of huge conflict in the home. Once, when the family was having a conservatory built, Callum's sister, who was twenty-one at the time, tried to stop him leaving the house. Fourteen at the time, Callum picked up an eight-foot section of the conservatory wall and raised it above his head. He threatened to smash the plastic and metal down on his sister's head. She backed off.

'It really was a shock to me,' says Helen. 'I just didn't think this sort of thing existed, but to actually be involved in it and see what it can do … it was a nightmare. That's the only way I can describe it. It could break your family very easily.'

Despite being the youngest member of the family, Callum became a terrifying presence at home. The anger was usually directed at himself, such as punching his fists through plaster walls, but his addiction soon became apparent too. Helen remembers being out searching for Callum on one of the occasions he went missing: when he spotted her, he tried to push her car back up the road. Her bleary-eyed son was so high that, even though he wasn't able to stand properly, he thought he could simply push the car away.

'I just remember the face of him,' says Helen. 'It was the first time I'd seen him on MDMA, and he just couldn't keep his eyes open. It was horrendous, absolutely horrendous. He thought he was Superman. It's frightening what drugs can do.'

Callum went to hospital three times over this period. Not through the drugs themselves but always because of things he'd done after taking the drugs, such as punching the walls. Once, he was being chased by police officers, so he jumped off a fifteen-foot bridge into a shallow river. He was lucky not to break any bones, but he twisted ligaments in his knee.

Even though he was supplying for the gang, Callum wasn't earning enough to feed his habit, so he took to shoplifting. Helen remembers picking him up from the police station after he'd been caught. She described her son as 'completely broken'. At this point she became desperate to get him out of the area, as did the school – not because they thought Helen wasn't trying to look after her son, but because they knew, and she knew, that whatever they did they couldn't protect him as long as he stayed in the family home. 'He just wasn't going to escape this ring if we didn't send him away,' says Helen. 'And we pushed and pushed. I actually went to the local authority and they didn't want anything to do with it. They said I needed to take more parental responsibility for my child. I couldn't make them see that I couldn't keep him safe. I said, "I am doing everything I can do, but I cannot physically keep him safe. So, I need your help."'

To begin with, social services registered Callum on what is called the 'childhood need level'. It doesn't require him to be relocated but they keep a closer eye on him. Only if it can be proven that a child is in imminent danger of harm do things go up a notch to 'child protection status'. This then allows the council to set up a relocation service. But Colette says that because Callum wasn't at risk directly from his family, social services couldn't understand why he was in danger. They didn't seem to comprehend the nature of the external threat. The fact that it was the people he was choosing to hang out with who were the danger – not his parents – didn't compute in the system. As Colette puts it: 'He was at huge risk. We are talking adults with guns and knives who were getting him to run serious drugs for them. But social care just didn't get it. They said to Callum's mum, "We will do you for neglect if you refuse to have Callum living with you." And she said, "I can't have him living with me because I can't keep him safe."'

What's more, Colette believes the local authority was in denial about the existence of county lines drug dealing in their borough. She tells me: 'They said: "We don't have a problem with county lines drug dealing or child sexual exploitation in Harrogate." So, they either didn't get it or they knew it was going on and chose to ignore it. And that means there's a lack of funding and resources. They are not prepared to go the extra mile that is needed to keep these children safe.'

Without locking him in his room twenty-four hours a day, there was little Helen could do to keep Callum from going out, and he was starting to disappear for longer and longer periods. Then, one December just before Christmas, he vanished. Days passed and there was no sign of him. It was a cold winter and Helen became frantic, calling friends, driving around the local area – begging the police to keep an eye out for him. He was gone. Staff at the PRU would call up offering help to look for him. Christmas Eve came and went. Things were desperate. A fourteen-year-old child who didn't want to be home for Christmas – how bad had things got? Even over the festive period, staff at the PRU were offering support. 'Christmas Day, Boxing Day, the school were on the phone. "Where is he? Do you need our help?" That network of us all working together, the school and the family, helped massively.'

Ten days passed before Callum was picked up by the police. He'd been taking drugs, selling drugs, and sleeping rough under bridges in sub-zero temperatures. He was lucky to be alive. At this point, Helen made a difficult decision. She would refuse to take him home. To allow him back would be the equivalent of just throwing him back out onto the street. He'd only run away again. She'd tried this tactic once before and had been threatened with arrest for abandonment, but this time she had the police on her side. They too told the council that this was something different. Callum was at high risk, living in fear of his obligations to the gang. He needed to be protected by the state, not just by his mother. Helen says: 'The police told the council, if you don't do something, this boy's not going to wake up one morning.'

Finally, social services agreed to step in and he was moved to a children's care home in North Yorkshire, two hours from his home. Helen signed away her parental responsibility to the council. 'We had to send him,' she tells me. 'That was one of the hardest things I've ever had to do.'

The PRU kept his place open and provision was made for him to make the two-hour drive each day to his school. He was given a new timetable allowing him to come into the PRU at 10am and go back to the care home at 3pm. He was being treated like someone in a witness protection programme, but his support network and school structure stayed in place.

The children's home got him away from the immediate problem – but when you are a fourteen-year-old drug addict, it's never a completely smooth ride back to normality. In care, he was still mixing with the wrong people, still going out after dark. Staff at care homes don't have the powers to keep the children inside locked up. All they can really do is the same as a parent, and call the police when a child goes missing. Colette says: 'It was sort of out of the frying pan into the fire – but on this occasion the fire was less dangerous than the frying pan.'

Slowly, things began to improve. The gang didn't know where Callum was and he started a programme to get himself off the drugs. He was less disruptive at school. Perhaps it was the relief that the gang couldn't get to him. He could have easily carried on his downward spiral, but, after seeing the efforts others had made to rescue him, he finally seemed to want to save himself. 'Deep down, Callum is a very decent boy with decent values,' says Colette. 'At some point, he knew that the time had come – he needed to sort himself out. He wanted to go back to Mum.'

After about a year, there was a phased return. He'd go home for a weekend and he'd be fine. He wouldn't go missing. Slowly, over time, he came back and things started to change.

When I met Helen and Colette, Callum was about to turn sixteen. He was regularly attending the PRU and thriving. That day, a teacher had taken him fishing and they returned with a massive pike. Callum's childlike excitement at the catch was far removed from the withdrawn, lost child of a year or two before. Now, three days a week, he'd do work experience and he worked hard enough that his employer offered an apprenticeship on the condition he got into college. To that end, he'd recently had an interview to do an agriculture course.

Callum had also built up a relationship with a police community support officer. He was one of the team who'd previously arrested him, and would sometimes keep him in custody to protect him from the gang. Now they'd started to go boxing together. But Colette reckons the thing that turned him around more than anything else was earning money. His work experience was pocketing him more than £100 a week. 'He likes his clothes, does Callum,' says Colette. 'He's got a good work ethic. Don't get me wrong – he's not totally clean-faced.

He's not the blue-eyed little boy. He still gets up to anti-social behaviour. He does have a drink, and he probably has the odd spliff, but he's not involved anywhere near the depth he was.'

She adds: 'He needed a lot of support to be able to say, "I don't want to do this any more." But none of these children – believe me when I say this – *none of these children* want to do this. They are just in too deep, too scared to get out of it. They are controlled by these evil, nasty people who wouldn't think twice about murdering them.'

Callum was extremely lucky. He clearly had a lot of multi-agency assistance. More importantly, his mum fought tooth and nail to protect him, even when that meant giving him over to the authorities for his own safety.

'Touch wood, we've come through it,' says Helen. 'He's a good kid now – a live wire, but a good kid. With children, you just want to protect them. But when they won't let you in, you're lost. It's very frightening. Fortunately, he came to Grove Academy PRU. And they supported him and helped him manage his aggression. And they helped us as a family dig a little bit deeper in our support of him. If he exploded, they wouldn't say, "Right, go stand outside", they'd try to understand why. He'd got involved very deeply in something I'd never heard of. I had no idea it even existed.'

There are over 350 pupil referral units in England and they have a reputation for disruptive classes and poor attendance rates. The standard of provision across the country varies wildly and research by education news website School's Week found some areas, such as Newcastle, Gateshead, Lincolnshire and Thurrock, could only offer units referred to by Ofsted as 'inadequate'. There have been calls to shut them all down, and a report in Parliament suggested that mainstream schools were using them as dumping grounds for poor-performing students, so they could improve the schools' exam results.

I put it to Helen that pupil referral units are often portrayed as being part of the reason children gravitate towards gangs. She answered: 'You know, people are looking for the vulnerable ones regardless of what school they go to.'

'And what would happen if the teachers and staff at this PRU hadn't stepped in?' I ask.

'Honestly, I don't think he would be here. He was taking MDMA, cocaine, and that, on a young body, isn't the best of things. I think his addiction could have taken him over. I don't know. I dread to think.'

Now, here's the sting in the tale. The PRU that helped save Callum is now battling to save itself. The council decided to re-jig its high-needs education budget, and by re-jig I mean cut around 50 per cent of the funds to the school, making it near impossible for it to stay open. The series of inspirational and caring teachers I met at Grove Academy at the time of writing are all looking for new jobs.

A few weeks after I met them, they were forced to go on strike with placards saying 'Save Our School' and 'What's The Plan For The Future?' Without Grove Academy, there will not be a safety net for excluded children in the town.

On the day teachers went on strike, the Grove's head teacher John Warren told local reporters they had been forced to take such a drastic step to get their voice heard. He said: 'Staff, parents and other professionals are deeply concerned at the impact of these cuts and fear Harrogate will be left with a black hole of alternative provision for the most needy children if the Grove is unable to continue.'

Despite the school being rated 'outstanding' in its last Ofsted inspectors' report, the local authority needed to claw back a £5.5 million overspend in the high-needs sector. Councillors also decided they should 'redirect' some money towards mainstream schools, so they could do more to prevent exclusions of students in the first place. I agree with the idea that, where possible, difficult children should be kept in mainstream schools. It's just that sometimes this doesn't happen. I'm not sure any mainstream school would have accommodated Callum, and plenty of headmasters I respect have told me that if they don't expel for drugs or violence, then where do they draw the line? How many children can be saved for bad behaviour by making an example of one? I'd say that if you're going to address the expulsion issue, don't start by pulling away the safety net.

In a statement reported in the *Harrogate Advertiser* in June 2019, Jane Le Sage, the county council's director of inclusion, said: 'We recognise the negative impact of exclusion on educational attainment, life chances and increased vulnerability of young people. We remain committed to reducing the numbers of permanent exclusions across the county by ensuring schools have access to high-quality, alternative provision for young people, who will benefit from a more personalised curriculum and higher levels of support.'

Across the United Kingdom, the level of exclusions in the years 2013–2017 rose by 70 per cent, and mainstream schools have been accused of 'off-rolling' difficult children so that their GCSE results don't reflect badly on their institutions. The idea that school league tables might be a motivation to ditch kids from a proper education is shocking – but head teachers have told me they think it happens, and this thorny issue of exclusions is something this book will delve into again later.

When it comes to Grove Academy though, there seems to be a wilful blindness to its obvious benefit to society. Helen credits the PRU for changing the course of her son's life. 'They were fantastic. I can't praise them enough,' she says. Let her story be a warning to what might happen if it is forced to close.

The Grove Academy battle is by no means unique. Across the country, over the last decade, the Conservative government's austerity measures have cut into children's services. The consequences are incalculable.

In February 2019, the five biggest children's charities produced findings showing that between 2010 and 2018 there had been an overall cut of 29 per cent in children's services. That's equivalent to £3 billion, and this was impacting on everything from family crisis support to child protection. More than 1,000 children's centres and 600 youth clubs had closed. The situation was worse in the places we have focused on so far in this story. In Haringey – the borough that includes Tottenham – they were spending £39 million less than they had 8 years ago: a 38 per cent reduction.

In Yorkshire and the Humber, which includes Harrogate, the per-head funding was down 33 per cent. Charities warned that the cuts were unsustainable and putting thousands of children at greater risk of sexual and criminal exploitation.

Julie Bentley, the chief executive at Action For Children, said children's services were 'at breaking point', describing the cuts as 'dangerous and devastating'. And this against a backdrop where there has been increased child poverty and a growing demand on paediatric mental-health services. You almost don't need any other explanation for the growth in county lines.

In April 2019, North Yorkshire police delivered a stark message to Harrogate Borough Council's overview and scrutiny committee. Inspector Steve Breen told them that around thirty people had been arrested over four months in relation to county lines drug dealing, including a sixteen-year-old boy who had been reported missing 'for some time' from Birmingham.

A police report said there were five 'county lines' operating in Harrogate, coming from Leeds, Bradford and Birmingham, but a series of arrests had stopped a gang coming in from Manchester in January and February. Of the thirty arrests, the majority were for drug supply offences, with arrests also for possession of bladed weapons and stun guns. Despite their best efforts, police said the gangs continued to operate in the area and make 'significant amounts of money' – up to £5,000 a day in Harrogate alone.

On the day I visited the PRU, there had been a drug-related stabbing in the town, and two others the previous week. 'These people will stop at nothing,' said Colette Munro. She'd also been told by police that a number of vulnerable people had had their homes taken over, or 'cuckooed', by drug dealers to create drug preparation and storage houses. Officers told her: 'Now this has started, we will not be able to stop it. The bottom line is county lines is based on the supply-and-demand business model. While there is a demand, there will always be a supply.'

So, the council was clearly wrong when it asserted a few months previously that county lines didn't exist in Harrogate, and it appears to be misguided again in its decision to pull funds from Grove Academy.

I didn't get to talk to Callum directly – those around him said he was still too vulnerable to talk about what happened – but other children I met in the school told me their lives had been transformed for the better. And teachers said the myth that these units are breeding grounds for criminals is unfounded.

A fourteen-year-old friend of Callum's called Toby tells me: 'People think these things only happen in big cities but it's happening here as well. I know a lot of people who carry knives. I don't think it's a big deal until you actually get stabbed.'

Despite having lessons about the dangers of knife crime, Toby said that most of his friends carry knives because they think it makes them safer. 'I know some people who've got machetes, samurai swords, crossbows,' he says. 'They sometimes carry them around with them. Sometimes it can be helpful, if you get what I mean … you pull it out, most people will start walking backwards, and then you've got time to either run or fight.'

'Isn't it better just to run?' I suggest.

Toby shakes his head. 'Not if you get cornered,' he says.

Toby ended up at PRU for 'quite a lot of reasons'. He lists fighting, smoking, vandalism and an assault on a teacher who he punched and elbowed after being shut in a classroom. He thinks the PRU is 'ten times better' than his mainstream school.

'I like smaller groups, it's better for my concentration. I still don't concentrate but they give you a chance here. Mainstream schools, if you do one or two things wrong, then you get kicked out. Here, they actually give you warnings, and they give you a chance.'

Being given a chance seems to strike Toby as something rather special. And it strikes me as something that shouldn't be given up too lightly. The expertise of the teachers could too easily be lost. As well as kids who've been trafficked for county lines, I met a girl in the classroom who'd been trafficked for sexual exploitation. How on earth this school could be under threat of closure truly baffles me. And, of course, its biggest endorsement is Callum and the life he might now lead, as opposed to the direction in which he was heading.

Helen knows she's lucky and she's also hugely grateful – how awful that other parents in her predicament might be left without the support offered by Grove Academy. There are, of course, parents elsewhere in the UK who don't have that specialist support, so what do they do? I'm reminded of how Helen described her darkest moments: *You either pull together, or you end up falling apart.*

I fear society is making the wrong choice on this. But there is one specific group who've been accused of making the wrong choice – a section of society that has been roundly criticised for the hypocrisy of pretending to have a social conscience whilst funding all of this misery with a recreational drug habit – the middle class.

12

THE MIDDLE-CLASS USER

'It's an open secret, cocaine is everywhere.'

Sarah was raised in a stable middle-class family in Winchester. She started taking cocaine when she was fifteen years old. Recovering from glandular fever, she was just coming up to her GCSEs and feeling exhausted all the time. Her friends were going out and she was always having to go home early. She just wanted to keep up. 'Someone suggested cocaine, and I just ran with it.'

It was the first drug she'd ever tried, and from that point, for more than a decade, she would steadily increase her consumption levels. Over the course of fifteen years, she would pass all her GCSEs, get good grades in her A levels, go to university, get a degree and afterwards a good management job in the fashion industry. She'd have a house and a car and a boyfriend. But in that time, Sarah was falling deeper and deeper down the rabbit hole. She was what you might call a high-functioning addict. Externally, for all to see, she was an achiever, but inside she was spiralling out of control.

Everything that she built up would eventually come crumbling down, until finally she found herself where I met her – sitting on a plastic chair in a town hall near Bristol waiting to attend a Cocaine Anonymous (CA) meeting. The Bristol CA group, which meets nearly every day, agreed to let me come to a session on the obvious agreement that no one was identified.

'I think for me cocaine and drink went hand in hand,' said Sarah. 'The taste of alcohol would trigger that response into wanting to get some cocaine, but I also think it's socially acceptable, like other drugs, like weed is just socially acceptable these days, and it doesn't seem to have that stigma that heroin does. But cocaine absolutely, absolutely is a class A drug and I found out the hard way, the really hard way.'

Sarah had been attending CA for more than two years when I met her. This was my second meeting, as CA London had also let me sit in as a guest in one of their gatherings. I'd come to get an insight into drug addiction, but also the stories of the so-called 'middle-class user', and their attitude to what Sarah describes as a 'socially acceptable' drug. These recreational drug-takers may have more of a problem than they realise, and are, through their drug habit, contributing to the industry of child trafficking and violence that we've found in county lines.

In recent years, the middle class has been specifically targeted by politicians and senior police officers, who believe this section of society needs to take a hard look at itself. London's Mayor, Sadiq Khan, said that 'middle-class parties' are helping to fuel drug-related gang violence on the streets of London.

Answering questions on his LBC radio phone-in show in July 2018, Mr Khan said: 'There is a definite link, which has been shown to me by the police, of drugs and criminal gangs and knife crime and crime going up.'

The mayor believes some of his fellow Londoners think taking cocaine is a victimless crime but, as far as he's concerned, the users, or the middle-class ones at least, are no better than the dealers. He added: 'We have got to make sure we take action among those young people who are involved in criminal gangs as well as those who are buying them at middle-class parties.'

Next to blame the 'hypocritical' middle classes was Metropolitan Police Commissioner Cressida Dick. A week after the mayor's comments, the UK's most senior police chief said: 'There is this challenge that there are a whole group of middle-class – or whatever you want to call them – people who will sit round … happily think about global warming and fair trade, and environmental protection and all sorts of things, organic food, but think there is no harm in taking a bit of cocaine. Well, there is; there's misery throughout the supply chain. Middle-class cocaine users are guilty of causing harm.'

The Tottenham MP David Lammy had more to say on this. He cited reports from Interpol and Europol, saying the white middle-class market for cocaine was booming, and they should think about the killings that were associated with the movement of drugs.

In May 2019, the then justice secretary David Gauke also said middle-class people who used cocaine 'should feel a degree of guilt and responsibility' when they saw stories of teenagers being murdered in Hackney, east London. And, in the same month, Simon Kempton, who leads on drug policy for the Police Federation, also said middle-class drug users were to blame for the drug trade and related violence.

Speaking at the federation's conference in Birmingham, he said: 'The big market is people with money to spend and they are often oblivious to the misery they cause, because it is not on their doorstep. Middle-class drug users do not come across the radar of police because they are consuming it behind closed doors.'

Sarah, who I met in Bristol, was definitely consuming behind closed doors and she's definitely middle class. She agrees that the drug was commonly used by her peers, and for her that was part of the problem. But she was much, much more than a recreational user. For Sarah cocaine rapidly became something beyond a party drug. I chatted to her ahead of the Bristol CA meeting in August 2019. She agreed to be interviewed before the others arrived, so we sat in a room of empty chairs and she told me her story.

'It started out as a lot of fun and I was partying a lot with it,' says Sarah. 'I think it really hit me really hard when I was at university. It was a socially acceptable drug to be using, because everybody was doing it and it's that kind of middle-class drug. But then, suddenly, I was the one chasing the party all the time and those friends that were recreationally using it, I left them behind. My social group started to change.

'I started to realise I had a problem when I was eighteen years old and I was standing in the middle of central London and I called up my mum. I couldn't pay yet another phone bill and she had to bail me out yet again, as she did throughout my using. I knew at that point I was in trouble with it. But there's a big difference between knowing you are in trouble and being absolutely on your knees and prepared to do something about that problem.' It would take a long time for Sarah to reach this point.

After leaving university the drug habit came with her. Sarah found there were just as many like-minded cocaine users in the workplace as there had been in higher education.

'A lot of us, we'd go for a drink after work and be absolutely convinced we were just going for a drink. A couple of pints, or a couple of glasses of wine and then that idea comes. Somebody round the table says, "Shall we get a bag of coke? Shall we get an eight?" And then you would be calling the dealer and a few would leave the party.'

'How easy was it to get a bag of coke?'

'Very easy. I would have a list of numbers in my phone and I would call one, and the fact that it is a middle-class drug just normalised it in my mind. I picked it up at such a young age and everybody in my social group was using it, very normal people. My denial was so strong because I had a job and I had the car and I had the boyfriend, I thought I was alright – and that actually made me ill for a very long time. In the workplace I was paranoid I was going to get caught out. I was having heart palpitations all the time. I was making doctors do ECGs on my heart because I was convinced I was going to die of a heart attack due to the sheer amount of cocaine that I was using by my twenties. I got to a point where I was basically using chronically throughout the day. And ultimately, if you're up all night using cocaine you're not functioning.'

I decide to press Sarah on this idea that cocaine is socially acceptable in certain circles, illegal but an open secret. 'You wouldn't get it out and start doing it on the pub table, would you?' I say. 'So, there is still that sense of, this is naughty, but is it like being at school and going out and having a cigarette behind the bike shed? Or do you feel, no I'm breaking the law here, this is a class A drug?'

'It was more the former rather than the latter, definitely. I felt like it was a naughty thing to do but it was definitely a treat. It was a reward at the end of a hard-working day. But when you're an addict you think of excuses – you know it could be that the sun was shining and that would be my reason, or it could have been raining and that would be my justification.'

'When did you hit rock bottom?'

'Many years later. I was twenty-seven when I ended up in hospital, overdosed. My boyfriend left me. The house we were renting … without him, I couldn't pay the bills, so I lost that. I lost my job and I went to live with my mum and then my mum said, "I just cannot watch you killing yourself and enable this process." She said I needed to find somewhere else to go. That was a really tough decision for her and I'm sure she didn't make it easily.'

Sarah went into a 'dry house' in Bristol, where she lived for two years, on benefits, slowly tackling her demons. Tenants in these council-run houses are not allowed to use illegal drugs or alcohol on or off the premises. It's often a place that people go to after a period of intensive rehab. It's a halfway house between treatment and independent living. Councils see it as a good investment, to stop people relapsing and having to go through the process again. As well as a bed space, the addicts get support such as counselling, help with benefits, training and help to look for employment.

It's a worrying fact that while drug addiction seems to be a growing problem in the UK, the number of dry houses is diminishing. A study by the Inside Housing website in May 2019 found that 13 out of 32 London boroughs have had no dry house provision for a decade. Responses to a Freedom of Information request also found there were no dry houses in Birmingham, nor across the whole of Scotland and Wales.

The councils blamed the government's austerity drive, causing cuts to local budgets. For example, the Royal Borough of Kensington and Chelsea, which funds its dry house provision out of its housing budget, has lost 50 per cent of its funds in the past decade. It now supports one dry house as opposed to the two it had in 2009. An RBKC spokesman told Inside Housing: 'We do a huge amount with our partners to support people struggling with addiction but local government funding is being reduced. We are being forced to save over £40 million in the next two years alone.'

For Sarah, the dry house certainly wasn't an immediate fix. She relapsed a number of times. But eventually she found Cocaine Anonymous and that was really where her journey to recovery began.

'I was the most isolated person in my addiction. By the end of it, it wasn't social, it wasn't fun,' says Sarah. I wanted to be on my own in a room with my bag of cocaine so nobody else was getting their hands on it. I was crippled with anxiety. CA has given me courage and I've made friends here and it gives me a place that offers a solution on a daily basis.

'I struggled with confidence a lot when I was younger and I can still go back into that same place of suffering with the lack of confidence now and lack of self-worth, and CA gives me tools to deal with it. I can fall on the programme – the Twelve Steps of recovery – and it's giving me just so much more than that; it's giving me the opportunity to seek refuge, I guess, from my own emotional condition, which can still sometimes be really extreme.'

At the time of talking, Sarah has been clean for more than two years. I have to ask, 'Do you think you'll ever take it again?'

'So, this programme teaches me that I will absolutely use again if I don't keep coming and that has been proven to me. I got sixteen months clean and sober, and, you know, I got all of those things back. I got the car back. I got the job back. I got out of a dry house. I got into a privately rented flat and I got some savings in my account. Finally, after living in the red all the time, I was in the black. But I just found CA a bit of an inconvenience, having to go to meetings. So I stopped doing the thing that made me better.'

Sarah discovered that without the treatment she was back on the drugs. Talking to other CA addicts I found this was a universal fear. They can never say never. This final question 'Will you ever take drugs again?' is the one that cuts deepest. The thought of going back is so monstrous – but the pull is something they learn to deal with on a day-to-day basis rather than extinguish.

While researching a story on cocaine for Sky News I went to Cocaine Anonymous meetings in both Bristol and London. I have to say they were like nothing I've experienced before. Having seen AA meetings depicted on TV, the CA meetings were far more upbeat than I expected. In attending, you are joining a group of people who have done incredibly foolish things in the pursuit of their habit, who are brutally honest, open and often amusing about their shortcomings. I'd recommend it to anyone. The stories you will hear in the space of an hour! You will laugh and cry in equal measure and there is a buzz of optimism in the air that is infectious. Yet, in the room in London was a banker who admitted standing on the edge of a bridge considering suicide only the week before.

Cocaine use has been linked to higher suicide rates, as persistent use causes deep paranoia and depression. It took a while for the banker to open up, but perhaps he was encouraged in part by hearing from another member, a DJ who admitted he'd bought himself night-vision goggles because he was so paranoid he was being watched in his bedroom. Or the smartly dressed woman at the front who talked about the hours spent staring under the crack of her bedroom door, convinced someone was coming to get her. And brilliantly, no one is able to pass judgement on the others, only listen and, through a mentor programme, guide each other through what they call the 'Twelve Steps' to a drug-free life.

But I would add that the social mix in the Cocaine Anonymous meetings was diverse, both in London and Bristol. The suicidal banker, for example, was sat next to a tattooed bricklayer. Sarah has described a culture where cocaine use is prevalent among her middle-class peers – but there's more to it than this.

Cocaine was used by an estimated 875,000 people in 2017–18 according to the latest crime survey for England and Wales – the highest number in a decade and a 15 per cent year-on-year rise.

Use of cocaine in England and Wales is higher than at any point in the past ten years and the EU drugs agency has said purity of street cocaine is at its highest level in a decade. But it's no longer the reserve of the middle class, and they are not even necessarily the dominant users.

I recently spoke to researchers at substance-abuse charity Addaction, who say the UK's cocaine habit is classless. In the largest study of its kind, the charity put out a survey on social media in Scotland and found cannabis is used by almost 80 per cent of drug users, while cocaine or crack cocaine is taken by 70 per cent. Previous studies suggested that only 30 per cent of drug users used cocaine regularly.

Andrew Horne, director of Addaction in Scotland, told me: 'People think it's a middle-class, middle-aged dinner-party drug, but our experience is that it's everywhere. Cocaine is seen as a party drug, across all sections of society, but also has a stigma around it and is widely used yet no one is talking about it. It's an open secret. We talk about alcohol oiling the conversation; well my experience is that cocaine is that drug now.'

Filming in Bristol, I went looking for cocaine users on a Friday night. At a pub in Corn Street I found students, teachers, health workers and bar staff who all admitted taking coke. One gym instructor in his thirties, who lives on a council estate in Bristol, told me: 'It's usually just a weekend thing, when I'm out with the lads, in a pub or club or festival or something like that. It's more a recreational thing. I don't do it every day or anything. But when you go out on the lash, you have a few pints, you know, you have a bit of coke to bring you back. It wakes you back up. That's it really.'

This man admitted that, in his local working-class pub toilets, cocaine use was rife. 'I'm telling you, it's sixteen-year-olds, seventeen-year-olds, eighteen-year-olds doing it in the toilets. With me and my generation it was more of a taboo than now, that's why we didn't do it. When we were younger, [we'd see it] in films like *Pulp Fiction* – all them sorts of things, you'd associate coke with druggies. Apart from business guys or bankers and that. But now coke is looked at as another form of weed almost. It's not like the old days, where you have to spend £100 on a gram; there's kids doing £10 of this, £20 that, so they cater to all pockets and prices.'

The manager of one Bristol pub told me she was spending an additional thousand pounds a week on security to keep out what she calls the 'eau de Bristol'. She believes a new tide of drug users is rising up in Bristol. It was her view that austerity and stretched public services is what has made the problems escalate in recent years.

Once a 'yuppie drug', it now transcends geography, profession and class. Author Dr Gabor Maté, a world-renowned expert in addiction, said this in a Sky News interview in autumn 2019:

'Really, it's a product of childhood experience combined with worsening social circumstances, which here in Britain have been exacerbated by three decades of the breaking down of the social network, of austerity, of cutbacks. Margaret Thatcher famously saying there's no such thing as society; those people are totally on their own, they're just individuals. The current cocaine 'epidemic', you might call it in the UK, is really a social malaise that's totally related to larger social, political and economic factors.'

This anecdotal sense that the problem is becoming 'epidemic' is supported by scientific research. Tests of the sewerage water in Bristol found a very high concentration of benzoylecgonine – the substance produced by the body after it has broken down cocaine – as mentioned in the first chapter of this book. The levels of this substance in Bristol, at 969.2 mg per 1000 people, is higher per-head of population than the amounts found from similar tests in 73 European cities, including London and Amsterdam.

What's also interesting about these tests is that because they've been repeated over several years, we can see emerging patterns of drug use. In London, cocaine usage doubled between 2011 and 2016 – however, the figure has started to plateau in the last few years. In Bristol, they only started the tests in 2013. It began at quite a low base but has rapidly quadrupled over five years and continues to rise, overtaking London in terms of its per-head of population cocaine usage.

This adds weight to the theory put forward by drug dealer Cody, and by former drug cop Tony Saggers, that the London market has plateaued, and that smaller towns are becoming growth areas. But there's another interesting fact from these tests. Leon Barron, the scientist who tested the sewage in London (and also did the shrimp tests at King's College lab) has calculated, from the waste product, that the daily cocaine intake of Londoners measures at 23 kilograms a day. I can tell you, because I've measured it out in flour, that it fills a two-metre-square palette in a huge pyramid of white dust. But this measurement is for pure cocaine. In reality, the cocaine consumed would be anywhere between 10 and 50 per cent pure, because it would be diluted with cutting agents (usually anaesthetics such as lidocaine and benzocaine), used by suppliers to increase their margins – so the actual pile would be much bigger, perhaps two or three times the size. And based on 40 milligrams being enough to give you a hit, the number of doses in 23 kilos comes to more than half a million. That's the amount of cocaine consumed every day in our capital city and it is nearly double the amount recorded in any other European city, making London the unassailable cocaine capital of Europe.

Now, just to add to that, the annual consumption in London would be over 8 tonnes, and if London per-head of population represented the country (and we've established London has lower numbers of users per-head of population than Bristol) then we could estimate that the UK consumes 70 tonnes of pure cocaine a year. That's several lorries full, and more than double the estimate Tony Saggers suggested at 30 tonnes (which he agrees is probably low). None of this is an exact science, of course, but we definitely get through tonnes and tonnes of coke in the UK, every year.

Several of the people I spoke to in the pub in Bristol were clearly on something as I was talking to them, including one of the bar staff who spoke as if it was a race to get the words out. Another bar worker admitted she took cocaine to get through her late-night shift. 'How else do you think I stay up till 2am every night?'

'It's everywhere,' said a punter called Victoria, repeating the expression used by Mr Horne from Addaction. Victoria admitted that she was a recovering addict who'd used a number of drugs when growing up in an isolated and deprived area of Cornwall. She'd become homeless because of her dependency on crack cocaine. She was helped to recovery by an addiction centre in Bristol, which she said had since been closed down. 'If I had my addiction now, I'd have nowhere to go,' she told me.

So, if cocaine is now 'everywhere', is it fair to point the finger at 'hypocritical middle-class cocaine users' just because they happen to care about fair trade and organic food? It might once have been the wealthy man's drug, but now it's an everyman drug, indeed an everywoman drug too. There's no doubt it is prevalent on the middle-class scene – but there's more to it. I've even seen it being taken on a Football Lads Association march in Sunderland. Try calling them anything other than working-class to their faces. The powder cocaine market is growing, but a big proportion of it is going up working-class noses. The more addictive crack cocaine side of the market also tends to consist of people from low-income backgrounds, and these, along with generally low-income heroin users, are the lifeblood of any county lines operation. Shouldn't they also get a telling-off from the London mayor and the Met commissioner?

I think the point they are trying to make is that the middle class often assumes the position of having the moral high ground. Probably the most sensible voice on this comes again from Tony Saggers. It was while he was head of the UK's drug threat at the NCA that he coined the phrase 'responsible society' in relation to cocaine. He told me, 'I stand by that phrase, but unfortunately the headline was: "Middle-class cocaine users". And that stuck. And I think it skews the picture, and how it's been applied skews it again.

'I used two examples: the dinner party, which of course may draw that idea of a middle-class group; and young people at university. Both sets of people will be responsibly condemning the world for the wrongs that occur. University students in particular will then often put some sort of campaign together against whatever the abhorrent nature of that exploitation is. But then, both sets of people may well snort cocaine at the end of their evening's discussion. And my point then, several years ago, was that whether you're a manual worker living a crime-free life with a family and playing football on a Sunday, or whether you or someone in high society, all of those people are deemed generally responsible. Yet, they subscribe to a powder drug that's long since been proven as not being glamorous, that puts money into the hands of a supply chain that knocks on to making cocaine markets buoyant, and wholesale values are kept low.

'Gangs can afford to buy cocaine at prices that allow them to make big profits. And it comes back around that way. So, what you're doing is subscribing to something that you're not thinking about the consequences of.

'I've gone to great lengths over the years to educate on that point. I'm getting a little bit impatient with people saying, well, I just didn't know. People do know. So, it's not that cocaine users are causing violence in London and it's not that cocaine users are funding county lines and gang crime. They're not. Directly. What they are doing is putting money into a supply chain that crosses over and interacts with those markets. That makes cocaine cheaper and more accessible to those that are perpetrating county lines and gang crime in London.'

Sometimes people don't see, or want to see, the association between the trade in powder and the more harmful crack cocaine. The truth is all crack cocaine is made in the UK using imported powder cocaine, so the two markets are intrinsically linked by the base material. If you buy powder cocaine you are also putting money into the supply chain for the highly addictive crack cocaine. Middle class users who may feel they have a relationship with their dealer still don't know who their dealer's supplier is, or how they may be connected to trafficking and numerous other crimes further up the supply chain.'

Tony Adds: 'My main point, a few years ago, was actually – for every £40 you spend on a gram of coke, percentages of that go into sexual exploitation, human trafficking, modern slavery, firearms trafficking, money laundering, cash smuggling, the list goes on because all of those crimes are intertwined with the cocaine trade.

'The cocaine trade does not sit in isolation. If someone said, "Give me £40 for a gram of coke, and, by the way, I'm now about to invest three pounds of this into a large pot that's going to bring a seventeen-year-old Romanian into the UK to be exploited for sex and raped five times a day for six months", I would genuinely like to think that many of the people handing over that £40 would withhold it at that point. And just because that's not being said to them, doesn't mean that that's not the reality of where their money's going.'

I think that's probably the last word on this issue. But there is another matter that is under-discussed. That is the extent to which so-called 'recreational users' – from whatever background – are actually not recreational at all.

The most concerning aspect of the Addaction survey in 2019 was that a high proportion of the users admitted to behaviour that would indicate they were problem users. The survey included standard DAST-10 (Drug Abuse Screening Test) questions. DAST-10 is used identify problematic substance use and whether intervention would be recommended.

DAST-10 questions are as follows:

1. Have you used drugs other than those required for medical reasons?
2. Do you take more than one drug at a time?
3. Are you able to stop using drugs when you want to?
4. Have you ever had blackouts or flashbacks as a result of drug use?
5. Do you ever feel bad or guilty about your drug use?
6. Has your partner/parents/friends ever complained about your involvement or use of drugs?
7. Have you ever missed work/school/college/uni as a result of drug use?
8. Have you engaged in illegal activities in order to obtain drugs?
9. Have you ever experienced withdrawal symptoms (felt sick) when you stopped taking drugs?
10. Have you had medical problems as a result of your drug use?

Nearly 80 per cent of cocaine users had more than three indicators – three indicators suggest hazardous use. But, what's more, a third of users were even worse, with six indicators, which suggests a potential dependence problem. So, of those people using cocaine, the majority need to seek help. Even so, only 14 per cent had approached healthcare professionals or charities to ask for help.

You could attribute this failure, in part, to the fact that, like Sarah, they are often working professionals and fear the consequences of admitting their reality. But it is also perhaps due to what Sarah points to – the normalisation of cocaine use in society. The study found 90 per cent of users who responded to the survey were employed or in full-time education.

My profession, the media industry, is particularly infamous for having a cocaine culture. Author and columnist Bryony Gordon has famously written about her addiction. She told me her cocaine habit crept up on her while living a hectic social life as a journalist – and nearly destroyed her when it took a grip.

She said: 'It destroys lives. It tends to lead to people searching for the next high, and all normal reservations come down. It makes you inherently risky and you don't care about the consequences until the next day.

'The problem is that it's seen as a party drug. Obviously it is vilified, because it's a class A drug, but not on the same level as heroin or meth or crack cocaine, which is the same thing but taken a different way. I suppose it's that celebrities take it, middle-class journalists like me take it, politicians take it, and people think it's okay to take it, either it's okay to take it or it's not as problematic … it's recreational. That's the word, recreational. It destroys lives.'

In the spring of 2019, Tory leadership candidate Michael Gove admitted taking cocaine in his younger days working in the media. And this again set the rabbits running about middle-class users and their lack of social conscience. But there is another way of looking at the demographics of this.

In 2017, Addaction launched an online live-chat service for drug addicts and users. Mr Horne said they immediately noticed this discreet, anonymous helpline was attracting a high proportion of cocaine users. But interestingly, the online help service attracted a 60/40 female to male ratio, whereas the drop-in centres tend to be the other way around. That would suggest that women are less likely to seek help face to face with a professional. When I raised this at the CA meeting in Bristol, a number of the women concurred that they were extremely reluctant to seek help. They were afraid, not just of the stigma but of having their children taken away if they told anyone in authority about their addiction.

I suspect women, who are generally on lower wages, sometimes feel they can't afford to go through rehab – because it is associated with footballers' wives going to The Priory. In actual fact, Cocaine Anonymous is a free service, run by the recovering addicts themselves.

CA isn't for everyone – and there is a frustration among a number of agency workers I've spoken to that we are simply not joining up our approach to drug addiction. One police officer told me that while a heroin addict might get picked up several times a week for shoplifting to pay for his habit, and will eventually go to prison, they will still come out a few weeks later an addict. He argued it would probably be more cost effective for the state to give that addict their heroin in a consumption room, then help wean them off through controlled methadone intake. That way the shoplifting stops and the dealer is cut out of the equation. The cycle of criminalisation comes to an end. 'There's no point the health workers and police dealing with that individual separately,' he told me. 'One giving him methadone every day, the other arresting him every day.'

Decriminalisation, or the state supply of certain drugs, is a controversial idea and this police officer didn't condone it for all class A drugs. But he did see an advantage with immediately addictive substances like heroin. I've met a number of senior officers who agree. But, even if that is a politically unacceptable solution, the underlying point is a need to focus on the user. As Tony Saggers put it: 'The NCA recently had a huge success, intercepting two tonnes of heroin at Felixstowe – now, is that going to stop a single heroin addict from getting their hit tomorrow? No.'

County lines, like any drug-dealing operation, relies on demand. And where it exists there will always be supply. We spend a fortune trying to police the supply – but reducing demand needs an even greater focus and investment.

Cocaine Anonymous might be a cost-free service but it relies purely on an individual's determination to change, and the assistance of other recovering addicts to see them through it. Like Alcoholics Anonymous, CA has been incredibly successful and there are hundreds of meetings held around the country every day that help thousands to escape the shackles of their addiction.

I suspect that the secret to its success is that the meetings themselves are somewhat addictive. My view, from limited exposure, is that they hit the spot, by giving people with an addictive personality a new addiction to clean living.

'This is my medicine,' Sarah tells me, as the room we are sat in begins to fill with other addicts. 'If you have epilepsy you take medicine on a daily basis to stop yourself having fits. I'm an addict, so I need to come to these meetings. I don't have to come every day, but I practise the principles of the Twelve Steps on a daily basis and I go to two or three meetings a week. That's my medicine. That's what keeps me well, and I now know categorically, from my previous experience, if I stop doing this then I will use again. It seems a very small trade-off compared to the life that I was leading before.'

The twelfth step of CA is to help others – become a mentor to the never-ending influx of newcomers. And every mentor I met said that this too is part of the treatment. Unless you've experienced it, it's perhaps hard to understand how a roomful of other addicts, all of whom have similar stories, can somehow offer the support that Sarah needs. But it does appear to work. Those damaged people are her salvation, and she is theirs.

Next, we shall meet someone who believes he is beyond salvation.

13.

THE SAVAGE

'What can I do?'

Handsome is a hitman. The sort of guy you wouldn't want to meet down a dark alley, which is exactly where we do meet. He might have been handsome once, had his cheeks not sunk into yellow pits and his dark-brown eyes not turned to bloodshot marbles. Over a decade ago, the Iraqi Kurd escaped northern Iraq after being held captive by Islamic extremists who shot him in the leg for punishment. He crossed into Turkey on foot. He crossed the Mediterranean in a boat to Greece. He was a year in Greece before he travelled to Italy in a farm lorry full of sheep. Then he got a train to Paris and made his way to the so-called 'Jungle' in Sangatte, where he stayed for six months, looking for a route across the Channel. Then, one day, a lorry driver bound for Dover went to pay for petrol and failed to notice Handsome on the forecourt, unlocking his back door and sneaking into the cargo. The teenager had finally made it to the UK. But for what? Having survived all

239

that, his worst demons awaited him at his destination. It was the drugs that got him in the end.

'This place has destroyed me,' he says. 'Look what I've become.' Not-so-Handsome, now in his thirties, is ravaged by drugs. The crack helps him do his work. It dulls the senses. It takes the pain away. But it has left him beholden to those who feed his addiction. He has become a 'savage', a collector of debts, an administer of punishment – a cog in the wheel of a brutal operation.

I have written a lot in this book about how the county lines drug industry exploits and brutalises children. But just as often it does the same to addicts. I don't expect you to sympathise with Handsome in the way you will have with the runner Lucy, but his story shows how even a hardened immigrant can become seemingly powerless. There are different ways that dealers use an addict's habit to their own advantage. We saw how in Ipswich an addict was used as a driver in the planned attack on Tavis Spencer-Aitkens. The driver ended up in the dock with the gang members and, thankfully for him, he was acquitted by the jury. Handsome, however, knows he's done bad things. A slave to his addiction, he has been walked down a dark path by his suppliers, into people trafficking, gun smuggling and conducting casual acts of violence for gang members. He is a man who hates drug dealers, despises drugs and loathes what he has become.

Handsome left Iraq in 2001 when he was just fourteen and Saddam Hussein was still in power. As a Kurd, his people were in conflict with the government. The regime had committed atrocities against the Kurds, including the use of chemical weapons that killed 5,000 people in Halabja in 1998. That happened when he was just a boy, and during his childhood the Ba'athist authorities continued to persecute the Kurds, organising large-scale displacement and colonisation projects in northern Iraq, aiming to shift demographics and thus destabilise Kurdish power bases. The place was lawless and full of fledgling Islamic extremist groups. Handsome says: 'They had so many criminals there. If you wanted to buy gun or bomb, you buy gun and bomb.'

As a teenager, he was captured by a group called Jihad-Islami and kept in a small dark room. He'd often hear people being tortured. He had no idea why they held him; nor why one day they took him from his cell and shot him in the leg. 'They did it for no reason,' he says. 'You don't ask why, in case somebody kill you.'

He adds, 'I had to escape. I heard them shooting and beating people in the room next to me and I thought I was going to be next.' One night his cell door was left unlocked and he took a chance to escape, even with a wounded leg. By morning he was on his way to the Turkish border, determined to get to a safer country where he could live a normal life.

It took nearly two years and $20,000 to get to the UK, but when he arrived life started well. Declaring himself an asylum seeker in Dover, he was initially housed in Birmingham. It was his first permanent home since he'd been kidnapped by the Islamists. But, still young and struggling with the language and lack of qualifications, it wasn't easy to find employment, so he came to London – the great melting pot that can make or break you. With Handsome it was the latter.

His accent is still difficult to follow at times, but he makes himself understood. It was in London where his addiction began. 'In 2003 someone give me some hashish and I started smoking,' he says. 'Then someone give me cocaine. First, they give me free. After I started, I buy. It was in my blood. I took one line and I was maniac – I said nobody could touch me. The guy gave me everything. I took crack, ketamine, miaow-miaow, crystal meth, heroin, everything. And for what? It has fucked my life.'

Even though Handsome now works for drug dealers, he immediately starts railing at the man who got him hooked while he was still a teenager, and the UK legal system for not being tough enough on dealers. 'If you smoke hashish in my country, you go to prison for twenty years. Here you go to prison a few months – it's like school. There are just more bad people. They show you everything. You come out ten times worse. It was too easy to get the drugs. The guy who sold me the drugs – he fucked my life. Then he gave me the gun. He gave me the knife. You come here for freedom but there is no freedom. Now, in 2019, there are too many criminals – for what? For drugs.'

He'd escaped a world of daily violence, and somehow found himself involved in something just as sinister, here in the UK. Handsome says once he got hooked he found jobs with 'bad people'. It was easy money. 'I started to do everything: killing, robbing.'

Having successfully made his way to the UK, he had contacts in the trafficking business, so his first work was helping criminals to get out of the country. 'I had a contact to get people out of the country, if they are in trouble with the police,' he tells me. 'I take them to Dover in a car and I put them in a lorry. And I send people to Europe.' I'm surprised that there's a business in this, but he assures me. 'So many people here are trying to get out – in secret. They are trying to avoid the courts or whatever. I get a contact. People tell me how many people and where they need to go. So, it might be ten people to France, ten people to Italy. I arrange it.'

'Is it easy?' I ask.

'Money,' is his reply. 'Money is power. It depends on money. If you have money you have family. If you don't have money – no honey.'

Handsome also helped people to get into the UK, which he describes as 'easy' but dangerous if you use the wrong traffickers, who sometimes use refrigerated lorries, as they are less likely to get picked up. 'So many people end up getting killed because they don't have money and they don't pay. So, they take risks. These people, not me, but these people push people inside [refrigerated lorries]. You put ten or twenty people in a fridge – some of those people die. It's a risk.'

This interview took place several months before 39 people were found dead in the back of a lorry trailer in Essex. Bodies of the Vietnamese migrants were discovered inside the container on an industrial estate in Grays in Essex in the early hours of 23 October 2019. The discovery opened everyone's eyes to the risks taken by people desperate to find a new life in the UK.

Handsome is just on the finges of this horrific trafficking business and clearly has associates more heavily involved in it. As we talk about the perils and how people are putting their faith in criminals who can't be trusted, he shrugs and uses an expression I will hear him say a lot: 'What can I do?' As if this is just how life is. But sometimes, when he uses this expression, the answer to me seems obvious: 'Don't get involved.' 'Put down the baseball bat.' 'Get help.' But I'm not here to judge him, just to find out about his life and how it has come to this. He is quite difficult to interview, as sometimes he doesn't

COUNTY **LINES**

understand the question and he often returns to the thing that upsets him most. 'The government here, more than anything, they need to stop the drugs,' he says again and again, and even though he's just been talking about people dying in fridges, he quickly turns back to this topic. 'For my life, I don't care – but for the kids. I see kids come out of school and someone go up to them and they get them smoking weed. And these are nice kids, but people are encouraging them and give them knives.'

He goes on, getting quite angry. He seems to find it hard to regulate the pace of his conversation, and once the tap is open random stuff just splutters out. 'I would die for this country. It's the first country I would die for. They gave me a house, they gave me a job, they helped me. I want to stop the drugs. There are too many traffic police and wardens putting tickets on cars. We need to focus on drugs. And if you are caught selling drugs you should go to prison for a long time, fifteen, twenty years. You get two months – and there's drugs inside. In prison, the wardens are bringing in the drugs. So, they are taking drugs in the yard.'

I want to get on to talking more about what he does for the gangs. So I tentatively ask a little bit about his work. Again, the answers come in strange bursts. 'Rob, fight, beat people, break leg, arms, hands. One leg five thousand pounds, one hand two thousand. The face – that's different again. What can I do?'

'So, there's a different price for different damage you can cause?'

'Yes.'

'That's extraordinary.'

'What can I do?'

'If you are going to break someone's leg, do you stab them first or…'

'I have a baseball bat or maybe hammer. Maybe somebody shoot them, or maybe kick them. We have technology. You go to your phone. Click on Facebook Messenger, they show you the picture, the address and everything. What can I do? You have the GPS, you have the tracker ... put in your car ... follow you. They might say, "He has a car like this, here's the number plate, the colour red." You put a magnet tracker under the car like that. [He gestures leaning down and putting a magnet under a car.] They go – they are connected to my phone. So, when they drive. I follow them.'

'Have you been asked to kill people?'

A pause.

'No answer.' His eyes are dead. He did say earlier he had. He doesn't seem to like the direct question. So I bring the subject back to him.

'If you attack someone like that, aren't you in danger? Aren't they going to fight back – or maybe send someone to attack you?'

'If I take drugs I don't feel nothing,' he says. I notice he has heavy scarring on his arms, so I ask if he has been stabbed.

'Yes, I've been stabbed. The drugs ... you don't feel anything. Then, after two or three days – then after, I know.'

'Because of what you've been through, where you are from, are you desensitised? Do you feel anything? If you are asked to break someone's leg?'

'To tell the truth, I grew up in a place where every day there was a *ta-ta-tat*. [He gestures as if holding a machine gun.] Every day I saw people die. I woke up, and one and two people beside me had died. I see their blood. When I came here life seemed easy. Nobody had guns, nobody touched me. I come outside of the fire.' Then he says something I can't quite understand,

245

perhaps talking about drugs again. And he finishes: 'So now I don't feel nothing, man. It's easy. I don't feel a thing.'

So, Handsome is a jack-of-all-trades for the gangs – people-smuggler and hitman – but he also traffics weapons into the UK. From his time as a refugee he has contacts in Belgium where he says they have 'too many guns' and it is 'very easy' to get them into France. Weapons experts back up this view, and if you've ever wondered how guns get into the UK, the answer is that a fair number come through Belgium.

Back in 2016, after three terrorists exploded a bomb at Brussels airport killing thirty-two people and themselves, I spent some time exploring the criminal underworld of that city. It's where a number of Islamic terrorists originate from and also where they acquire their weapons. Nils Duquet, a senior researcher at the Flemish Peace Institute, has authored more than forty publications on illicit firearms trafficking and gun violence in Europe. Back in 2016, he told me: 'There has been an increase of heavy firearms – military-style weapons such as Kalashnikovs – among criminals in Belgium, and it is mainly linked to smuggling from the Balkans.'

After the Balkan wars of the 1990s, hundreds of thousands of military weapons stayed in the hands of civilians and found their way to Western Europe, smuggled in small quantities but creating a steady flow of unlicensed guns into black-market circulation. It has been estimated that 90 per cent of the illegal arms in Belgium probably originate from Balkan countries, including Bosnia and Albania.

Nils said that Belgium had a particularly bad record-keeping system for guns coming into the country, along with a complicated legislative structure. The Weapons Act, which regulates possession and use, is a federal matter, but the control of the import and export of firearms, as well as hunting and shooting regulations, are a regional concern. Cooperation and data-sharing between the country's administrations wasn't as you might expect. Most record-keeping, in 2016, was still done on paper rather than computer databases for all to access.

For a long time, Belgium also had quite a liberal domestic gun legislation, making the country a European hotspot for the arms trade. In 2006, it was made stricter, after two innocent people were gunned down, and now ordinary citizens must meet strict criteria before they can legally own a firearm. But a lot of the weapons had already arrived. What's more, the black market in Belgium had become well established, so it retained its reputation as a place to get guns.

Handguns are in high demand because they are easy to conceal, but Kalashnikovs are also said to be popular due to their easy availability. Despite their size, once they cross the EU's external borders, they are easily transferred from one European country to another within the Schengen zone – an area comprised of twenty-six European member states that have officially abolished passport and border controls and introduced a common visa policy.

Handsome tends to import handguns to the UK, and says that although they were purchased in Belgium, he would often collect his weapons from his old contacts from the so-called 'Jungle' in France. Of course, migrant camps on the north coast of France have been constantly evolving since Handsome passed through. He lived in the original Jungle, established in the woods around the Port of Sangatte in 2002.

In April 2009, there was a raid on the shantytown and French authorities arrested 190 people and used bulldozers to destroy tents. But just two months later, a new camp was established with around 800 inhabitants. Since then, there have been numerous incarnations of these shantytowns where conditions are typically poor, without proper sanitary or washing facilities, and accommodation consisting of tents or shelters made out of scrap. Food is usually supplied by charity kitchens, but the French authorities have always grappled with the dilemma of addressing humanitarian needs without attracting additional migrants.

The most recent camp of immigrants in Calais was dismantled in 2016, but many smaller versions have since emerged. Within these groups Handsome has a network in which he gets guns from Belgium to the UK. He says the lorries heading to Dover are not just targeted by desperate migrants as they pass through the French ports. 'We find a lorry,' says Handsome. 'Someone will hide the gun in the lorry and put a tracker on the lorry. That gives you the postcode and everything. We have the number plate. Then somebody this side picks it up.'

'Does the lorry driver know?'

'Some lorry drivers don't know. There are places we can hide the guns.'

He continues: 'I might go and collect five or ten guns. There are lots of guns. Holland and Belgium, it's very cheap. But you can make money here. Guns more expensive in UK.'

There have been a number of recent significant seizures on the route that Handsome uses. In August 2019, a man from Dublin – thirty-seven-year-old Robert Keogh – was stopped at the Port of Dover and found to have sixty guns hidden in his car. It was the largest ever seizure of lethal weapons at a UK port. A Sig Sauer P226 blank-firing handgun, with a barrel converted to fire live ammunition, was the first weapon to be discovered in the car's rear-left quarter panel. Specialist search officers then unearthed another fifty-nine firearms hidden inside the car's bumper and both rear quarter panels. Border Force said the discovery 'undoubtedly saved many lives'.

Another man, Emmanuel Okubote, aged twenty-seven, from Peckham, was found guilty of conspiracy to supply firearms with intent to endanger life in November 2018 after being stopped going through the Channel Tunnel. As well as two handguns, he was travelling with ammunition, and 990 grammes of high-purity cocaine.

In 2018, the NCA asked all forty-three forces in England and Wales to put greater focus on gathering intelligence about firearms. Simon Brough, NCA's head of firearms, said: 'The majority of guns being used are new, clean firearms, which indicates a relatively fluid supply.' He added that shotguns were 40 per cent of the total. Handguns are the next biggest category, with ferry ports such as Dover being a popular entry point into the UK for organised crime groups.

The level of gun crime in the UK is one of the lowest in the world. But Chief Constable Andy Cooke, the national police lead for serious and organised crime, said law enforcement had seen an increased supply of guns in recent years. In late December 2018, Cooke told the *Guardian*: 'We in law enforcement expect the rise in new firearms to continue. We are doing all we can. We are not in a position to stop it any time soon.'

He said that more weapons were coming in from eastern Europe and the western Balkans, and added that the dynamics of the streets of British cities had changed and that criminals were more willing to use guns: 'If they bring them in people will buy them. It's a kudos thing for organised criminals.'

Handsome agrees. He told me: 'People here want to kill people, to make money. I don't sell guns to my friends. Because if they killed someone and went to jail, then they'd say fuck me. But if the kids want to buy them, I'll sell them to the kids. They want to kill their friends, their mum and dad – I don't care. For what? Money.'

He has a strange way at being angry with pretty much everyone who does all these bad things, but I genuinely think he also reserves some anger for himself. In a way he is dead to himself. He has no respect or liking for the man he has become.

'Have you tried giving up the drugs?' I ask.

'No.'

'Do you think you will?'

'I wish.'

I ask if anyone has offered him, or if he has sought out, professional help to rid himself of the addiction, but I think he interprets this as a question about seeking help from God, because that's what he starts talking about. Clearly he's never considered any form of rehab beyond a morning prayer. But his eyes show he doesn't anticipate any divine intervention to fly him out of these depths. My next question seems almost pointless.

'If you could change your life, what would it be?'

'God – he made me clean. No drugs, no smoking, nothing. I wish I could go back clean. I promise I'd go back. I'd be strong. I'd be controlled. Every day I pray to God. I wish.' But again, his dead eyes tell me that won't happen.

'If you weren't doing what you do – what would you do?'

'I would want to find a good family, a good house, a good job.'

'Did you have dreams about what you wanted to be when you were in Iraq?'

'I don't have a future. I don't know. I don't have a life for nobody.'

And he smiles. He does have a charming smile – and his nickname does, sort of, make sense. He still has thick dark hair, and a certain rugged appeal to the woman who helped arrange this meeting, and who genuinely refers to him as Handsome. But Handsome recognises that my line of questioning has reached a level of pointlessness. He is fidgety. One or two people are milling about. It's time to leave. Handsome will remain a savage. Brutalised by the drugs industry and his addiction. What can he do?

14.

THE CUCKOO

'Think of anything bad, it happens here.'

Clair heard her phone ping and looked at the text: '*Come now.*' It was from her son Adrian. What did he need at this hour? She checked her watch. It was gone eight o'clock in the evening. What a strange text – why not call? She waited a moment for some additional information but nothing came. Did he really expect her to drive for half an hour to his new flat in Gravesend, for the sake of a two-word text? She picked up the phone and dialled. Adrian's phone rang out.

Now what? He'd been a difficult child. Adrian suffered from ADHD, autism, anxiety and emotional behaviour disorder. It was unusual for him to do something like this, but he was prone to some odd behaviour. Usually this would be displayed towards people who didn't understand him and thought him too direct, too mouthy and a bit confrontational. Sometimes he caused problems, but Clair was close to him. The only other strange thing in combination with this text was that she hadn't spoken to him in about twenty-four hours, and it was unlike him not to have been in touch all day.

He'd moved out of the family home only a few months earlier, aged eighteen, into adult social housing. He'd been quite disruptive to his siblings and he was socially complex to deal with. His family had been on the wrong end of him 'winding up' some unsavoury characters, and his brother had once been threatened because of something he'd said to a gang member in his home area of Bexleyheath in the south-east of Greater London. He didn't mean to cause trouble; it was just how he was.

A few minutes later came another text: '*Don't call.*'

This was too weird. Clair responded: '*I'm coming to you.*'

The text came back: '*Don't come.*' The opposite of his first text. Clair sat looking at her phone. Then she began looking for her car keys. What else could she do but go to him? Still thinking this was probably just a wind-up, she got in the car and began driving. She sent one more text: '*I'm coming.*'

One final aspect of county lines we have yet to explore is the cuckooing of vulnerable people. Clair and Adrian's story gives a frightening example of how it works. It was November 2018, and Adrian had for the most part been enjoying his new life, independent from his family. Twenty-four hours before sending the text he'd been having a laugh with friends and had then set off home on his moped. His new place was a bedsit with its own bedroom, bathroom and a small living room with a fridge. But the large communal building also had a shared living space and a kitchen used by all the residents. A private landlord rented it to the council as temporary housing for people who were registered as homeless or waiting for more permanent accommodation.

The main entrance opened out on to a busy road. But Adrian would always take his scooter up a dirt track that led to garages at the back. That's where he first spotted the gang. There were four of them: black, aged sixteen to nineteen, their heads covered by hoodies and enveloped in puffs of cannabis smoke. One of them held a muscular pit bull on a metal chain.

'Hey man, nice bike.'

'Thanks.' Adrian could talk to anyone. He was apprehensive but he liked talking about bikes. He was good at wheelies. Indeed, he was known in the local area as a bit of a tearaway when it came to noisily riding his bike around the high street.

But of course he knew he could be in trouble here. They could be about to steal the bike. He was familiar with gangs – he'd been on the fringes of one when he was younger. He'd made the mistake in secondary school of telling a teacher about a girl who was self-harming. Only the girl also happened to be going out with a gang leader, and Adrian paid the price for snitching on the girlfriend's habit of cutting herself. It resulted in a blow to the head that hospitalised him with a haematoma bleed to his skull. He never snitched again.

The four hooded teens continued to chat. 'Do you smoke weed?'

Adrian did. 'Yeah, you got some?'

'Do you want some?'

'Maybe.' It didn't seem that they were interested in the bike after all. He locked it up and, part through politeness, part genuinely wanting some weed, he allowed the gang to walk with him towards his flat. The dog snuffled along, too.

The conversation kept up till he reached the door. There

was nothing of value inside – he may as well just open it and hopefully they'd give him some weed and leave him alone to chill out. He would wonder later whether perhaps, somehow, he'd invited them in – but he certainly hadn't expected them to bundle through the door the moment he unlocked it. The second they were inside the mood changed.

Out came a gun, money and drugs, thrown casually on his living-room table. Adrian was informed that the gang was going to start working from his flat. There was nothing he could do. He watched as they began cutting up drugs. They helped themselves to food and drink from his fridge and pretended Adrian wasn't even there. After a while they even took out his Sony PlayStation and started playing video games with the pit bull curled up at their feet.

The four stayed in the flat all night, preparing drugs then going out in pairs to make deliveries. They kept conversation with Adrian to a minimum, but he worked out they were from a larger gang in south London – and for them this was 'out country'. The next morning, everyone was still in the flat, some sleeping, others getting the morning's round of crack ready for delivery. It wasn't until the following evening that all four of them had different reasons to leave – but they would be back by 10pm for the next round of night-time dealing. At this point Adrian sent the text to his mother – *'Come now'* – and warned the gang they couldn't come back, he had company. 'My mum's coming over,' he said.

'Tell her not to come,' said one of the gang.

'But—'

'This is our place now. Tell her not to come.'

Adrian's phone rang. It was his mother. He let it ring out.

'Don't call,' he texted.

'Tell her not to come.'

Adrian sent another text – '*Don't come*' – and switched off his phone.

'If she turns up, get rid of her by ten o'clock,' said one of the gang. He didn't turn his phone back on again until they'd all left. Then he received the final text from his mother saying she was on her way.

What if they came back while she was there? What would they do to her? He'd have to get rid of her quickly.

Clair arrived to find her son curled up in a ball.

'Mum, I've been taken hostage in my flat,' Adrian told her, sobbing. He explained how he'd been followed back to his flat and the gang had busted in when he'd opened the door. They'd said he needed to get rid of her by ten o'clock. He'd agreed to do it. She'd have to leave.

Clair said she would call the police, but Adrian begged her not to, remembering what had happened the last time he'd snitched on a gang member. He wouldn't let her. 'You have to leave.'

'I'm not going anywhere,' said Clair. 'If they come, they come.'

'They've got guns.'

Clair was deeply worried. But there was no way she was leaving her son. They just needed a strategy for keeping them out and stopping Adrian from freaking out.

'Okay – look, here's the plan,' she said. 'We turn off the lights, we lock the doors and we don't answer. We stay quiet. If they break in, if they kick it in, then I'm sorry, Adrian, I'll have to call the police.'

Adrian didn't agree to this at all. 'You can't stay here.'

'I'm not going.'

'They've got a big dog,' he told her. 'It'll smell us. They'll know we're here.' But there was nothing he could do or say – his mother wasn't going anywhere. So, at a quarter to ten, they turned out the lights and waited.

Clair lay on the bed and felt a buzz of fear, but also a long-forgotten rush of excitement. It had been a long time since anything like this had happened to her. Now in her forties, she had her own photography business and was married to an accountant. But in another life she'd been closer to this world than most people knew. Young and silly perhaps, but as a teenager she'd fallen in love with a Yardie gangster, Adrian Jr. Adrian Jr was her son's father. And, just to add confusion to this story, Adrian Jr's father was also called Adrian, and he had been one of the most notorious gangsters in north London.

A reggae musician, he owned a club in Dalston in which he sold crack, cocaine and cannabis. All of his thirteen children worked in the business. Clair remembered that even his twelve-year-old son carried a weapon and sometimes wore a bulletproof vest as he progressed around the club into the small hours selling cocaine. Aged nineteen, and a regular clubber, Clair had found the whole thing exciting. When she was invited into the family's inner circle, there was something intoxicating about the flash money, the nightclub glamour, the 'high-profile' gangster lifestyle. Her boyfriend's father was known, respected and feared. But she knew what came with it. She'd seen people get shot and stabbed. She'd seen a man battered with a claw hammer and watched another wet himself as he begged for mercy from the boss.

'He had a reputation to keep up,' said Clair in an interview for this book. 'People needed to respect him.'

Her boyfriend's father was an intimidating presence. Six foot three, he added to his height with a top hat. He always wore a smart suit and waistcoat, although his dreadlocks hung down to the backs of his knees. He had gold teeth, and on his wrists, from cuff to elbow, were thick gold bracelets that could deliver a nose-busting blow if anyone dared cross him. His business had made him rich and he owned a mansion in Hertfordshire. He had 'a main woman' and other girls who'd come back for orgies. He was proper bad.

The police knew who he was, but every time they got close, someone else would take the fall. A girlfriend went to jail for him. Clair was approached by undercover police and asked to inform on him. She wouldn't. He never was convicted of his drug-dealing crimes, but was eventually arrested and charged with the rape of a fifteen-year-old family member, whom he'd got pregnant. His club was raided and closed down. He emerged from prison years later, bankrupt. He now lives in a small one-bedroom flat. Life moves on. Adrian Jr managed to break away from the gangster life when Clair became pregnant. They left Dalston and Jr got a 'legit' job. Sadly, he died of a brain aneurysm in 2007.

Clair remarried an accountant and now had two younger children at home. Yet here she was in a bedsit with her eldest, waiting for a new set of gangsters to enter her life. And indeed they came, their arrival announced with a loud rap on the door.

'We're back.'

Silence.

'WE'RE BACK. Open up.'

Silence.

Convinced that Adrian was malleable and would let them

back in, they hadn't thought to insist on having a key. Clair could see their shapes outside the window and hear the dog barking. 'I know you are in there,' said a deep voice.

Forty-two-year-old Clair clutched the phone waiting for her moment to call the police. But her younger self, nineteen-year-old Clair, wanted to open the door and confront them. That's who she was. She was from a gangster family. She knew more about this life than the kids outside. She'd dealt with ten times worse.

'I'm going to open the door and tell them what for,' she said to her son.

'Don't,' he said.

'They need a talking to,' replied Clair, the anger and confidence rising.

'You shouldn't have come,' said Adrian, real alarm and panic in his voice.

BANG, BANG. 'We *know* you're in there.'

'I wasn't going to leave you, was I?' whispered Clair.

BANG, BANG. The windows shuddered.

'I'm going to tell them to bugger off.'

'What if they hurt you?'

'They won't.'

'What if they do?' insisted Adrian.

They sat in silence. The gang outside still goading them.

'We're not leaving,' they said.

Adrian wasn't sure if they'd left drugs on the property, but they were determined on coming in.

'If I'm on my own, I've only got myself to look after,' said Adrian. 'But if someone did something to you, I'd have to kill them. Do you get it?'

Clair was suddenly forty-two again. A helpless mother.

Could it be true, that she was a liability to her son? Was she more of a burden than a help?

BANG! BANG!

'Do you have a cigarette?' Adrian asked suddenly.

'Yes.'

'Give it here.'

'Why?' This wasn't a time to start smoking. They might see it through the window.

'Look.' Adrian pointed at the smoke alarm on the bedroom ceiling. Clair retrieved a pack of 20 Silk Cut from her handbag, along with a lighter. Adrian lit up and took a drag on the cigarette. As the gang outside began to kick at the door, he puffed smoke into the sensor. It took only a few seconds, then suddenly the alarm was ringing.

The banging stopped. Now the only noise was the blaring siren and the sounds of neighbours stirring in the communal areas. Clair and Adrian waited until they were sure the corridors outside were full of baffled and slightly frustrated residents from the communal building. 'Bloody alarm!' came the voices. When they finally peered outside the gang had gone.

Clair stayed with Adrian that night, and the next day she called the police and Adrian was immediately moved to new accommodation. He recounted later how he'd met one of the neighbours earlier in the week, another vulnerable adult who'd been living on his own. And, when he dropped in on the man's flat, he'd noticed a big Jamaican man who appeared to have made himself at home in the older man's house. He was preparing drugs on the living-room table. Perhaps, thought Clair, this man had clocked that Adrian was autistic and living across the hall from a property they had already cuckooed.

Perhaps then he'd told the others of the potential opportunity to take over another flat.

Clair's son Adrian is safe from the cuckoos now. She knows they were a gang from south London but doesn't know if they've been arrested.

I asked Clair to draw on her own experience of being linked to gangs and, having seen her own son become a victim, what she thought the solution might be.

'Better parenting, more social workers, get kids off the street. My fourteen-year-old son, he can go to the park for an hour but that's it. Some of these kids are twelve or thirteen and they're out all night.

'There's a lack of family morals, principles and nurturing these days. There's pressure on all of us to work, work, work. Parents are tired. But they are also tied by the government on how to discipline their kids. They might get done for abuse. Obviously, sometimes there is abuse, and that's a problem too. And it seems way too many parents just don't give a damn. So it's getting worse. And the police are just going around picking up the pieces. No one is getting to the root of the problem. That needs investment.'

As discussed already in this book, cuckooing is part of the county lines phenomenon, where drug dealers from metropolitan areas befriend vulnerable people in smaller towns and turn their homes into places to keep, prepare and sell drugs. Adrian was lucky that he was cuckooed only for one night. The scale of the crime is unclear, although last year Commander Simon Bray, the National Police Chiefs' Council lead on drugs, said the number of people having their houses taken over could be in the thousands. There's no doubt Clair and Adrian's story is becoming increasingly common, and I recently discovered an extreme case of cuckooing in Swansea.

Close to the city centre, there are a series of tall, time-stained tower blocks called Griffith John Street. Here, residents say drug dealing and prostitution are a part of visible daily life. Speaking to locals on a visit to Swansea, I was told some shocking stories about this notorious block of flats. Firstly, it was a place where women had been seen standing on a stairwell offering sex. The ten-storey staircase is visible through a glass wall, and the sex wasn't just being offered there – it was happening. A shop owner also told me of a woman naked from the bottom down who had recently called out from a nearby bridge offering her services.

WalesOnline reports that between March 2018 and March 2019, fifty-eight crimes were reported in one single street that runs through the estate. Armed police and ambulances are a common sight. One resident from the block told me simply: 'Everything that is bad happens here. Think of something bad and it happens here.'

He said that the block had got increasingly worse over the ten years he'd lived there. A new group of people had arrived in the block that he thought were from eastern Europe. He described them as 'drug rats, scuttling around the corridors'. It sounded to me like a horrific place to live. This resident put it like this: 'I'm frightened twice a day – once when I leave my flat and once when I go home.'

Another local woman who overlooked the estate told me that she had been threatened with acid and wouldn't dare cross the street to walk on that side of the road. The woman described visible prostitution, sex workers seen at all times of the day in the court area or on balconies. She added that the men carried guns and knives, and it was common for people to get beaten up or for her to hear the smashing of windows.

It had already been voted Wales's ugliest building complex in 2011, but as word spread that it was also the most dangerous, Sainsbury's banned its delivery drivers from taking goods to the block, citing 'issues over driver safety'. Most telling of all, a refugee from war-torn Eritrea who'd been housed there went to court to appeal for relocation, describing the place as a 'hell-hole'. His flat was broken into twice and he felt 'violated' and pleaded to be allowed to escape the 'disruptive and rowdy behaviour, and bad people'. So, you get the picture.

After touring the block and meeting locals, I had a chat with a charity worker at a homeless drop-in centre. Deborah told me that at Griffith John Street, the county lines dealers are not just bringing in drugs but also working girls.

Deborah is particularly worried about this because, unlike the local sex workers, these girls stay under the radar of charities and local authorities that can offer help and access to medical services such as health checks. 'We don't know who they are,' she says. 'We've got no access to them and they've got no access to us. They don't speak English. For example, Women's Aid vans that go around offering condoms and health advice, they don't get to see them.'

There has been a concerted effort by police to stamp out street prostitution in the city centre, but Deborah describes this as 'bleaching the streets' when actually bigger problems hide behind closed doors – prostitutes installed into homes that have been taken over from desperate drug addicts. Essentially she is describing a diversification of county lines drug dealing into a potentially complementary business of sex trafficking.

'It's frightening,' adds Deborah. 'It's a residential area – there's a school just across the road and a playground a bit further up. But there are girls in the glass-fronted stairs. I've been told of girls there with nothing on, in the stairwell, calling out for business. But they don't speak English. They've got nowhere they can go for help. They are trapped. Monday last week someone told me they were having sex in the stairwell in view of everybody.'

Swansea has been plagued by county lines coming in from London, Bristol, Birmingham and northern cities, such as Manchester and Liverpool. Those working in addiction services believe the drugs being sold are stronger than before, and that itself leads to a risk of people overdosing.

'What's happened to the local dealers?' I ask Deborah.

'The local dealers are small fry. The people we're talking about are gangsters. These are nasty people, very nasty – they wouldn't think twice about barging in here with guns. That's the type of people they are. And that's why we won't go there. As concerned as we are for the working girls, we can't afford to take that risk. So the services we offer – condoms, wet wipes, testing for HIV and Hep C, just general support – they haven't got it. It's got gradually worse,' she adds. 'There's always been outsiders but this year [2019] it has got worse.'

The addition of imported sex workers into the county lines mix is a worrying development, but this new breed of dealers have been using the classic modus operandi of cuckooing the homes of addicts. There is a plentiful supply of vulnerable drug addicts in the city – and the ones with homes in Griffith John Street are easy targets.

'What happens is they give what's called a "lay-on",' says Deborah. 'They give them the drugs and then the users have to pay them later, when they've got money. But when they go back the price has tripled. So they are always in debt to the dealer, and this is where the trouble starts. People get beaten up. People commit crimes to get money for the dealers, but they'll never get out of debt. With the working girls, they have to work for free to pay for the drugs.

'They will take over a vulnerable person's property – usually a drug user. They befriend them, give them a little bit of what they need and take over the flat. The person is suddenly stuck. Now there's someone living in their flat. They can't get rid of them because they're scared of what they'll do if they did, but secondly, they are giving them what they need. So the addiction gets worse.'

'I suppose it's like a drunk living in a pub – the drugs are always there?' I suggest.

'Yes, and then what happens is the person whose flat they've taken over is the drug person's mule if they get stopped and searched. It's the mule that's got the drugs on them – not the dealer. And the mule never says who the dealer is.'

Deborah then tells me the story of a man called Gareth, who quite recently started coming to the homeless centre. He was cuckooed and lived with the dealers for several months as they fuelled and escalated his drug habit. Neighbours noticed there were people always going back and forth and it was reported to the council. When they checked the property they found that somebody had been in and stripped out all the copper pipes. There were some young men in the flat, and police officers found drugs, but the owner wasn't there. It was assessed that Gareth had allowed his property to become a crack den, and the decision was made that it should be taken away from him – but in truth he was already sleeping on the streets four or five weeks earlier, because he didn't want to go back. The council threw him out, but actually, the cuckoos had beaten the council to it. Gary had been so terrified of his new housemates he'd decided he preferred sleeping rough. So, the consequence for him was that he lost his home.

In September 2019 the *Guardian* reported an increase in the number of 'closure orders' related to drug dealing. The newspaper said the orders preventing access to local authority homes for a period of time – issued for antisocial behaviour and drug activity – had quadrupled nationwide in four years.

The data was obtained via Freedom of Information requests to which 20 police forces responded. A total of 186 local authority homes had been closed in 2018, up from 46 in 2014. Bedfordshire alone closed 42 homes, up from one in 2014; the majority of these were linked to drug use. Experts told the paper this number was likely to be a significant underestimate but expressed concern that the surge was due to county lines drug activity.

Paul Andell, a criminologist from the University of Suffolk, told the *Guardian* the rising number of closure orders showed that 'the phenomenon of cuckooing in itself is increasing, therefore increasing numbers of properties of vulnerable people are being used as the county lines drug business model expands.'

Many police forces have now acknowledged cuckooing as a major concern. North Yorkshire police said that by the end of June 2019, they had identified 90 victims of cuckooing. This compared with 39 victims in total the previous year.

Devon and Cornwall police said that as of 22 August

residents of about 200 homes were known to be at risk of cuckooing and were being safeguarded by police.

Chief Inspector Rachael Glendenning of Bedfordshire Police said the sharp rise in closure orders used was 'a means of taking positive action against drug criminality and anti-social behaviour.'

Kim Warner, an area commander with Suffolk Constabulary, said cuckooing was adaptable. 'So, if an address is being cuckooed then we have tactics to disrupt that. For example, by issuing a warrant. When you do that you displace the line but it will adapt, so they move to more street-based dealing. Then we react to that and then there is a resurrection of cuckooing – so there are peaks and troughs in the activity.'

He added: 'You have to work hard with the council to think about what to do long term to prevent it.' Warner said closure orders were not always the best way to deal with the problem. 'With some cuckooed addresses they will move in, and by the time you respond they have moved. A closure order can take months to obtain, so it would work better if an individual was repeatedly getting involved in that sort of activity.'

Back in Swansea, I ask Deborah whether she had a sense of the scale of the cuckooing problem in the city.

'It's happening a lot,' she says. 'Especially where you've just been. In the block, the girls are working; there are children, fourteen, fifteen, sixteen who are taking drugs. They don't care who they sell to and who they use.'

'What can be done to deal with all this?' I ask.

'If steps were taken to get rid of this lot, another lot will come in. I honestly can't see how it can be dealt with.'

Somehow, I'd hoped for a more positive response. I'd imagined someone like Deborah, with her nose pressed right up against the coalface, would see the thing that we are all missing. But my trip to Swansea just made me feel like the whole thing is spiralling downwards, and that county lines is spreading its tentacles more widely and taking an ever firmer grip in towns across the UK. We are not struggling enough to loosen its grip – not nearly enough. So how do we end this?

15.

THE SOLUTION

'The answer to the million-dollar question.'

Mahir had been stabbed twenty times and was being hauled towards an ambulance as I drove past in a taxi on my way home from a night out with my wife. On that January night in 2006, I was just another passer-by catching a snapshot image of chilling gang violence, while sitting in the warmth of a black cab. There were young men holding his floppy frame as upright as possible, but his head lolled to one side revealing a gruesome gash. One of them pressed a balled T-shirt to his neck as a makeshift plug. A paramedic, new to the scene, rushed in with rolled bandages and it looked, from my brief glimpse, as if he was stuffing the wound. Even this couldn't prevent the catastrophic bleeding that left Mahir limp, as they tried to steer him through the open doors at the back of the ambulance. And beyond the horror of it, and the sympathy anyone would naturally feel for a fellow human being in such peril, teetering on the edge of life, my first thought, as father of a young child, was: 'I need to move out of this area.'

It's a natural reaction. We all want to distance ourselves from what is happening. But the solution to our problem is going to take something else. We not only have to open our eyes and understand what is going on; there also needs to be a combined and profound effort to tackle it. In this book I've raised a whole heap of problems that require our attention: drug addiction, exploitation, dwindling police resources, a crisis in social care and school funding, poor parenting and a youth subculture that glorifies crime and violence. So how to deal with it?

We are all susceptible to the apparent glamour of criminality. It's perhaps why you are reading this book, and I'm writing it, and there are so many successful crime dramas on TV. It was part of the attraction to a thirty-year-old me that Camden was edgy. The bars were cool. Amy Winehouse hung out in my local pub, so it didn't get much cooler than that (except so too did Liam Gallagher). But it wasn't somewhere I wanted to raise my children. Sometimes there were syringes on the street, and every day I was offered drugs as I walked home from work. Once, while walking my toddler down the street, a drug-addled tramp stood up and urinated in front of us. At one point, there were police signs at either end of my road asking for information about separate violent assaults, and one morning I woke up to see police officers and blue tape two doors down from my house. There had been a domestic murder.

A crime correspondent at the time, I used to say that I was living my beat. Camden was perhaps the most famous area for buying drugs in a city that was, and remains, the biggest illicit drug market in Europe. So, more than a decade ago now, I lived in the thick of a problem that was slowly seeping across the country. But as a crime correspondent, I did have another thought, as we drove away from the flashing lights and the limp body of Mahir. I thought to myself, What the hell is going on?

Since that day in January 2006, I've taken an interest in gang culture and I've watched it spread like an illness to other towns and cities, and today, more than ever, I still ask myself that same question. But I think with county lines the first thing we need to ask is what is changing? Is this a new threat and, if so, what conditions have created it?

After Mahir's murder, over a decade ago, I set out to make a film for 5 *News* studying gangs in different cities across the UK. I began with the Somalis in Camden. I met Mahir's grieving mother and some of his friends, who had known him as 'Smiley' because he always smiled. At that time, the Somalis were considered to be among the most violent gangs in London, and there was an obvious reason for that.

Even though you couldn't get a house on my street in Camden for less than half a million pounds, the Somali community lived on some of the borough's roughest, ugliest estates, a stone's throw from my home, and this was true of all the Somali communities in London. They were located in the most deprived pockets of a city that was otherwise gentrifying and watching property prices rise £50k a year. The Somalis were mostly refugee families that had fled civil war in their homeland in the 1990s, and in one way or another each individual carried the scars of that trauma.

Now they were bottom of the food chain – newcomers cut off socially and culturally – an invisible community. The parents spoke very little English, the children struggled at school and a high proportion were excluded, which rapidly spiralled into anti-social behaviour, truancy, and substance abuse and gangs. Very few could see any prospect of jobs and integration into our society. If you are looking for a lethal absence of hope – I've never seen it more profoundly than there, right on my doorstep.

In Camden, the Somali gang was called the Centric Crew, and in Tottenham they were the NLS (North London Somalis). I discovered there had been escalating hostilities between the two groups, and a recent incursion in Tottenham by the Centric Crew had prompted a gang of 40 NLS to come south on a bus to attack someone – anyone – on that January night in 2006. They arrived with wooden bats, bottles, hammers and screwdrivers. What knives they didn't have already, they stole from a nearby Sainsbury's. It was strikingly similar to the later murder of Tavis Spencer-Aitkens in Ipswich, only on a bigger scale. Mahir just happened to be in the wrong place at the wrong time. He was the first person NLS spotted – so they killed him. Afterwards, a number of the attackers foolishly tried to escape by hijacking a London bus, and it was easy for the police to intercept it and contain them. Twenty people were eventually charged in connection with the murder.

After studying London gangs, I went to Manchester and Glasgow, both cities with serious problems. But only after visiting Los Angeles did I find the same kind of isolated communities creating a similar type of violence drawn along ethnic lines that I'd witnessed in my own backyard.

There was then a gap of twelve years before I properly returned to the subject. In 2018, I made a short film for Sky News about county lines, which in turn led to me writing this book. In those twelve intervening years things have changed a great deal. The first thing to say is that, with county lines, the whole thing feels more of a business than it did before. Also, there's an almost emotionless brutality, which has evolved from the kind of tit-for-tat gang warfare that led to Mahir's murder in Camden.

There seem to be fewer single-ethnicity gangs like the Somalis playing out imported feuds and bearing the scars from countries of origin. Much more of the modern gangs' energy seems to be devoted to self-image and the calculated accumulation of money, and this appears to be intrinsically linked to the violence. But the levels of violence that were once the reserve of alienated communities such as the Somalis now seems to exist within homegrown communities. One way to regard the violence is as a symptom of a disease called alienation. And if that is spreading – and more young people are behaving like traumatised refugees – the obvious question is why are they becoming alienated?

My second observation is that ten years ago it seemed obvious that a lot of the young people I met joined gangs for a sense of belonging – and perhaps to fill a gap left from being brought up in an unstructured home life or lack of a father figure. But with county lines it is very different. Here, you are involved in something that takes you away from your community. It banishes you from your home life, sets you outside of any reliable structure, and leaves you further exposed in an unfamiliar environment. That's a massive reworking of the old-school gang structure.

Cody, the Tottenham dealer, was the first person to really alert me to this increasingly callous nature of gang life, but everything he said has played out in what I experienced while researching this subject. The operations I came across, such as Uncle's, are more brutal and ambitious than the protection of local turf. And the idea that youngers are protected by their elders – that is long gone. Uncle puts them in harm's way. They protect *him*.

Some, such as the Tottenham postcode gang, still operate within their estate and hold territory, but even here identity and belonging is less of a motivation – money is everything. It was all the postcode gang talked about: the desire for wealth – and maybe escape through wealth. This, it seems, outstrips the desire for belonging. And there is something different about their attitude to violence too.

Even among the Somalis I met a decade ago, a brutal act such as Mahir's murder was rare, but it now seems common. It is expected. It is even encouraged. It is part of the game of life. Is it happening more, or it is perhaps just perception? From speaking with these marginalised kids up and down the country, it would seem these groups have adopted a belief that the violence is everywhere. Remember Lee, who got stabbed in the head: 'Everyone gets stabbed in Southend, bruv.' That's the perception of the kids caught up in this. And with the postcode gang and Uncle, there was something far too casual about their relationship with violence. When they talked about a knife attack on someone, it was just business. It was functional. They were utterly lacking in empathy. Violence is such a part of their regular digest that it no longer shocks them.

And, with social media, if a gang member happens to miss an act of violence happening on their street corner, it's okay, because someone will have filmed it and they can watch it at their leisure. They get to see it in slo-mo. They get to *share* the violence, or *like* the violence, or *comment* on the violence – or make drill videos where they can *rap* about the violence, and threaten more. As a result, tensions rise much more quickly and intractably. An argument that might have been settled in

the street, in one bloody fight – possibly even in a murder –
seems to perpetuate even beyond that. Disputes are both real
and virtual, and in the online space can take on a new life: on
Snapchat, on Messenger, on Instagram, in a high-production
video on YouTube. It appears to have contributed to young
people becoming desensitised to violence.

It is quite chilling to hear them speak about it. As Chris
Preddie and others have said in this book, it isn't any different
to the *Call of Duty* violence they control on their Xbox games.
In the film I made in 2006, I remember a group of Somali
children reflecting with genuine shock and sadness on the
fatal stabbing of their friend Mahir. They wanted the world
to change as a result. One of them was so deeply affected
that, twelve years on, he has a clothing brand and runs design
programmes for children from disadvantaged backgrounds in
Camden Market.

Nowadays, that kind of killing is sometimes talked about
with a shrug. Or treated as points on the scoreboard that need
to be evened up. And what's worse, this attitude is wafting on
the breeze of county lines. It is being exported to smaller towns,
such as Ipswich, where ten years ago you'd never imagine gangs
aping what they see in London, making drill music videos
about selling drugs, scoring points and murdering rivals, and
then actually doing it. It's cancerous.

Or maybe it's just me. I decided to put this to Tony Saggers,
who I've quoted throughout this book. In 2017, Tony retired
from his role as Britain's most senior anti-drugs cop after two
decades investigating high-end distributors and traffickers
for the National Crime Agency. He has watched this industry
evolve. I wondered, from his expert perspective, what he thinks
has changed since his early days in policing.

'There's always been violence associated with drug markets, but it has changed,' he says. 'A decade ago there might be the occasional ruthless drug dealer at street level who would carry a knife or even a gun, because they have a reputation for it, and just like a county lines gang they might let people build up debts and use a weapon to enforce the debt. But now there are more people carrying and prepared to use knives, and sometimes guns,' he says. He adds that this is partly because dealers are 'more paranoid' that everyone else is carrying a weapon, and partly because, in some instances, they are right to be paranoid: 'The business has become more brutal.'

I decide to offload and talk to Tony about the things that have been bugging me since I met Uncle in his crack den, and the postcode gang. Was this desensitised attitude to violence something new?

'Yeah, definitely,' says Tony. 'It has changed, and I often find myself thinking about what's the difference between child soldiers in Central Africa, being desensitised by being forced to watch killings, sometimes of their own families, and what's happening in county lines at the moment. I think there's very little difference. This is about desensitising a child to use a knife to plunge into someone else and kill them if you need to.

Tony recalls working with the military, delivering pre-Afghanistan deployment briefings to British troops. He says of the soldiers: 'They go through a lot of training to teach them to kill and give them the mentality and the ability to kill in hand-to-hand combat. No one is training these young people involved in county lines and yet, almost every week, someone of that age is stabbing someone else of that age to death.'

He struggles with this a bit, in the way I do. 'I don't fully understand it,' says Tony, 'but we do need to understand what drives a fifteen-year-old to even be able to plunge a knife into the body of someone else in twenty-first-century Britain. I've thought about it more than most, and it's a difficult one. I think ultimately there's a sense of, "I'm in a very fearful position here and bottom of the supply chain. The only way that I stop myself from being exploited is to prove that I'm prepared to exploit someone else." And when they've proven that, the only way to get on the next step up the ladder and to get out of the sights of someone else, is to perform an act that actually would have been incomprehensible to them twelve months earlier. I think if there is an answer, it's about escalation. Being less vulnerable by being prepared to exploit others more.'

I tell Tony about Cody, who talked about how gangs used to be a family but the love and protection had gone.

'There's a lot less trust,' agrees Tony. 'Maybe a consequence of that is it's becoming more fractured and more dangerous. There's a lot of debate over how much drug crime is the cause of violent crime. Some people are saying it's not linked; it's about deprivation and social economics. But you can't get away from the fact that drugs are lucrative. They're the quickest way to elevate yourself out of a position of poverty in the UK. With that comes distrust and violence, because it's simply that sort of environment, and county lines have enhanced that.

'If your runners are in sight, in the local area, they need to be controlled less. If they are out in the counties you need to make sure they do as they're told. That's where the violence and exploitation comes from. Because if someone oversteps the mark, and your reputation is, "I will stab people if they let me down", and then you *don't* stab the first person to let you down, where do you go from there? Who respects you and does what you tell them from that point onwards? It becomes a vicious circle, because if one gang controls its drug markets through brutality, others need do the same in order not to look weak.'

When it comes to policing the problem, we've had recent advances. We've now got the National Crime Agency Coordination Centre – a central hub that is helping to pull together national-scale investigations and support local police forces. In October 2019, the Home Office announced a surge of activity and an extra £20 million investment to increase its capacity, which up to that point had coordinated four separate weeks of action resulting in over 2,500 arrests and over 3,000 safeguarding measures for vulnerable individuals caught up in the trade. The Offensive Weapons Act, which received royal assent in May 2019, gives police extra powers to seize dangerous weapons, making it illegal to possess knuckle dusters and zombie knives – even in private – and harder to buy online. Modern slavery legislation has come into force and proven effective in the prosecution of child traffickers, as we saw in The Castro Line chapter.

But is this enough to reverse county lines and the associated violence? Every time there's a focus on knife crime in the news, usually after a spate of stabbings, you can be sure that a politician will talk about increasing powers of stop and search, or increasing sentences for people carrying knives. This could have an impact, or it could have no impact whatsoever. All I can tell you is that none of the police officers I interviewed for this book once mentioned stop and search. I refer you back to DCI Mike Brown, the Ipswich murder investigator, who I asked for his solutions.

'Whoever finds that has got the answer to the million-dollar question,' he said. He talked about 'early intervention'; of parents 'knowing their kids' and asking questions. He talked about schools and support, volunteers and charities, but he added, 'You have to put yourself in the shoes – or the trainers – of these young men.' For them, he suggested drug dealing seemed like the 'opportunity of a lifetime' because the choice was set against poverty or abuse and isolation. How to deal with that?

I think back to what Uncle said in his crack den: 'The best way, in my opinion, is to target the little kids while they're young. When they're young their minds are vulnerable and they can be corrupted.'

Tim Champion from the National County Lines Co-ordination Centre agrees. He told me: 'Unless we turn off the tap there is a sausage factory of children who will be exploited by this. And it's not just kids from metropolitan areas and from the estates – they've started using local kids. Kids in grammar schools. The methodology is evolving. So, the first thing, if we can stop kids being used, that would be a major step forward, because that means the organisers have to get their hands dirty. They have to get closer to the user and the point of arrest. We have to look at what is pushing kids into this. How do we prevent and divert them? There needs to be a lot of early intervention.' We have to accept too, that children recruited into dealing now will grow up to be recruiters of the future.

On top of this, psychologist Carlotta Raby's extensive research tells us that intervention could be better targeted – and if it was done at a young age might be highly effective in diverting young people away from gangs. There has to be a way of breaking what she calls the 'toxic web' that's trapping the UK's most disadvantaged children into a life of violence and exploitation.

We've already seen that school exclusions are on the rise and the fallback facilities such as pupil referral units are struggling to stay afloat and are sometimes blamed for exacerbating the problem. Recently, however, I visited Redbridge Alternative Provision (RAP) in Essex. It caters for the most challenging children from the area: those expelled from local mainstream schools. Despite this, the facility was given an 'outstanding' rating by Ofsted. This school has a reputation for kids walking in as gang members, drug-takers and county lines dealers, and walking out as students on a path to college and contributing to society. If there is a sage-like character at the end of this journey, then perhaps it is Sam Walters, the executive head teacher who oversees the unit and three other schools in the area.

This former police officer, who has also worked in mainstream secondary education, has a wiry athleticism, and as he walks through the corridors of his architecturally modest two-storey block, he seems to command respect from his uniformed pupils. As we chat in the snooker room, he acknowledges there has been an increase in young people becoming excluded for drug- and knife-related offences in his catchment area. All of them end up at his door.

I put it to Sam that his school is a basket for bad apples. 'It's literally like saying, "All right, here's the most difficult children in this area. Deal with it."' It's worth pointing out that every child who comes to his school is screened by metal detectors for weapons on entry.

'And we're saying, "Thanks"', responds Sam, with a grin.

'But surely, when someone new arrives here with those kinds

of issues, you must be bracing yourselves for what's coming?'
I suggest.

'Sometimes you read the referral paperwork and you create this image of what's going to walk through the door the next day. But they're all kids. Some are eleven years old, twelve, thirteen. I think there's two ways of looking at it. We get a referral through for a young person who may have been permanently excluded for having a knife and distributing drugs in school, let's say. And on paper it can read particularly badly. But the truth is behind each person that comes to us, there's a story. I think our job here is not to continue where they left off and put them straight into an English lesson or a maths lesson – it isn't going to work, and it hasn't worked, which is largely why they're here in the first place. So, it's about trying to rewind that story and strip back some of those layers to identify the root cause of some of the problems. If you want that young person to move on, to either a future education or employment, we need to understand why things went wrong. And when you strip back, you find commonalities within those issues.'

'Such as?'

'Just to put it into perspective, if I'm honest I can say that a lot of these kids have been through more than most adults would in sixty, seventy years of living. I think that for a young person to go to bed one night and wake up in the morning and one of their parents has passed away in the same house as they're in, or for a young person to witness the levels of domestic violence that are taking place in their home, or for a young person to be out on the street and witness one of their friends die in front of them, that's not something most adults will ever experience.

283

'And when we understand and strip it back to really identify the traumatic events they've been through, I'm not saying it *excuses* the behaviour we see later, but it sure as hell provides some form of reasoning as to why a young person may behave in a way that's not considered normal.'

Now, this shouldn't be huge revelation, having spoken to Carlotta Raby about her work, but somehow, when I hear it from Sam, it suddenly hits me that, despite my blaming everything from computer games, to drill music, to social conditions and social media – as I have throughout this book – surely the most influential factor on the behaviour of our children is the behaviour of their parents and surrounding adults. Did I once, for example, mention during the chapter on the Ipswich murder that one of the killers who was humiliated in the soap shop – his father was a notorious violent drug dealer who was himself in prison? How could I not touch on that while blaming the lyrics of a music video?

I'm not saying that all the things Sam listed are the fault of parents, and it's all too easy to simply blame parents and dismiss this as not our problem. It is still our problem. That child is still left with a trauma that will come to bite us if we don't help him. And we can't expect kids to be living day-to-day with alcoholism or domestic violence and assume they'll be okay.

We also need to acknowledge that some parents or carers themselves have mental-health problems or learning difficulties or addictions that are difficult to combat – or they may have simply lost control of a child outside of the home. An emerging approach to children at risk is called 'Contextual Safeguarding', which recognises that young people form a range of relationships outside the family, including with peers, schools and online, which can feature violence and abuse. And that parents and carers may have little influence over these spaces, but they've become a critical part of safeguarding practices with adolescents. So, the trauma Sam refers to may not always be in the home.

'I'm not saying every young person carrying a knife or every young person drug dealing has had this high level of trauma,' continues Sam. 'But from my experience of the two hundred or so young people that come through this provision every year, the vast majority have experienced things similar to what I've just said.'

I ask Sam if he feels mainstream schools could do more to deal with some of those challenges, before it gets to the stage of kids getting kicked out. Sam doesn't feel they have the resources.

'It's just not always possible,' he says. 'With schools losing a lot of their government income they have to make decisions about what goes. The English teacher can't go, the Maths teacher can't go – they need to be in class, teaching young people. So what you then lose is that pastoral wraparound care; whether it is the educational psychologist's hours, learning support or assistance, mentors or extracurricular activities such as boxing and sports programmes. That's what goes – and unfortunately that's the support that those one or two per cent of really highly complex young people rely on.'

In Redbridge Alternative Provision, Sam tries to foster an environment where young people feel open and confident to talk about their problems. A lot of time is spent talking about drugs and violence in a non-judgemental way. Here, you won't get expelled for having a drug problem. The relationship between teacher and pupil is at the core of everything they do.

If they can gain trust from the pupil, they hope in return the pupil will be honest about what's going on in their lives, be it gang membership or selling drugs. As the child settles in, there are still sanctions for children who misbehave, but Sam believes a ten-minute detention in his facility has the same impact as an hour detention would in a normal school. His teachers and mentors instil the idea that there is a consequence for every action. However, at the same time, anger-management issues or drug taking will also be treated as a child welfare problem rather than simply requiring punishment.

'The fact they're quite happy to speak to us, whether it be about drugs, whether it be about gangs, means that we can give them the appropriate advice and put the appropriate support in place to try and prevent incidents occurring.'

'Do you have children here who are involved in county lines?' I ask.

'Yes,' replies Sam, and he recounts the story of a gang turning up outside his school with weapons looking for a pupil, and of one of his children being involved in a stabbing outside of school hours. In the course of spending a day at the school he introduced me to children who'd been involved in going OT.

'And how do you deal with that? Because you know you could say they are being exploited, or you could say they're breaking the law.'

'I think there is a fine line between being groomed into county lines to when suddenly *you* are now the groomer. And, unfortunately, they have that sense of belonging within the gang structure, and in turn they recruit younger people into that gang. And we do a lot of work with young people running county lines, warning them of the consequences – and I think in a mainstream environment they wouldn't necessarily have the resources to do that, and many young people would be permanently excluded for being involved in things such as that. But here it's about using those relationships that we've fostered, exploring the reasons why young people are doing county lines, and trying to put the support in place to get them out of it.'

The system seems to work. I met a number of young people who were now in classrooms preparing for their GCSEs rather than preparing drugs in a trap house. But I do wonder why this kind of focus can't be offered in mainstream education. The default tactic in schools seems increasingly to be to kick out the troublemakers. Not every kid ends up in a PRU, and if they do they are lucky if it's a good one. I've been to several referral units where the discipline doesn't seem to be on the level of Sam's school. Children wander in and out of class, or they don't turn up at all. I'm not suggesting everything at Redbridge is perfect, but it's the best I've seen, and few PRUs perform at this level.

I spoke to one of the students who was expelled from his mainstream school for smoking weed in the bathroom – his grades have rapidly improved since he came to Redbridge, but I asked Sam if he thought it was right to exclude someone for that offence?

'My personal belief is no. There is the potential to cause more damage to that young person's future than dealing with the issue in school. However, I do understand that schools are struggling to find teachers, let alone the support packages to put in place to support people like that young man. And they are not always asking the right questions. They need to be asking, Why? What's gone wrong? How can we try and change this?'

Sam has launched a programme called 'including the excludable'. It's a free course for senior leaders and behaviour leaders in schools. They come to Redbridge and look at how the system works, the different teaching and mentoring strategies. It feels like the kind of programme that should be rolled out across the county. He says, 'In theory we're trying to put ourselves out of business.' Sam believes, if there were the resources and the ambition, schools could avoid or prevent many exclusions from happening. Part of it is about trying not to stereotype children into good and bad apples. 'I think it's quite easy to paint a picture of a young person, and over a period of time that is very difficult to change,' says Sam.

Then again, why should quality mainstream schools really try to learn anything from referral units, which are considered the bottom rung of education? I put it to Sam: 'Some people say that pupil referral units are a conveyor belt into crime?'

'And I just completely disagree. Blaming PRUs for grooming young people into gangs is the same as blaming hospitals for having too many sick people. We are here to serve a certain area of the community, where they've had problems in their mainstream environment. I actually believe the opposite. If they were in a mainstream environment they would be far worse off than they are now.

'I think that if gangs are going to find a group of people, they're going to find a group of people. I mean, we're looking at kids as young as Year Five and Six in primary school. Kids from broken homes. So gangs are really picking up on the vulnerability of those young people. Another key time is the end of Year Six and that transition to Year Seven and often a new school. So, it's quite strategic in terms of how gangs are targeting young people. I think that the work that takes place in places such as this actually changes young people to the point where, if they *are* approached, they're in a better position to make the right decision rather than go the wrong way.'

If that were possible every school would do it, wouldn't they? I still don't really understand how he thinks he can achieve that? 'How do you even get them to stay in the classroom?'

'It's about raising ambition, having high expectations, and young people often will rise to that if the opportunity is there. It's about stripping back those traumatic layers. Addressing the problem, rebuilding and then moving them on with support. So, for a period of transition, they can learn from mistakes and settle in a new environment. I understand what you're saying, that it's difficult to even get them into a class. But we've got a cohort here today that are doing Maths, English Language and Literature, including Shakespeare, Science, plus three or four other GCSEs, who all aspire to go on to achieve bigger and better things. That wasn't their mindset when they turned up. And again, it's through no fault of the mainstream secondary school.

'You spoke to one young man earlier who had the most bad-behaviour points in a mainstream school of two thousand people. [He is referring to a kid called Tye who was expelled from his last school for among many other things, turning up with a knife.] But his outlook has changed,' continues Sam.

It's true. I went on to meet Tye's mother, who said he simply didn't get the attention he needed in mainstream education, but through the PRU and mentoring system he now has a place at sixth-form college.

'So, someone that suffers with severe anxiety now has the self-belief and self-esteem to achieve,' continues Sam. 'They believe that they can leave here at the end of Year Eleven with qualifications to go to college and make something of themselves. And I think that's really the difference. It's about installing a sense of belief and a sense of ambition into the young people we're working with. It's not okay for them to come in and do a crossword, that's not okay.'

I'm still not convinced. 'But in your classrooms are kids with anger management issues, kids who have a history of taking drugs, a history of disrupting the classroom – and yet you say they're now getting on with their studies? I don't get how you do that?'

'Because there's no barrier to their learning here. Negative behaviour in a classroom is quite often, for me, through a lack of understanding and a lack of self-esteem, and embarrassment. A lot of the young people admit that they didn't actually understand what was going on at all in class. It's about creating an environment where young people feel comfortable. That it's fine to make mistakes. I'm not going to kick you out. We're not going to have a go at you. It's about working with you to get it. Young people don't want to continually get things wrong. People want to do well and we're here to make that happen.'

It seems too simple – that talking and investing time in young people and instilling in them a sense of self-belief could be the answer to the million-dollar question. But even if it was, I'm not sure you could create a Redbridge for every failing child. It seems that Sam's magic cure needs to be instilled right across the education system and society as a whole.

'I believe that with time you can create a culture and an ethos within a school that permeates from the top to the bottom,' continues Sam. 'And that, like I say, comes with raising expectations. There isn't a single young person out there that wants to do badly. They may say they do, as a defence mechanism, but there is not a single young person who wants to be in a gang, who wants to go to prison, who wants to stab someone, who wants to drug deal, who wants to fail and mess up their whole education. They may say they want to, time and time and time again, because they're almost setting themselves up with an excuse. It's about changing that mindset. It's about making every young person here believe that they have the potential to achieve. If PRUs are done properly, they can work. I'd go a step further and say they don't just work – they can serve some of the most complex young people better than mainstream environments can.'

Beyond what we've already explored with Carlotta's study, there is surprisingly little research on how to steer children away from crime, but a study of adult offenders about what helped them to stop committing crimes suggested that someone 'believing' in them was significant. The 2015 paper, 'Lifelines: Desistance Social Relations and Reciprocity', by Beth Weaver and Fergus McNeill from Strathclyde and Glasgow Universities, found that persistent optimism, combined with opportunities to make progress, can be an incredible tonic. Pertinently, the paper mentioned how: 'Our social relations shape our behaviours, our identities and our sense of belonging ... It seems to us that unless policymakers and practitioners engage constructively with these relational contexts their efforts to influence individual behaviours are likely to be seriously undermined.'

Certainly Sam's level of belief in his children's potential is infectious. We need a Sam Walters in place for every struggling child out there and, to be fair, I've met numerous inspiring teachers and head teachers who fit that role. There just aren't enough of them to go around.

I don't believe you can end exclusions from mainstream schools, however. There has to be an ultimate sanction, as other children have to be protected. It's not okay, for example, for Tye to bring a knife to class – but that happened after months of disruptive behaviour that appears to have been treated almost purely with detentions and isolating him from the classroom. Indeed, the school became so used to issuing Tye with a detention, that his mother continued to receive emails telling her that he was in detention, even after he'd been kicked out of the school.

I came away from meeting Sam believing that, wherever possible, mainstream schools should try to instil some of his methods for confronting difficult children. But more importantly, there needs to be a focus on bringing PRUs up to the standard of Redbridge, rather than, as I saw in Huddersfield, having their budgets cut.

However, even if with great levels of investment you could foster a more pastoral approach to disruptive behaviour, there does also have to be opportunities at the end of it. When I made my venture into gang activity in Los Angeles, I stumbled across a priest called Father Greg, who, having seen a thousand gang murders in his community in a single year, set up a charity focused on directing gang members into the workplace.

He said that while law enforcement tactics and criminal justice policies were based on 'suppression and mass incarceration', he'd taken what he called 'a radical approach; to treat gang members as human beings'. He trained them and found them employment. He set up social enterprises. I visited one, where muscular tattooed hulks worked in a factory making T-shirts. They said their lives had been turned around, just by having something other than drug dealing as an option for employment. Father Greg's ethos has stuck with me. He said: 'Nothing stops a bullet like a job.'

I've recently seen similar projects start up in the UK. The YMCA could play a big role here. It's a national organisation – mostly known for a song by Village People – but a recent project in Ipswich called 'Designed By You' has an air of homeboy industries about it. They started with a simple competition among children from the estates that produced the killers of Tavis Spencer-Aitkens, to design a piece of jewellery. The winner's pendant design was then made and sold in F. Hinds jewellery branches around the country. All profits from sales of the pendant will go to YMCA to fund further initiatives. The plan from here is to go into clothing design with a big sports retailer and hopefully create apprentice projects in these and other industries where young people can learn skills and have access to employment opportunities they might not have thought possible.

While these projects are commendable, it's still not going to solve the problem. According to Tim Champion: 'We have to recognise that there are often mental-health issues and the problem isn't simply going to be solved by finding that person a job. You have to provide the necessary support around the individual. Obviously the family has a role to play, but it might require one-to-one support, and that's expensive. But then again, how expensive is a murder investigation?'

In the 2015 general election, mental health appeared to become a political priority, with pledges by all parties to increase funding and bring spending in line with that of physical health – and that year the new government under

David Cameron pledged an extra £1.4 billion over five years to transform child and adolescent mental-health services. There has been an uptick in funding made available, but according to the charity Young Minds, it wasn't used properly by councils. The charity sent Freedom of Information requests to clinical commissioning groups and discovered that two-thirds of respondents had diverted the money to other priorities or used it to backfill previous cuts.

It's not just mental health but youth services in general that are falling short of much-needed investment. In May 2019, a committee of MPs found that English councils had slashed funding on youth services by 40 per cent, on average, in the previous three years alone. Some had made cuts of up to 90 per cent. The all-parliamentary group on knife crime also found there had been a 50 per cent drop in the number of council-run youth centres in England. Chair of the group, Sarah Jones, MP for Croydon Central said: 'Youth Services cannot be "nice to have". Our children's safety must be our number one priority.'

Furthermore, the committee found that those areas with the biggest cuts had the sharpest increase in knife crime. Take Cambridgeshire, as an example: the youth budget fell from £3.5 million in 2011 to £0.7 million in 2018, while knife crimes rose from 220 cases in 2014 to 430 in 2018. Cambridgeshire Council said it was 'focusing' its resources on more vulnerable children. Focusing, by the way, is a form of reducing the circle of vision.

Meanwhile, I think it's fair to say that in the months leading up to this book's publication, the government had been *focusing* on Brexit. There is no doubt that if we hadn't spent the last few years discussing whether 'Brexit means Brexit' or if 'no deal really is better than a bad deal', our parliamentary time might have been more devoted to this issue. Between one Brexit deadline and another, in April 2019, Theresa May did however host a summit on youth violence and the then Home Secretary Sajid Javid launched a consultation on creating a new legal duty to ensure public bodies, including hospitals, raised concerns about children at risk of becoming involved in knife crime. Teachers and NHS staff had a lukewarm response to this idea – putting the onus on them to report children – and the civil rights campaign group Liberty warned of 'dragnet surveillance'.

I'm not sure how teachers like Sam Walters would gain trust of his pupils if he knew he was obliged to report them to the authorities if they admitted a crime. This balance between treating children as criminals and victims is a tough line to tread, but it seems to me that they need somewhere they can talk to people in confidence who will lead them in the right direction – otherwise they'll get their guidance from the wrong places.

There is now increasing political interest in how to tackle county lines and, in January 2019, the Home Affairs Select Committee called senior police officers to give evidence of what they were doing to combat the problem. Nikki Holland, director of investigations at NCA, told the committee that more and more areas of the country were now becoming exporters as well as importers of county lines networks, citing twenty-three forces reporting that they were exporting.

Duncan Ball, the National Police Chiefs' Council lead on gangs, told the committee that the model was evolving not just 'urban to rural' but 'like a spider's web'. The biggest exporters remain London, the West Midlands and Merseyside. But the 200 street gangs in London, for example, have built up their own networks, which will sometimes choose collaboration over conflict with other gangs. 'They agree not to fight until supply overtakes demand,' he said.

Jackie Sebire, Bedfordshire Police NPCC serious violence crime coordinator, asked the committee if there could be new powers for Ofsted to regulate care homes that cater for children over sixteen years of age. She argued that the support levels in the homes are inconsistent. New powers would help ensure that children in care weren't easy prey to county lines gangs.

The senior officers told MPs that the £3.5 million invested in the National County Lines Coordination Centre was beginning to have success in shutting down lines and how they were using new telecommunication restriction orders, which meant they could essentially switch off lines – at least until another line emerged. And they were gaining the intelligence to identify the most harmful lines so they could focus their efforts.

But MP for Barrow and Furness, John Woodcock, warned they were in danger of portraying 'an overly rosy impression'. He said: 'You talk about twenty telephone lines being shut down but there are two thousand on record. You talk about a level of resilience in these gangs; you say if one gets shut down another four can be operated. The question is, why are we bothering in that case? There has been no tangible impact on the supply of drugs.'

He went on to give the example of his constituency of Barrow and Furness, where two fourteen-year-olds were picked up for being involved in a county lines operation, having been installed from one area of the country. Once they'd been taken into custody they were almost immediately replaced by children who came from an entirely different area of the country. 'We're not having an impact,' he told the senior officers.

'I would disagree with that,' responded Duncan Ball, and he listed a series of successes during a recent week of police action where nationally they had arrested more than 600 people, interviewed over 1,000 adults and juveniles in a safeguarding position, raided 700 cuckooed addresses and seized over 150 weapons. These were all commendable successes, agreed the MPs, but he had to admit that, despite this, they were failing to restrict the supply of drugs.

There have been significant drug seizures in the past year. In September 2019, 1.3 tonnes of heroin with a street value of £120 million was found concealed in towels and bathrobes on a container ship after it docked in Felixstowe, Suffolk. It was the UK's largest ever seizure of the drug. National Crime Agency officers removed the heroin and returned the container, before tracking it to the Netherlands and making arrests.

It came in the same month that £40 million of heroin, about 400 kilos, was also found at the port. But even police officers are cynical about whether this will mean that UK heroin users will in any way be restricted from getting a fix.

Lawrence Gibbons, the head of drugs threat and intelligence at the NCA, says: 'The key focus, in terms of policing, needs to be looking for those organised crime groups that are causing the most harm economically and physically to the UK and targeting them. If you took out the right person – and he only had five kilos of coke or heroin on him, and he got ten or twelve years in prison – that's a major success, as opposed to a tonne or two tonnes taken out with some couriers. It's about trying to have a strategic approach. So, even if we seize sixty tonnes of cocaine, we can't automatically start feeling like heroes.'

A number of police officers have told me there is too much focus on the supply side of the drugs problem and not enough on demand. 'We need to know more about users,' says Detective Superintendent Champion. 'Users as we define it now, are not just people seeking help. There are regular users not seeking help. There are casual users, weekend users and chronic users who don't get treatment.'

To properly reach out to users there may have to be a softer approach to drug use. Not necessarily legalisation, but it seems to me that Cody shouldn't have got a criminal record for smoking weed when he was a teenager, and the kid in Sam's PRU who smoked weed in the toilets probably shouldn't have lost his chance of a mainstream education because of it. But on a wider scale we are clearly failing to even properly assess the amount of drug use in the UK, and health services and police need to work together on this.

In Scotland and elsewhere there are calls for drug consumption rooms. The needle-littered woodlands and derelict buildings where heroin addicts go to shoot up just off the streets of Glasgow provide a compelling argument for why these monitored drug rooms are an idea worthy of consideration. Some addicts will be suspicious of them, but sterile environments, where professionals are on hand to help, have worked in other countries to dramatically reduce drug-related deaths – and it's a daily opportunity to offer information that may help steer people away from their addiction.

We saw in a previous chapter how addiction services are in decline, while the number of users appears to be increasing. With the wholesale price of cocaine and therefore crack cocaine being reduced – combined with the growth of county lines – one would expect this is adding to the number of drug users, creating new markets, and possibly increasing consumption by existing users. The increased availability and purity will make addicts more tolerant, the general rule being the more heroin and crack you use, the more you want.

Tony Saggers says: 'When I was on drug squads a few years back, people would be supplied their drugs in the morning and in the evening, and there was a fairly strict pattern to that. Now, with county lines, the drugs are available twenty-four hours a day, so people can build up their tolerance quicker and move from one ten-pound bag of heroin to two, and from two to four, and of course what that means is those people are sometimes having to turn to crime to pay for their habit; maybe become dealers or work in the trap house to alleviate the cost, or some women sell themselves for sex. So I think county lines is potentially increasing the scale of the problem in terms of volume.'

The other change for the user is that they are dealing with someone less invested in them. 'What we are hearing is that drug users are being treated less respectfully,' says Tony. 'This might sound like a strange thing to say but local dealers had relationships with their customers and now it's very much a commercial enterprise, where there's very little care.'

According to Tim Champion every police force and local authority needs a better understanding of its user market. 'Demand is where it starts and finishes,' he says. 'Activity on recognising the levels of demand is non-existent. But knowing the number of users in your area is important. If you don't know the number of users compared to the number of dealers, then you don't know what your saturation point is. And, therefore, you don't know when the violence is coming.'

From a policing perspective, we've already seen that county

lines throws up a series of new challenges. For one, it's harder to get to know who the dealers are. Forces have to react more quickly because of the faster turnaround of dealers.

'You need to understand the business model they're running in your town,' says Tony Saggers. 'And you need to put a lot of time into understanding the bigger picture. Policing is very good at policing its own environment. County lines demands that you work at a regional and sometimes national level with the line that you're targeting – and that means going out of your patch, liaising more with other parts of police services.'

A line from London to the east of England is likely to have other lines in the centre of England or in the south of England. Bringing together the intelligence picture of which gang is where and who's doing what is absolutely crucial. Therefore, local forces and the National Crime Agency are having to take a much more joined-up approach. But Tony says the other key element to this is the money.

'I've been monitoring drug markets for the best part of twenty or more years now,' he says, 'and no one sends drugs anywhere in the world, or in any country or town, if they don't think they'll get the money back.'

Those in charge of county lines are strengthened by their displacement and anonymity in the area – but they still have to collect their money. Tony's view is that if you want to stop drugs coming to your town, it's just as important to stop the money getting back as stopping the drugs getting in.

'That for me is key,' he says. 'Anonymity and money. The drugs, of course, you've got to keep targeting, because that's what's causing some of the harm. But that's not the sole response to this problem.'

I ask if he thinks county lines is a national emergency?

'I *do* think it's a national emergency. It's already established as a very strong and efficient method of getting drugs to dependent users – but we cannot accept this as the new way. Undermining that is absolutely crucial and no one police force, no one agency, or one safeguarding institution can do that on their own. I think the time has come, and it's an appropriate time, we need to evaluate it properly. And now the resources are being put into it.'

'Do you think enough?'

'I don't. I don't think you can ever put enough resources into the drugs threat and into the county lines. My main point on that is you need to drive out county lines and then address what is actually success. You know, we didn't have all of these problems when drug markets were local. The first stage for me in the success of the county lines response is to make local drug markets local again. And when you're doing that you can then start to address demand and try and reduce demand for dependent drugs.'

Some of the most radical suggestions for tackling this problem come from the Children's Commissioner, Anne Longfield. She believes county lines *is* a national emergency and has produced a number of reports that have shed light on gang activity. One, in February 2019, found that 27,000 children in England identified as a gang member. It also reported that those children were much more likely than other children known to social services to have emotional and mental-health issues and be self-harming, misusing substances, have a parent drug abuser and to have witnessed domestic violence.

After producing this report, Anne got together with experts from various local authorities' Children's Safeguarding bodies, and she asked them what proportion of local gang activity was connected to county lines. 'No one could tell me,' she said in an interview for this book. 'No one even had an idea – no one had any intelligence about it. There was just nothing.'

Anne agrees that the levels of violence are increasing. 'If you look at the level of violence around county lines, it is extreme. Probably that wasn't there ten years ago. There's a big group of children who are increasingly marginalised. The county lines gangs use violence to control the kids, or as an initiation and requirement of proof that you can be part of it. The stakes have escalated so much and a new norm has been created over this five- to ten-year period.'

She identifies a series of problems that have come from changes in education, social provision and policing: 'There are more kids at risk because exclusions have rocketed, there aren't youth clubs, the police have stopped local patrols – they are all in a centralised office that has no connection with the local community. There's a lack of other influences in the street, in the way you had before. If you have a youth club, there is somewhere to go, you have youth workers, people know what's going on; there are people who have relationships with those kids. There are chances to notice what's happening and have an influence. It's the same with the police being there on the street gathering intelligence.

'If kids are chucked out of a mainstream school, the teachers who know them lose their relationship with them. At best, they go to a PRU where often there is a twilight timetable of maybe two hours a day, and some have a 75 per cent absentee rate – so there is no other influence. Our new government needs to reverse that – they need youth workers wandering the streets looking for these young vulnerable kids to inspire them and reassure them, rather than leaving them to those guys out there who want to exploit them. The safeguarding boards too have been stripped of the people who would know what is going on. We found only one in four gang members were known to the authorities.'

I'm surprised by this figure, but Anne continues: 'The authorities only know about these kids when it gets to "crisis intervention point". Now, you and I might think it was a crisis if you've been stabbed or you're selling drugs, but that isn't always the case.'

Here is Anne's solution. She says: 'If you took the thirty or fifty hotspots or areas of highest risk in the UK, I'd put them into emergency measures for a year. You would keep schools open after school and during school holidays. We have schools everywhere. We pay for them. They are designed for kids and they are often shut. You'd repopulate those areas with good things – you'd have youth workers who could use school premises to run sports and activities in the holidays. You'd work out which kids were at risk, for a start, which is not difficult to do, and you'd provide help for those families at risk. Help them keep their kids safe – and help them prevent the younger siblings getting into that situation. You set up a fund to create youth workers – to grow the numbers fast.' Here Anne is thinking along the lines of the Teach First programme, to fast-track new recruits into teaching, but applying it to youth workers.

She continues: 'Then you put information in schools – lots of primary kids going into secondary schools need help with resilience. That would change the balance completely in an area. You combine all that with a package of support, so that, for example, the moment a child comes into hospital with knife wounds it should trigger all sorts of interventions around the child and the family – but it doesn't at the moment.'

There is considerable evidence that the kind of interventions Anne suggests are effective for the prevention of violence. Home-visiting programmes such as family nurse partnerships have helped improve parenting skills, maternal mental health and have reduced child neglect and abuse. Recent evidence, including that provided by Carlotta Raby, suggests that targeting these programmes towards families with a history of domestic abuse would protect a great number of children and be very cost-effective. One review found that the largest impact on long-term crime reduction could be achieved by creating programmes that focus on conduct problems in childhood. But what exactly does Anne mean by 'emergency measures'?

'Emergency measures means you can't have schools saying, "I'm not opening", for whatever reason. Because, actually, there is a bigger issue here and it's the fact that in this community kids aren't safe. It's like this: *we need your school*. Obviously all this requires serious money, but I think this government is going to have to introduce a new programme around reducing youth crime. A year ago, people were questioning whether this was real. Now people are saying, "It's not good, is it?" It has got to the point where more people are experiencing it themselves and it feels like a tipping point. Government polling must show youth crime coming up as a high concern – they're going to have to do more than just stop and search. They need to move into serious planning.'

I agree. The attitude that we cut funding, then, when problems emerge, we increase police powers, is unsustainable. If we ask ourselves why we have a drug violence issue, the answer might well be the same reason that the UK has a drugs habit; that Bristol consumes more cocaine per head than any other city; that Glasgow has the European record for drug deaths; and Suffolk shrimp eat cocaine in the dirt of our riverbeds. We have the wealth to indulge in the recreational use of powder cocaine, but at the same time the extreme poverty that drives people into the addiction of heroin and crack. That same poverty drives children into the clutches of the dealers, who are constantly trying to expand their businesses. This has to stop.

In some respects, the county lines phenomenon is being used by politicians as the new buzzword that provides an explanation for the increasing violence – and can be tackled with a focused investment on law and order, and tactics like stop and search. But that's not what it is at all. County lines is a symptom of the unravelling social fabric of the UK. In part, it is caused by austerity, reduced community policing, cuts in early years provision, dramatic reductions in youth services spending, parents falling through the gaps and leaving children living in more pressured and fractured homes. They are then dragged through the 'toxic web', vulnerable to criminal exploitation and corrupted by the only promise of a way out – the market for illicit substances. But here they are exposed to drug taking and brutalised by a world where disputes are settled with guns and knives.

In case you are wondering, I haven't found the solution to end poverty, but reinstating those previously mentioned lost services would be a start, as I do believe young people are currently an undervalued investment. Like a good pension, the sooner you start putting money in the better. It may not be the complete answer to the million-dollar question, but couldn't we do more to give children goals, skills, mentors, role models, education and hope? Otherwise we're just setting them up to fail.

Sam Walters puts it like this: 'If there is a two-by-four plank of wood and you put it across the floor and you ask these kids to walk from one side to the other it's easy. But as soon as you raise that plank of wood to a higher point the focus shifts to falling. These young people are trying to walk across a piece of wood that's 75 feet up in the air and there are so many reasons as to why they could fall, so they struggle to get to the other end. What we're trying to say here at this school is yes, the piece of wood may be 75 feet up in the air and there may be barriers, but we can hold your hand and get you to the other side.'

We've been so distracted by other things in our politics, but what could be more important than making this country a safe place for our children, and getting the ones who are up on the high-plank safely across it?

ACKNOWLEDGEMENTS

I couldn't have written this story without the help of Nevres and Azra Kemal – a mother and daughter act like no other. They have been my doorway into this world, gaining the trust of those at the heart of the county lines business. A thank you to all of the unidentified people who've spoken candidly about their lives and motivations. Be you classed as victim or criminal, we have helped to establish, I think, that there is often a fine line between the two.

I'm hugely grateful to Kerri Sharp, my commissioning editor, who realised a book like this needed writing and came looking for me. It's been wonderful working with you. Thanks for your expert help and guidance through this process. Thanks to all at John Blake, at Bonnier Books UK, for asking me to take on this story of our times, and I appreciate the team effort of senior editor Ciara Lloyd, publicist Lizzie Dorney-Kingdom, and copy editor Nicki Gyopari.

I'm incredibly lucky to have a loving family and especially my wife Kerrie, who supports me in my job, and my two children Charlotte and Mille, who put up with tapping noises in the kitchen, on holiday and elsewhere. I'm not sure they were delighted I was going to write another book, but they got behind it. They already forgive me the antisocial hours and unpredictable nature of my day job, and I'm exceptionally lucky they put up with me. My mum and dad have also always been there for me in ways I appreciate more and more every day when I see how others are neglected by their parents. I don't take anything for granted.

My second family is Sky News. Sometimes dysfunctional, but held together with grit and passion, somehow we roll out the UK's most trusted (according to a recent survey) 24-hour news service and find time to create original, award-winning content. I've learned from some of the great news reporters of our time, such as Alex Crawford, and have met important mentors along the way, such as my former 5 News boss David Kermode, my former boss at the Sky Politics team Esme Wren and my current boss David Mapstone. The job is a huge privilege. As Sky News correspondents, we meet incredible people who trust us to tell their stories. With county lines, this experience was more exceptional than usual.

For the original special report, which caught the publisher's eye, I'm grateful to my producer Andy Hughes, who came with me on much of the journey and was, as ever, great fun to work with. My cameraman on the story was Hedley Trigge, one of the best in the business and unflinching in the face of anything. My editors, Jonathan Levy and John Ryley have always had my back, giving me time to develop new material within the pressure of a 24-hour news cycle.

The National Crime Agency has been exceptionally generous with its time. My thanks to Lawrence Gibbons, Joshua Brookstone, Tim Champion and Natasha Bolton